THE NATURE OF POLITICAL THEORY

THE NATURE
OF
POLITICAL THEORY

EDITED BY

DAVID MILLER

AND

LARRY SIEDENTOP

CLARENDON PRESS · OXFORD

Oxford University Press, Walton Street, Oxford OX2 6DP
London New York Toronto
Delhi Bombay Calcutta Madras Karachi
Kuala Lumpur Singapore Hong Kong Tokyo
Nairobi Dar es Salaam Cape Town
Melbourne Auckland

and associates in
Beirut Berlin Ibadan Mexico City Nicosia

OXFORD is a trade mark of Oxford University Press

Published in the United States by
Oxford University Press, New York

© *Except where otherwise stated, David Miller and Larry Siedentop 1983*

British Library Cataloguing in Publication Data
The Nature of political theory.
1. Plamenatz, John 2. Political science—
Addresses, essays, lectures
I. Miller, David II. Siedentop, Larry
III. Plamenatz, John
320'.01 JA71
ISBN 0-19-827473-4

Library of Congress Cataloging in Publication Data
Main entry under title:
The Nature of political theory.
"Bibliography of the published work of John
Plamenatz": p.
Includes index.
1. Political science—Addresses, essays, lectures.
2. Plamenatz, John Petrov—Addresses, essays, lectures.
3. Plamenatz, John Petrov—Bibliography. I. Miller,
David (David Leslie) II. Siedentop, Larry.
[JA71.N34 1984 320'.01 84-17478

ISBN 0-19-827473-4 (Oxford University Press: pbk.)

*Printed and bound in Great Britain
by Billings & Sons Ltd,
Worcester*

*Dedicated to the memory of
John Petrov Plamenatz,
Chichele Professor of Social and
Political Theory in the
University of Oxford 1967–1975,
by former colleagues and pupils*

Contents

Introduction
David Miller and Larry Siedentop

In the last two decades, political theory has re-emerged as a distinct intellectual activity in Britain and the United States. It has developed out of two pre-existing academic traditions—'political thought' as studied in departments of government, and 'political philosophy' as practised in philosophy departments. While drawing on both traditions, it has come to differ from each. It differs from 'political thought' chiefly by being less historical in focus, less given up to examining the development of political ideas through time. Political theory differs from 'political philosophy', on the other hand, because it is less formal and atomistic, less concerned to establish logical relationships between individual political concepts. It does not, indeed, restrict itself to what are now often called 'second-order' questions, questions about the definition and use of the central terms of political argument—terms such as 'authority', 'liberty', and 'justice'. It can (and often does) undertake the revision or extension of purely normative theory, as well as exploring the links between political concepts on the one hand and the changing structure of society on the other.

Political theory is, therefore, an essentially mixed mode of thought. It not only embraces deductive argument and empirical theory, but combines these with normative concerns (in a way that we shall try to elucidate), so acquiring a practical, action-guiding character. This last feature brings its role in some respects close to that of 'ideology' as the word is usually understood. Yet few political theorists would accept that what they do is merely to restate or refine some class ideology or socially influential point of view. Most would hold that the criticism of ideas, far from defending or propagating the interests of particular social groups or classes, is the most effective means of leading such groups or classes to redefine their own interests. Political theorists would prefer to understand their role not as providing a sanction for interests or groups, but as acting as a goad—inducing people to reconsider beliefs previously taken for granted, to notice the fuller implications of their value-commitments, or perhaps to recognize the incompatibility between different goals that they espouse. Implicit in that

1

view is the idea that a political theorist should be able to move, with confidence and skill, between social conditions and political concepts. That suggests that political theorists should be adept at understanding how concepts are joined together in points of view or ideologies, and how those, in turn, spring out of particular social conditions and help to transform them. This ability to move between meanings or concepts and social conditions—to see how every stable social order necessarily implies widely shared beliefs, but also how those beliefs may contain the seeds of further social change—need not impair, and may in fact promote, advances in strictly normative theory.

To that extent, then, political theory is associated with a more active impulse than either 'the study of political thought' or 'doing political philosophy'. It involves, at least implicitly, the assumption that shaping social and political concepts is also, in the longer run, shaping social and political institutions.

The several modes of thought now combined in political theory were, of course, also joined together in the major works that popularly help to identify the tradition of political thought in the West—Aristotle's *Politics*, Hobbes's *Leviathan*, and Rousseau's *Social Contract*, among others. But until recently these modes were combined in a less self-conscious way, a way which reflected a less advanced division of intellectual labour than we live with today. The growth of self-consciousness about method did not, it should be emphasized, suddenly make it easier to write important books in this 'mixed' mode. On the contrary, the emergence of the distinctions mentioned above probably inhibited thinkers at first, and made it more likely that they would confine themselves to one of the three modes—doing, that is, formal conceptual analysis, 'value-free' empirical theory, or offering relatively brief defences of particular policies or values. Only in the last few years have more ambitious and synthetic works appeared, attempting, albeit with only partial success, to combine the modes—works like Rawls's *A Theory of Justice*, Nozick's *Anarchy, State and Utopia*, Oakeshott's *On Human Conduct*, and Dworkin's *Taking Rights Seriously*.

---

[1] J. Rawls, *A Theory of Justice* (Oxford, Clarendon Press, 1972); R. Nozick, *Anarchy, State and Utopia* (Oxford, Blackwell, 1974); M. Oakeshott, *On Human Conduct* (Oxford, Clarendon Press, 1975); R. Dworkin, *Taking Rights Seriously* (London, Duckworth, 1978).

The thirty or forty years before this outburst, the period, say, from the mid-1930s to the early 1970s, might be described as a period of 'regrouping'—a period when the several modes of argument drew apart and took each other's measure, before seeking new ways of combining. No figure loomed larger in the world of Anglo-American political theory during this period than John Plamenatz. Plamenatz, a Fellow of All Souls and then of Nuffield College, later became Chichele Professor of Social and Political Theory in the University of Oxford, a chair he held from 1967 to 1975. His first work, *Consent, Freedom and Political Obligation*, appeared in 1938, and his last, *Karl Marx's Philosophy of Man*, in 1975, the year of his death.[2] Thus Plamenatz's active career as a writer and thinker coincided almost exactly with this 'regrouping', and with the growing self-consciousness about method that accompanied it. Yet at first glance Plamenatz's work may seem to be insulated from the trends which, together, have led to the emergence of 'political theory' out of the earlier 'political thought' and 'political philosophy'. Some indeed have criticized him precisely for not innovating or putting his own point of view directly —for, as it were, 'hiding' among the classical texts of political thought.

That criticism is only partly true. Despite the fact that most of his published writings took the form of commentaries on the ideas of major political thinkers since Machiavelli, Plamenatz's handling of such thinkers was far removed from the conventional historical treatment. His most celebrated book, *Man and Society* published in 1963,[3] is a case in point. Successive chapters of that book reveal Plamenatz holding a conversation with the leading political minds since the Renaissance, a conversation in which he subjects their assumptions and definitions to a rigorous and subtle analysis. He wielded the principle of non-contradiction like a fine scalpel. That resolute probing led Plamenatz largely to disregard the context in which the texts he took up were written—to a point where he was severely criticized by Quentin Skinner and others who, following Pocock and drawing on the hermeneutic tradition, doubted whether concepts and arguments could or should be detached from a particular language that was tied to a place and a time. To such

[2] J. P. Plamenatz, *Consent, Freedom and Political Obligation* (London, Oxford University Press, 1938); *Karl Marx's Philosophy of Man* (Oxford, Clarendon Press, 1975).

[3] J. P. Plamenatz, *Man and Society*, 2 vols. (London, Longman, 1963).

critics, the apparently historical framework of Plamenatz's analyses was misleading. In their view, the tenor of his first book *Consent, Freedom and Political Obligation*—an attempt to identify inconsistencies in the use of basic political terms and to offer some improved definitions—would be a better guide to the nature of his enterprise. That book does indeed bear the mark of a kind of positivism, the philosophical imprint of the 1930s.

So we have two conflicting views of the work of this leading figure: he is seen on the one hand as relatively detached from the tendencies of his own day, and on the other as exhibiting certain features of the movement that was reshaping philosophical argument, in Oxford and elsewhere. Neither side would contest the extraordinary integrity of Plamenatz's enterprise, or deny the spirit of patient truth-telling which informs his examination of classical writers and texts. But the character of the enterprise is disputed. And that dispute itself throws light on the period of 'regrouping'.

Up to a point *both* views of Plamenatz's work are correct. His relationship to his own age and its intellectual currents was two-sided. Plamenatz reacted against some trends, but was deeply and permanently influenced by others. By looking both at the character of his *œuvre* and at his account of how he understood political theory as an activity, we can begin to understand some of the currents which have shaped political theory since the 1930s.

Perhaps the first thing to notice is the absence of any major *new* ideology, the extent to which disputes about values and concepts could still be placed within a framework of inherited ideologies—notably, Conservatism, Liberalism, and Socialism, which had been bequeathed to the twentieth century by the nineteenth. Of course, refinements within those ideologies took place, variations emerged, and the implications, both theoretical and institutional, of these ideologies were traced further than before. But the lack of any major new ideology—which may in itself have contributed to discussions about the 'end' of ideology in the 1960s—was a striking fact. No doubt, to be fully understood, that fact would have to be related to economic trends as well as political events. But it must also be placed against a specifically intellectual background. Now, arguably, the two most important features of that background in the Anglo-American world were the professionalizing of intellectual life and the prestige of the natural sciences.

The increasing division of labour in the intellectual world paralleled, of course, developments in society at large. But that did not make the effect of professionalizing any less important. Perhaps the most obvious consequence of the professionalizing of intellectual life was the felt need for those who thought and wrote to have a 'subject' or a 'field'—an area of concern which could be clearly marked out and contrasted with the areas 'covered' by other subjects. That search for a *raison d'être*, as much institutional as intellectual, powerfully reinforced interest in methodology in the academic world. The search was, moreover, made more urgent by the apparent success of the natural sciences in identifying their province, in holding up a method which yielded undoubted results. 'Method' therefore seemed to be the key to content, the guarantee of results. Positivism—in the sense of a philosophical standpoint that took an empiricist account of explanation in the natural sciences to be definitive, and then held up this account as a paradigm for knowledge generally—became an academic force to conjure with by the 1930s and 1940s. It began to leave a mark on the study of politics, creating strong pressures for a more quantitative and model-based discipline of 'political science'. At the same time it induced philosophers to redefine their role, as one of clarifying and defining the concepts which would then be used in the construction of positive science. The impact of this redefinition on political philosophy could be seen in the work of writers such as Weldon, who, in *The Vocabulary of Politics* (1953), saw his task as one of eliminating the verbal muddles which hindered the progress of positive political science.[4]

These two tendencies—the professionalizing of intellectual life and the impact of the natural scientific model on both social science and philosophy—form the backdrop against which Plamenatz's career at Oxford must be set. One of the reasons why his work is so interesting, and why examining that *œuvre* throws so much light on the emergence of political theory, now becomes apparent. Plamenatz strongly resisted the professionalizing trends at work, while at the same time accepting a philosophical position that regarded social science, interpreted in a positivist manner, as relatively unproblematic. Hence his writing displays two contrasting features. On the one hand, he disliked the move into professional jargon, a move towards 'special' languages which

[4] T. D. Weldon, *The Vocabulary of Politics* (Harmondsworth, Penguin, 1953).

might serve the interests not so much of truth as of the 'profession'. The standard of clarity and simplicity that he set himself was drawn from a much earlier period, especially from French writers of the 'great' seventeenth century, writers such as Pascal. The idea that political theorizing should continue to be an activity in which one man talks to another—in which that man looks deeply into himself as well as at the world around him—informed his writings more and more. He detested the pretentious. On the other hand, Plamenatz took it for granted that science itself was a relatively straightforward undertaking. He also assumed, as we shall shortly see, that there were no radical difficulties in applying the scientific model of explanation to the social world. In that sense, Plamenatz's work and conception of his own activity rested on a point of view that contained an element of positivism.

The grip of positivism on the social sciences has since been greatly weakened. This is due in part to the important debate about social explanation which Peter Winch, drawing on the later Wittgenstein, helped to create with his book *The Idea of a Social Science*.[5] That debate involved drawing a more careful distinction between explanation in terms of rules or reasons and causal explanation, as well as raising the important question whether, in certain circumstances, 'reasons' may also count as 'causes'. It helped to undermine the positivist view that the terms in which social activity is to be explained are external to that activity itself—in the extreme version, behaviourism, the social scientist's subject-matter is taken to be observable behaviour which can be identified without reference to intentions or beliefs. By contrast, the critics of positivism drew attention to the fact that ideas and beliefs play a constituent role in social life—that the identity of actions and practices depends upon the intentions of the agents concerned —and inferred that a social scientist's explanation of any human activity must begin from the participants' own understanding of their conduct, even if eventually going beyond it.

What is fascinating about Plamenatz's writings, viewed over his entire career, is that he moved steadily towards that view *de facto*— without fully revising his earlier view of the nature of political theory as an activity. Thus, his work became ever subtler, and was free of any trace of reductionism by the time of *Man and Society*—informed,

[5] P. Winch, *The Idea of a Social Science* (London, Routledge and Kegan Paul, 1958).

that is, by a sharp sense of the social nature of man, and of what we have called the constituent role of ideas. None the less, he still clung to the possibility of a value-free social science, and spoke of science as if the model of explanation thrown up by physics in the seventeenth century, and elaborated by empiricist philosophy since the eighteenth, did not need significant amendment to be applied in an appropriate way to the social world. In that sense, he broke with positivism in practice, while at the same time continuing to embrace certain tenets of positivism philosophically.

That admixture of positivism emerges most clearly on those rare occasions when he chose to explain and defend political theory as an activity.[6] Writing at a time when linguistic philosophy and empirical political science were still the dominant modes of enquiry in departments of philosophy and politics respectively, he avoided a direct confrontation with either school. He did not dispute that political concepts should be analysed philosophically; and he allowed that it was possible, in principle, to study politics in an empirical and value-free way. He believed it sufficient to say (in defence of his own activity) that there was another form of thought, distinct from analytical philosophy and from political science, that was both intellectually respectable and of great importance to human beings. Its purpose was to enable them to understand their place in the world, and thereby to help them decide which rules should govern their future conduct. Plamenatz called this form of thought 'practical philosophy', and regarded political theory as one of its main components. He claimed that practical philosophy met needs which neither philosophy in the technical sense nor science was able to meet, and he implied that it could not be reduced to ideology or to the mere expression of preferences as to how men should live.

For several reasons, the form of this defence is of great significance. Consider how much Plamenatz conceded to his opponents. Although he dismissed exaggerated claims made for conceptual analysis, he allowed that 'at the moment, because political thinkers still use ambiguous concepts, the careful analysis of these concepts is still needed to show that many traditional problems are spurious,

---

[6] See especially J. P. Plamenatz, 'The Use of Political Theory', *Political Studies*, 8 (1960), 37–47, reprinted in A. Quinton (ed.), *Political Philosophy* (London, Oxford University Press, 1967) (page references to the reprinted version); and Plamenatz, *Man and Society*, Introduction.

arising only because the men who put them have fallen victims to the confusions and intricacies of language.'[7] In granting this he did not make it clear whether the concepts central to traditional political theory can be fully understood through the kind of analysis proposed by linguistic philosophers. He observed that the concepts in question were ambiguous, but he did not ask whether the ambiguity was of the familiar kind that can be eliminated by careful definition and attention to the use of terms, or whether it might not be more recalcitrant, arising from the fact that such concepts take on different shapes in different political traditions. Thus, he did not reject 'ordinary language' as a sufficient basis for analysis. He accepted the linguistic philosopher's own definition of his task, as an under-labourer who tidies up political discourse without needing to engage in substantive political argument: whereas if political concepts are more deeply ambiguous in the way just suggested, the philosopher who wishes to give a full account of any of them must explore their relations with different points of view or ideologies, and probably also abandon the veil of political neutrality if he wishes to defend a preferred conception. In the latter case the division between political philosopher and political theorist would be eroded if not dissolved.

Furthermore, although Plamenatz insisted that political science as understood by his contemporaries could not replace political theory—since unlike the latter it was unable to provide men with practical guidance—he also largely accepted the political scientists' own description of their role. Indeed, in one of his later books, *Ideology*, he argued at length against the thesis that the social sciences are inescapably value-laden in a way that the natural sciences are not. He allowed that the terms in which social behaviour was explained necessarily changed as society itself changed; he admitted too that many of the concepts used for explanatory purposes had, in fact, both descriptive and evaluative functions. But none of this meant that the social sciences could not be value-neutral and objective. For 'thought is objective where there are definite, consistent and relevant criteria of truth or probability which it satisfies; it is value-free when it describes or explains without passing value judgements, overtly or covertly. Thought about human behaviour, merely because this behaviour is purposeful and

[7] Plamenatz, 'The Use of Political Theory', p. 22.

is often affected by how men think about it, and often gives effect or expression to judgements of value, is not thereby precluded from being objective and value-free.'[8] Changes in the language of social explanation did not mean that the criteria of explanation changed as well: moreover the fact that the words used to explain social behaviour often had, in other contexts, both descriptive and evaluative roles did not imply that they could never be used descriptively without also being used to pass value-judgements. Thus the social sciences, although more likely than the natural sciences to be influenced by the value-stances of their practitioners, could, at least in principle, emancipate themselves from this influence and become entirely descriptive and explanatory in nature.

The danger of these concessions, which in effect sharply separate the formal study of political concepts from the empirical study of political life, is that political theory will be left without the requisite intellectual credentials. Plamenatz himself was at pains to argue that political theory was not merely free-floating speculation or the expression of personal feelings. Practical philosophies, he said, 'should aim at self-consistency and at taking account of the facts'; again, 'political theory . . . is not fantasy or the parading of prejudices; nor is it an intellectual game. Still less is it linguistic analysis. It is an elaborate, rigorous, difficult and useful undertaking . . . it must be systematic, self-consistent and realistic.'[9] These remarks suggest that he had in mind criteria which political theory must satisfy, even though he did not spell them out explicitly. What is now striking is that the criteria which are hinted at in these passages—logical consistency, empirical adequacy, and theoretical scope—are precisely those acknowledged in analytical political philosophy and in empirical social science. Thus the intellectual credentials of political theory, assuming it to have some, are no different from those belonging to the disciplines from which Plamenatz allowed it to be separated. This suggests that a satisfactory defence of political theory must involve a reassessment of the claims made on behalf of analytical political philosophy and social or political science.

Let us consider analytical political philosophy first. The relevant claim here is that political concepts can be analysed in a formal

---

[8]J. P. Plamenatz, *Ideology* (London, Pall Mall, 1970), p. 65.
[9]Plamenatz, 'The Use of Political Theory', p. 29.

manner, that is without introducing either empirical evidence or any evaluative commitments. It is assumed, for instance, that the formal question 'what does "democracy" mean?' can be separated both from the empirical question 'How may the ideals of democracy be realized?' and from the evaluative question 'Why is democracy valuable?'. But this assumption is open to challenge.[10] The concepts used in political argument are typically contestable concepts, in the sense that each may be interpreted in a variety of incompatible ways without manifest absurdity. Such contests cannot be resolved by formal means. There is no unequivocal 'ordinary use of language' to which appeal can be made to settle disputes about the meaning of a term like 'democracy'. Instead we find that any given speaker's use of the term depends on that speaker's overall political outlook—on the meanings he attaches to other terms, and on his political commitments. Thus, establishing a preferred meaning for such a term involves engaging in substantive political argument, bringing forward both empirical evidence and moral principle to justify the general perspective to which the preferred meaning corresponds. This does not imply that there is no such intellectual activity as 'analysing political concepts': but it does imply that the boundary between political philosophy (if the term is reserved for this activity) and political theory is extremely porous, consisting at most in a difference of emphasis. It also implies that the criteria employed in political philosophy are by no means purely formal: questions about the moral acceptability and empirical realism of proposed political arrangements intrude upon the business of conceptual clarification.

Next let us consider social science. Plamenatz's account of political theory was developed against a view of social science as a descriptive and explanatory activity, whose theoretical claims were judged by their success or failure in accounting for observed social phenomena. Although, on this view, a social scientist's moral and political preferences might influence his choice of subject for research, his explanatory claims themselves would be value-neutral; they would neither be influenced by, nor would they influence, his political standpoint. The challenge to this view stems from two connected observations. First, contrary to the thesis of

[10] For more detailed criticism, see David Miller, 'Linguistic Philosophy and Political Theory', below.

value-neutrality, the explanatory framework adopted by a social scientist has what Charles Taylor calls a 'value-slope'; meaning that, although it does not strictly entail any prescriptive conclusion about the kind of social and political order that should be realized, it does *support* such conclusions.[11] It does so because each framework embodies a certain view of human needs and potentialities. This in turn limits the range of political possibilities—many conceivable states of affairs are ruled out immediately by adopting the framework—while, of those that remain in play, some will appear better than others at meeting human needs as identified by the framework. By this means the positivists' radical separation of facts and values is called into question. Second, the choice between alternative explanatory frameworks cannot be made entirely on empirical grounds. For several reasons, some unique to the social sciences, others shared with the natural sciences, a given body of evidence can be accommodated by alternative theories without providing decisive support for any one of them. This does not mean that there is no progress in social science, or that no theory is ever finally discredited by the evidence, but it suggests that at any moment there may well be several theoretical frameworks competing to explain any given set of facts.

Taking these two observations together, we are led to the conclusion that the theoretical position adopted by a social scientist must be value-related, inasmuch as it supports a political standpoint of a particular kind, while its choice is not wholly dictated by the evidence to hand. This is not to say that every social scientist has political considerations consciously in mind when developing his theoretical position; he may be a-political, or he may believe, under the influence of a positivist philosophy of social science, that his political commitments are completely independent of his explanatory framework. The point is rather that the two-way link between explanatory framework and political standpoint means both that evaluative criteria may influence theory-construction in the social sciences, and that these sciences always have implications for practical questions of political conduct which go beyond the selection of the optimum means to previously chosen ends. The distinction between social science, whose function is descriptive

[11] C. Taylor, 'Neutrality in Political Science' in P. Laslett and W. G. Runciman (eds.), *Philosophy, Politics and Society*, Third Series (Oxford, Blackwell, 1967).

and/or explanatory, and political theory, whose function is practical, is thereby eroded. Instead, we may think in terms of a spectrum of theoretical activity, at one end of which stand those practitioners whose aim is to account for a body of evidence without much theoretical elaboration, and at the other end of which stand sophisticated theorists whose contact with empirical evidence is indirect, and whose chief interest lies in developing or revising normative theory.

This reconsideration of the character of analytical political philosophy and of social science bears out Plamenatz's suggestion that political theory is not to be distinguished from these other activities by the criteria of truth that it employs; but it does so without leaving political theory in the position of a poor relation. Since formal criteria are not sufficient in political philosophy, and empirical criteria are not sufficient in social science, it is no disgrace that political theorists use a complex mixture of empirical, formal, and evaluative criteria in developing their positions. At the same time, it is clear that political theory cannot be insulated from these other branches of enquiry. It both contributes to, and borrows from, analytical political philosophy and social science. Indeed we have suggested that the boundaries drawn between these three forms of intellectual activity are conventional in character, representing a convenient academic division of labour, but no clear-cut differences of method.

The account of political theory that we have just sketched goes beyond Plamenatz's. Yet this account often consorts better with his own practice as a political theorist than the one which he gave in the very different intellectual climate of the early 1960s. For one of the motifs that runs throughout his work—it is especially prominent in *Man and Society*—is the idea that man's nature is shaped by his social relationships, while those relationships in turn are shaped—indeed partly constituted—by men's beliefs about themselves. It was the presence of this idea in the thought of Rousseau, Hegel, and Marx, and its relative absence in Hobbes, Locke, and the English utilitarians, that eventually drew Plamenatz to speak with greater warmth of thinkers whose political sympathies were at times far removed from his own than of those with whom he had more in common politically. But the idea has profound consequences both for the philosophy of social explanation and for the analysis of social and political concepts. If beliefs play a constituent role in social relationships, how can a theoretical understanding of those relationships fail to have some effect—either supportive or subversive—on the relationships themselves? And how, in turn, is it possible to dissect ideas without understanding the social practices which they help to constitute? Plamenatz's work shows him to have been fully aware of this. Here, for instance, we find him chiding Marx for failing to take sufficient account of the difference between man's understanding of nature and his understanding of the social world:

In coming to understand society and in learning to control it, man recognizes it as a system of human activities in which he expresses what he is. He rises to a full understanding of what is involved in being human as he learns to understand and control his social environment. The activities that enlarge his understanding of society also enlarge his understanding of nature, but his understanding of society is related to his self-knowledge, and to his aims and the pursuit of them, in ways that his understanding of nature is not. His beliefs about society affect his behaviour in ways that his beliefs about mere nature do not; they affect his image of himself more directly. They are also more quickly changing and less easily defined.[12]

The insight contained in this passage accurately reflects Plamenatz's mature work. It also provides a better starting-point for political theory generally than his explicit discussions of method.

The essays that follow continue the methodological discussion that we have begun in this introduction. They also display political theory in practice, either in the form of an examination of concepts and principles or in the form of a critical dialogue with some political thinkers from the past. The first pair of papers, which are explicitly methodological, bring out two respects in which political theory as we have defined it is an indispensable activity. Alasdair MacIntyre suggests that political theories are essentially more systematic versions of the interpretive schemes that ordinary men and women use to make sense of their social surroundings. That being so, he maintains, explanations of historical events cannot be provided without at least implicit reliance on a political theory, the claims of empirical historians notwithstanding. David Miller examines the claim that political concepts can be analysed by

---

[12] Plamenatz, *Karl Marx's Philosophy of Man*, p. 79.

attention to the ordinary use of language. He argues that disputes over the use of political terms are simultaneously conceptual and substantive, and can only be resolved by taking up and defending a political standpoint. These papers reinforce the argument developed above that neither a wholly formal political philosophy nor a wholly empirical or 'value-free' social science is a coherent project.

The papers in the second group use particular concepts to explore methodological issues in political theory. Larry Siedentop argues that recent uses of the concept of 'the state' reveal the unacknowledged presence of an ideology, individualism. Contrary to a widespread view, the state is not equivalent to government as such, but is only one species of government. Equally the individual is only one type of social role. The concepts 'state' and 'individual' emerged together, and require one another. Siedentop suggests that political theorists may avoid the ideological contamination involved in universalizing terms such as these by developing a keener sense of the way in which concepts are embedded in traditions of thought, and ultimately in forms of social life. John Gray and Steven Lukes both deal, in different ways, with the concept of power. Gray uses recent discussions of this idea (including Lukes's) as a means of analysing the claim that political concepts are 'essentially contestable'. He finds that this thesis obscures the fact that conceptual disputes may have a number of different sources. His conclusion is that disagreements in social theory stem from philosophical differences and from the under-determination of theories by empirical evidence, rather than from the value-commitments which different theories bear. Lukes, by contrast, uses the contestability of the concept of power to defend Plamenatz's critique of historical materialism against an argument developed by G. A. Cohen. Cohen has suggested that the 'problem of legality'—the problem, for Marxists, of describing a society's economic base without invoking normative elements that properly belong in the superstructure—can be solved by specifying the base entirely in terms of powers. Lukes replies, in general, that all ascriptions of powers are theory- and therefore value-dependent, and, in particular, that those powers which themselves arise from the existence of norms cannot be identified without reference to their parent norms.

The third group of papers address themselves to particular

concepts, but do so in a way that emphasizes the connection between the analysis of concepts and substantive political issues. Brian Barry asks how, on individualist principles, the boundaries of states should be determined. An answer requires both a careful dissection of the various claims advanced by nationalists, and an analysis of different conceptions of individual interests. Barry's conclusion is that, starting from individualist premises, a good deal more can be said in defence of nationalism than is usually conceded, particularly if individuals are permitted to have interests in posthumous states of affairs. Peter Jones shows how disputes over the meaning of 'democracy' are connected with different justifications of democracy as a procedure for making decisions. He looks particularly at justifications which refer to the value of political equality, and then points out that, on this basis, there are serious objections to the system of majority rule, which is often assumed to be the only practical method of implementing democracy. He suggests that we should look instead for decision procedures that give each person an equal chance of having his interests satisfied. Geoffrey Marshall exposes the complexity of the notion of a rule— of what it means for a rule to exist or for someone to follow a rule—and uses his analysis to rehabilitate the model of law as a system of rules. Recent attacks on this model, he suggests, have interpreted the notion far too rigidly: in particular, the contrast that Dworkin has drawn between rules and principles becomes questionable once the elasticity of the former term is recognized.

Finally, we have two papers on three political thinkers about whom Plamenatz thought and wrote a great deal. Alan Ryan argues that Hobbes's political theory was less illiberal than is usually believed, in the sense that there is nothing in that theory which requires that private beliefs be controlled by the sovereign, and indeed a good deal to suggest that attempts at control would be unsuccessful. Robert Wokler asks what Marx might have learnt from Rousseau if (contrary to the evidence) he had read him carefully. He suggests that Marx might have come to understand, first, that men's ideas play a larger part in their productive and economic life than he recognized, and, second, that moral ideals are not merely the by-products of social change, but to a significant extent its driving force. Plamenatz would have been deeply sympathetic to both suggestions, and this paper, like all those collected here, attests to the continuing influence of his work on political theory in the 1980s.

The Indispensability of Political Theory*

Alasdair MacIntyre

Vanderbilt University

I

'Man, being rational and capable of self-knowledge, puts to himself two sorts of questions, and science answers only one of them. The sort of question which science answers he puts both of himself and of what is external to him; but the sort which science does not answer he puts only of himself or of creatures whom he believes to be in his own condition.' (*Man and Society* (London, Longman, 1963), vol. 1, p. xxi). Questions of the latter kind, on John Plamenatz's view, include the questions of political theory. And not only can science not answer them, neither can analytical philosophy. None the less they are not questions that can be waived or put permanently on one side. 'A hostile or perverse critic' may try to reduce the exercise of framing such theories to 'a statement of preferences or a laying down of rules or a defining of goals . . . and a whole lot of verbiage besides', but it may be pointed out to such a critic that 'it is perhaps a kind of verbiage in which he himself indulges when, momentarily, he forgets his opinions about it.' This inescapable character of political theorizing arises from the fact that it is one of the key activities by which man satisfies 'a need to "place" himself in the world . . . to take his own and the world's measure. This need is not met by science.' And it is not met by morality either, for human beings need a conception of the world and their place in it which will connect their morality with the nature of things. The thinker who understood this best, on Plamenatz's view, was Pascal, not at all because, as he always hastened to add both in his writings and in conversation, Pascal was a Christian. A modern secular thinker could, however, do no better than model himself upon Pascal (*Man and Society*, vol. 1, p. xxi and vol. 2, p. 457: my confidence that this is the view being expressed derives from more than one conversation with John Plamenatz).

*© Alasdair MacIntyre 1983.

17

Political theorizing is thus, on Plamenatz's view, an exemplification of the project of metaphysical self-knowledge. His defence of this project in the passages from which I have quoted was directed to what he took to be the hostile criticisms of 'analytic philosophy', an unsurprising stance to anyone who recalls the intellectual climate in Oxford in the nineteen fifties and sixties. But had he considered instead or as well the dominant attitudes of historians to political theory, the need for a defence of the project would have been quite as evident. Professional academic historians are notoriously suspicious of philosophies of history; and many political theories are or include just such philosophies. For where the philosopher of history looks for—and sometimes claims to find—patterns, generalizations, regular and determined development, the historian continually insists upon discovering the contingent, the irregular, the breakdown of pattern. Some academic historians do of course profess political theories or philosophies of history; Buckle, Bury, Beard, and Butterfield have their contemporary counterparts. But it is important to remark that the standing of historians *qua* historians in the academic community of their peers is based on considerations which disregard this fact; even the best of Marxist historians are usually evaluated by their colleagues as historians in a way designed to exclude consideration of them as Marxists. Moreover the compartmentalization of the conventional academic curriculum tends to assign Machiavelli and Hobbes and Rousseau and Hegel to one set of historical narratives and the Medici and Thomas Cromwell and Oliver Cromwell and Robespierre to another, in such a way that the history of ideas is presented with a minimum of political context and the history of politics as largely devoid of theoretical content. Both these characteristics of the professionalization of academic history are reinforced by the successful polemics conducted by Pieter Geyl and J. H. Hexter against the use made of particular philosophies of history. The dominant forms of contemporary historical understanding and those of theoretical or philosophical understanding coexist with at best lack of sympathy, at worse active mutual antagonism.

The professional historian can afford to regard this situation with some complacency; the political theorist and the philosopher of history cannot. For the latter are professionally bound to yield to the historian's findings in a way that apparently need not be reciprocated. Since the claims of the political theorist and of the philosopher of history do have empirical content and empirical consequences—for they are characteristically claims to the effect that the motives for striving after and the effects of obtaining power are of some specific kind (Machiavelli and Hobbes) or that projects of a certain kind are bound to fail (Burke) or to succeed (Marx) or that rationality in history emerges in certain specific forms (Hegel) —they are always open to at least prima-facie refutation by the empirical findings of the historian, even if the falsification of such theories is always in the end a complex matter. Consequently the serious political theorist always has to be concerned not only with the internal coherence of the theories which are his or her specific subject-matter, but also with the truth or falsity of a variety of historical claims about motives, institutions, and forms of development. Thus the serious political theorist must also *be* to greater or lesser degree a historian and the tension between the generalizing tasks of theory and respect for the particular contingencies which emerge from the study of history has to become internal to the study of political theory.

What I am going to argue in this paper is that if we are to allow this tension its due place in the studies which constitute political theory, then we shall have to recognize that history is more than a source of negative and falsifying constraints upon the theorist. We shall have to insist that the practice of history itself requires much more in the way of a relationship to theory than professional academic historians are apt or anxious to recognize. For in the practice of even the most implacably anti-theoretical historians, so I shall argue, there has to remain an implicit, even if unacknowledged, reference to philosophical theory. One fundamental reason why this is so is that historians, like those whom they write about, are human beings; and human beings, as John Plamenatz never allowed us to forget, are incurably theoretical and philosophical in their reflection upon themselves. It is therefore worth enquiring at the outset, even if in a manner that is necessarily too brief and compressed, in what way this is so.

II

Every society is constituted by members whose behaviour embodies a set of beliefs about the workings of that particular society: how individuals are to be classified and ranked, who owes what to whom under what circumstances, what the consequences are likely to be of breaking rather than keeping different types of rule. Those beliefs may be more or less systematic, and the more systematic that they become the more closely they approach the condition of a theory. It is of course rare for the ordinary members of a society to think of themselves as holding a *theory* about the social life which they enact in their everyday behaviour. But on the rare occasions when some of those about whom an anthropologist has written read the anthropologist's account and compare it with their own beliefs about how and why they do what they do, and on the somewhat more numerous occasions on which those who inhabit particular types of institution in advanced societies—industrial firms, universities, trade unions, hospitals—read theoretical accounts by sociologists or economists of how and why they do what they do, the ordinary members of a society become aware, sometimes uncomfortably aware, of the extent to which their own theory as to how and why they behave and the social scientist's theory of why and how they behave are rival and incompatible theories about one and the same subject-matter.

That there should be discrepancies between the theory of a given social order embodied in the behaviour of one particular individual and the theory of that same social order advanced in explicit and theoretically articulated terms by an observer is unsurprising for at least three different kinds of reason. The first is that although what constitutes the social order as an order, rather than a chaos, is the degree to which the theories embodied in the behaviour of different individuals overlap with each other and are compatible in such a way as to integrate the activities of each into the activities of all (if your understanding of what I am doing and of what you are doing does not to some degree match my understanding of what you are doing and what I am doing, then we will not be able to interact in an intelligible way), none the less there will always be discrepancies, discrepancies arising from the different vantage points from which the social order is viewed as well as from social conflicts. The views of social class taken by a duke, his butler, and the man who collects his rubbish will differ in significant ways; the view of urban–rural differences taken in the countryside is apt to differ from that taken in the town. The social scientific observer by contrast seeks to produce not a partial and one-sided theory of the social order, but one designed to overcome partiality and one-sidedness by presenting a view of the social order as a whole.

A second difference arises from the fact that the theories of the social scientific observer are apt to be constrained by the conventions of the curriculum to a degree not always recognized by the social scientist himself or herself. What the economist picks out as significant will not be the same as what the political scientist fastens on; anthropologists bring a professionally informed vision of social life to their field-work which is not the same as that which informs the observations and experiments of social psychologists. This second type of difference contrasts interestingly with the first, for here the partiality and one-sidedness are apt to belong to the social scientific observer rather than to those whom he or she studies. And this is so not only because of the different perspectives of the various social scientific professions, but also because the theory of society embodied in the behaviour of the inhabitants of a social order characteristically has dimensions excluded to greater or lesser degree by every kind of social scientific professionalism. For a social order is generally understood by those who inhabit it as standing in certain relationships to nature and to the divine. Nature is understood as providing some particular kind of environment, a source of fears, threats, and hopes, of material for enjoyment or domination or awe; the divine is either an important part of the natural and social orders, altogether distinct from either or both, or absent or non-existent. Ordinary members of almost all societies are metaphysicians in their implicit and explicit theorizing, a luxury which the Western academic tradition denies to social scientists.

Thirdly the theoretical constructions of the social scientist are of course just that: theoretical constructions explicitly spelled out in whatever idiom may be intellectually and professionally appropriate. But the theories which inform the behaviour of the ordinary member of a social order are often tacit and at best partially articulated schemes of thought and action, providing a set of maxims which are simultaneously instructions for interpreting the behaviour of others and prescriptions as to how to behave oneself if one's actions are to be susceptible of some particular interpretation. I have already suggested one reason why we should none the less think of such schemes as *theories*—their more or less systematic character. And to this I now want to add two other perhaps more important reasons. The first is that the ascriptions of actions and passions to others which are warranted by such everyday schemes of thought and action always in an important way go beyond the evidence provided by the bare observation of behaviour. And they must so outrun the evidence if they are to provide the kind of characterization of the actions of others which will enable us to respond to those actions in what we ourselves do and say.

Consider three different possible characterizations of one and the same segment of behaviour: 'His finger pressed against the trigger, the revolver went off and John fell down dead'; 'He shot John with the revolver'; 'He murdered John.' The first lists three successive events, but ascribes no causality. The second ascribes causality, but imputes no intention; its truth is compatible with the truth either of 'He killed John accidentally' or of 'He killed John in self-defence' and so with the falsity of the third characterization. It is only at this third level of characterization that we find a type of action description on the basis of which others can judge what type of response on their part to what happened is appropriate. And that is to say, it is only by characterizing the social life around us in terms of the intentions embodied in it and their effectiveness or ineffectiveness in producing either intended or unintended changes in that life —including changes in the intentions of others and in the effectiveness of *those* intentions—that we are able to find in that social life matter for our own intentional responses.

Such characterization requires that we go beyond the evidence afforded by the observation of the externals of behaviour in at least two ways. The thoughts and feelings which are partially constitutive of many of our intentions are often not manifest in the behaviour which is the expression of those intentions, and sometimes at least this is the result of an additional intention to disguise or withhold some of our intentions. And moreover the question of whether a particular intention was or was not effective in making it the case that someone did what he or she did can often only be answered by making a claim about the truth of some counterfactual conditional. For to assert of someone that they did or are doing such-and-such because it is their intention to do so-and-so always implies that they would not have done or be doing such-and-such if it were not their intention to do so-and-so. (This is too simple, for we need to add some clause to the effect that they might still have done such and such *if* some other causal agency had operated to that effect. Happily for my present purposes all that I need to note is that, however that type of clause is worded, the commitment to the truth of some set of counterfactual conditionals remains.)

It is these two features of our characterizations of the actions of

others which give point to the assertion that at the level of characterization which enables us to respond to the actions of others—that is,
at the level of characterization which makes all social transactions
possible—we are inevitably engaged in a task of theoretical interpretation. But where there has to be interpretation, there always
arises the possibility of rival, incompatible interpretations. And
indeed a good deal of social life is constituted by the coexistence and
sometimes the conflict of such interpretations.

It is important to notice that our systematic interpretations of the
actions of others and of the transactions in which we ourselves are
involved are not and cannot be neutral with respect to the solutions
of certain well-established philosophical problems. The relationship of intentionality to causality, the role of intention in the
constitution of action, the types of reasoning appropriate for
supporting counterfactual claims, and the nature of our knowledge
of other minds are all recurrent topics in the journals of professional
academic philosophy. Thus the everyday activity and experience of
plain men and women presupposes the truth of certain philosophical theses in these particular problem areas and the falsity of
others, even although this often goes unrecognized; and when such
everyday activity and experience is partially constituted by rival
and contested interpretations, one source of such conflicts is the
coexistence of rival philosophical presuppositions.

I am going to suggest that political theories are, by and large,
articulate, systematic, and explicit versions of the unarticulated,
more or less systematic and implicit interpretations, through which
plain men and women understand this experience of the actions of
others in a way that enables them to respond to it in their own
actions. If this is so, then the force of John Plamenatz's remarks
which I quoted at the outset becomes immediately clear. For if there
is any substance to my suggestion, then political theory is indeed
just the central kind of human activity that Plamenatz took it to be.
Moreover the grounds for disagreement with the kind of analytic
philosophy which Plamenatz identified as one of the antagonists of
classical political theory also becomes clear. One of the central
theses of that particular kind of analytic philosphy was that the
philosopher is a second-order commentator on 'ordinary language'
and the sciences. The ordinary language user is thus portrayed as
essentially a pre-philosophical being whose common-sense beliefs
are innocent of the sophistications of theory.

This was never plausible. The remark that common sense is

always the graveyard of past philosophical theories encapsulates part of the case against it; and my present argument supplements that remark, by suggesting that the ordinary agent is able to act in relation to others only because he has theoretical and philosophical commitments of the same kind as those expressed in classical political theory. This is most evident on the occasions when the political theorist articulates his systematic views in the course of his political activity and when therefore the theorist's interpretations and consequent actions are matched against the interpretations and consequent actions of those ordinary non-theoretically-minded agents who are caught up in the same set of political transactions. To turn therefore to an example of the theorist as political agent may help to lend force to an argument which, it may be rightly complained, has been too brief, schematic, compressed, and in consequence oversimplified. Before I offer such an example, however, it is necessary to make one further point.

When rival interpretations of one and the same set of actions and transactions become available, they characteristically become available after the event as rival narratives of those happenings. Before and during the event they function as dramatic scripts in terms of which each person understands both his or her own role and that of others; and as the drama is more and more fully enacted, those who persist in their allegiance to rival and conflicting interpretations necessarily tell different and incompatible tales of what has occurred. The disagreements embodied in such conflicts of interpretation are of course compatible with a wide range of agreement in the characterization of events at the level of what I have called the observation of the externals of behaviour. Who married whom on what day, the sentences uttered in someone's oration and the numbers of the units engaged in a battle, the size of the crowd and whether it rained or not: every party may well be able to agree on all of these points without mitigating the conflict of their interpretations to any degree at all.

To illustrate my thesis I need therefore to show how rival political theories have on some particular occasion functioned as articulate and systematic versions of the rival interpretative standpoints of ordinary men and women, in such a way as to function either as rival dramatic scripts before and during the event or as rival justificatory narratives after it. To this task I therefore turn.

III

The great events of history are rarely staged with an eye to the convenience of political theorists. What happened in France, and more especially in Paris, from February 1848 to December 1951 is exceptional in the number of theorists who were at or near the centre of events. Marx, who had been expelled from France by Guizot's government in 1845, returned to Paris at the invitation of Ferdinand Flocon, a member of the revolutionary government, in March 1848. He left for Cologne in June, but returned to Paris in June 1849, where he stayed until his departure for London in late August. He published *The Eighteenth Brumaire of Louis Bonaparte* in German in the second number of Joseph Weydemeyer's review *Die Revolution*, published in New York in 1852. Proudhon helped build barricades in Paris in February 1848, was elected to the Constituent Assembly in June, and supported the workers after the June days in his newspaper, *La Représentant du Peuple*. The newspaper was closed down and later Proudhon was imprisoned, but he managed to write not only his *Confessions of a Revolutionary*, but also *The General Idea of the Revolution in the Nineteenth Century*, which was published in 1851. Seven months after Louis Bonaparte's *coup d'état* he published *The Social Revolution Demonstrated by the Coup d'Etat*.

Alexis de Tocqueville was a member in turn of the Constituent Assembly and of the Legislative Assembly. From June to November 1849 he was Minister of Foreign Affairs in Odilon Barrot's Republican government. He remained a member of the Assembly and was imprisoned for two days after the *coup d'état*, but not before he had sent a letter of protest on behalf of his colleagues and himself to *The Times* in London. This letter was published on 11 December 1851. Walter Bagehot had been in Paris for several months before the *coup d'état*; his reports of and reflections on it—the first is dated 8 January 1852—appeared in an English Unitarian journal, *The Enquirer*.

Collect together four political theorists and the chances are that you will be presented with at least five rival interpretations of one and the same set of events. The events of 1848 to 1851 in France are no exception: for Marx, Tocqueville, and Bagehot each present us with a clear and distinctive view of events, while Proudhon presents us with two such views, in one of which Louis Napoleon is the subverter of the revolution, while in the other he is its potential leader. Of these five I shall concentrate attention on two only, that of Tocqueville and that of Marx. I shall do so in a way well designed, I hope, to bring out how each of these theories is an articulate version of just that kind of interpretation which everyone has to rely upon in his or her everyday social transactions. I shall try, that is, not only to show that each of them embodies some systematic method for interpreting the evidence of behaviour by ascribing intentions of a certain kind and by ascribing a certain kind of effectiveness or ineffectiveness to those intentions, but also that in so doing they are providing in their theories an explicit version of what ordinary non-theorizing participants in and observers of the very same events are providing in their actions, reactions, and transactions. It is very much to the point, of course, *both* that Marx and Tocqueville were themselves to varying degrees participants as well as theorists *and* that each aspired to represent in articulate form the point of view of some large body of participants. It is even more to the point that, at the level of what is available to the observation of what I have called the externals of behaviour, there is no significant or extensive disagreement between Marx and Tocqueville or between either of them and Proudhon or Bagehot as to what happened in France between 1848 and 1851. Disagreement arises at quite another level of characterization.

A central question to which Marx and Tocqueville address themselves is: why did an outcome which none of the original parties to the revolution of 1848 intended emerge in 1851? And since the answer to that question necessarily depends in part on what the intentions of the participants in the revolution of 1848 were, it is not surprising that the different answers to that question given by Marx and Tocqueville turn out to depend upon their different answers to the question of how the intentions of the participants are to be identified. It will clarify those differences if I first turn to consider two problems that characteristically arise whenever questions about the knowledge of intentions are raised.

The first is connected with the counterfactual claims associated with ascriptions of causal effectiveness to intentions. In many situations there are a number of equally truthful and appropriate answers to the question: 'What are you doing?' 'Digging the garden', 'Taking healthful exercise', 'Pleasing my wife', 'Making sure that we shall have vegetables in the summer'. An action at one level may be informed by a number of intentions. But these intentions may not all be equally powerful in the agent's life. It is only when we know the answers to such questions as 'Would you still be digging the garden if it did not please your wife, although you still believed it to be healthful exercise?' 'Would you still be digging the garden if it was cheaper to buy vegetables at the supermarket, although you still believed it pleased your wife?', and so on, that we are able to rank order the intentions that we ascribe in terms of causal effectiveness. And effective understanding of the behaviour of others always involves not only the ascription of intentions but also the role of these intentions in bringing it about that the agent acts in one way rather than in others.

Secondly short-term intentions are often nested within longer-term intentions. 'What are you doing?' 'Writing a sentence', 'Finishing a chapter', 'Completing my book', 'Trying to get tenure'. All these intentions clearly may be embodied in one and the same action. And effective understanding of the behaviour of others always involves understanding how and how far the short-term intentions of an agent are dependent for their existence and character upon his or her longer-term intentions.

When, therefore, someone sets out to decipher the intentions of those around him or her, he or she always has three types of question to answer: (i) What are they doing now? How many different intentions are embodied in their present behaviour?; (ii) If they had to choose to implement one rather than another of these intentions in a situation in which the implementation of both was or appeared to be impossible, which would be the dominant intention?; (iii) How do their present intentions relate to their longer-term intentions? What kind of bridge between a believed-in past and a projected future is their present intention? It was in the systematically different ways in which they answered these types of question, framed as specific questions about the major participants in the events of 1848 to 1851, that the systematically different political theories of Marx and Tocqueville—and indeed of Proudhon also—functioned as action-guiding interpretations of political transactions. Notice that *no one* could have participated in these events in an effective way without making practical judgements which would presuppose highly specific answers to all three types of question. Plamenatz was quite right in asserting that political theory is not an optional discipline for human beings.

Consider one particular episode. In May 1850 the party of

Order, the party of the monarchists, succeeded in having a law passed which, by requiring a particular kind of evidence of residence for voters, deprived a large minority of the electorate of the vote, while technically not violating the constitutional protection of universal adult male suffrage. When Louis Bonaparte as President agreed to this law, he did so in such a way as to make it appear that he had not foreseen or intended this outcome: 'all France', wrote F. A. Simpson, 'believed that the Royalists had tricked the President' (*Louis Napoleon and the Recovery of France, 1848–1856* (London, Longman, 1923), p. 95). Later, however, the Royalists came to believe that the President had in fact tricked them: that he had intended both the disfranchisement of three million voters, mostly peasants, *and* that that disfranchisement should appear to have been the work of the Royalists who had exploited his unsuspecting and innocent good will. 'They thought he would be a tool and a tool that they could break,' wrote Tocqueville of a similar earlier misjudgement; 'The folly of clever men is wonderful.' (*Correspondence and Conversations* (London, Henry S. King, 1872), vol. i, p. 195.) In November 1851 when Bonaparte restored universal suffrage he therefore appeared to have been its consistent friend. From the standpoint of the Royalists—as from that of almost all Republicans and Socialists—the story of Bonaparte is that of an unprincipled opportunist, whose overriding intention is to take power; from the standpoint of Bonaparte's apologists—Bagehot is an early example, but De Maupas in his *Mémoires* gives the semi-official Bonapartist view—Bonaparte appears as a principled lover of his country who is almost forced into taking power by *coup d'état* as a desparate remedy for the disorder produced by every other party. The partisans of the rival inter-pretation disagreed about the character of Bonaparte's actions precisely because they disagreed both about the character of his causally effective intentions at earlier and later stages and about the relationship of his short-term to his longer-term intentions.

I choose to begin with this episode because at first sight these particular rival ascriptions of intention may not seem to embody or presuppose any systematic theoretical standpoint. But we have only to notice the way in which both modes of ascription are incom-patible with that practised and defended by Marx to understand that there must be *some* tolerably systematic theoretical presupposi-tions at work. Both Royalists and Bonapartists agreed after all in believing that it was Bonaparte's intentions which were causally effective, that it was his agency which dictated events; their disagreements arose within the context of this agreement. It was Marx's fundamental thesis that Louis Bonaparte was an effect rather than a cause and that his success was an unintended consequence of the actions of others, actions which he interpreted very differently from either Royalists or Bonapartists, let alone from Tocqueville and Proudhon. In his introduction to the reprinted edition of the *Eighteenth Brumaire* in 1869 Marx wrote 'For my part, I prove that the class wars in France created circumstances and relationships that enabled a grotesque mediocrity to strut about in a hero's garb.'

The core of Marx's interpretation is his contention that in periods of bourgeois revolution, although men and women conceal from themselves their class roles and the way that their actions embody intentions intelligible only in the light of those roles, it is these latter intentions which are causally effective. The individual *qua* representative of the bourgeoisie characterizes what he does in terms of an ideological misrepresentation of himself: 'Thus Luther donned the mask of the Apostle Paul, the Revolution of 1789 to 1814 draped itself alternately as the Roman republic and the Roman empire, and the Revolution of 1848 knew nothing better than to parody, now 1789, now the revolutionary tradition of 1793 to 1795 . . .'. Hence there is a crucial difference between what individuals say about the meaning of their actions, to themselves as well as to others, and the real substance and effect of what they do. What such individuals treat as their own primary and effective intentions Marx takes to be secondary ideological disguise; what such individuals treat at first at least as merely incidental aspects of their actions Marx treats as the intentional substance of their basic, that is their class, roles. I say 'at first at least' because it is also Marx's contention that in the end individuals lose the need for such illusions. Bourgeois society comes to recognize itself for what it is: 'Wholly absorbed in the production of wealth and in peaceful competitive struggle, it no longer comprehended that ghosts from the days of Rome had watched over its cradle.'

The Revolution of 1848 in France had, however, created a quite new type of situation, one in which the bourgeoisie confront for the first time a rising and threatening proletariat in the face of whom they are prepared to hand over the powers of government to whomsoever will protect order and property, even to someone whose power involves the overthrow of their own elected political representatives. It is in fact Marx's thesis that the political role filled by Bonaparte after the *coup d'état* is one in which he must simultaneously represent and oppose the middle classes, and also one in which he must be the representative of 'the peasants and the people in general' *against* the middle classes. 'Bonaparte would like to appear as the patriarchal benefactor of all classes. But he cannot give to one class without taking from another.' Bonaparte thus has to become a political trickster, an opportunistic performer of conjuring tricks designed to conceal political realities. This is how circumstances and relationships 'enabled a gross mediocrity to strut about in a hero's garb'.

Louis Napoleon as a successful power-seeking individual is then intelligible only in the light of his relationships, especially those with the bourgeoisie who, in the course of seeking to protect their material economic power, sacrificed their political power to Bonaparte who 'looks on himself as the adversary of the political and literary power of the middle class. But by protecting its material power he generates its political power anew.' Thus Bonaparte's detailed intentions are intelligible and effective only as a response to the schism within the bourgeois character. And this schism derives from the contingently incompatible projects and intentions embodied in the class role of the bourgeoisie. Thus the bourgeoisie are essentially self-defeated and, given the contingent incompatibility of their political and their economic projects and the circumstances of 1848–51, things could scarcely have gone otherwise.

Whether they could indeed perhaps have gone otherwise was one of Tocqueville's central questions. By January 1851 he had already become highly pessimistic. But his pessimism was not rooted in any belief that the economic role of republicans would subvert their political intentions. It was rather that Tocqueville saw only a narrow prospect for what he called 'regulated liberty', a liberty whose enemies included both the revolutionary egalitarians of the Left and the autocratic ambitions of Louis Bonaparte. The parties in the Assembly 'failed to come to an understanding; this gave to the whole body an uncertain and sometimes contradictory policy' (Letter to *The Times*, 11 December, 1851). This contradictory character was rooted in the basic contradictions of the republican ideal, an unstable amalgam, as Tocqueville envisaged it, of the incompatible requirements of liberty and equality. Thus where Marx interprets the political intentions of the republicans as an ideological disguise, Tocqueville reads them as internally unstable. For Marx the explanation of the political is in the end to be found in the economic; for Tocqueville the explanation of the political is to be found in the political itself. Both see a schism within republicanism; but they locate it at very different points.

Thus according to Tocqueville—although he does not of course put it in any way remotely like this—a quite different set of counterfactuals is true of the republicans from that which Marx ascribes in deciphering their behaviour. According to Marx their economic role set limits to what the republicans could have done under *any* political circumstances; the only limits that Tocqueville identifies arise from a lack of clear political perceptions which a more adequate understanding and a firmer loyalty to regulated liberty might have provided. Thus Tocqueville's diagnosis warrants in retrospect a very different response to one and the same situation warranted by Marx's diagnosis; and this quite apart from —indeed it is logically prior to—the differences in their political ideals.

It is thus not too difficult to see that rival accounts and interpretations of political action at the day-to-day level are rooted in the rivalry of more comprehensive theories of human nature and action. There can then be no account of the events in France in 1848 to 1851 which is not theoretically committed at this more comprehensive level. For even if an empirically minded historian is dismissive of Marx *and* Tocqueville *and* Proudhon, he is at least committed, implicitly if not explicitly, to a set of negative theses about the nature and interpretation of human action at a more comprehensive level of theorizing. There is no way of characterizing the historical facts which is both theoretically neutral and capable of rendering the events thus characterized intelligible.

At once it may be remarked that the problem set us by the empirically minded historians has not been solved but only rendered more difficult of solution. For the negative theses to which the empirically minded historian finds himself committed may surely leave him without any systematic theoretical view of his own. His theoretical commitments may be and remain *only* negative.

To this, two very different kinds of response may be made. The first would be in a narrow way philosophical. Beginning perhaps from Spinoza's dictum that 'Omnis negatio est determinatio' an argument could be constructed to show that there are no purely and only negative theses in this area. All negations are the logical shadows cast by positive commitments. But, although I would be prepared to defend such a conclusion, I want here to consider another type of response, one that is a little closer to the historian's own immediate concerns.

IV

If the argument so far is correct, then ordinary agents are able to act politically and socially only in virtue of abilities to characterize their own actions and those of others in ways that presuppose, usually implicitly but sometimes explicitly, bodies of theory. The political theories which are expounded in the classical texts of academic political philosophy are, on the view that I have taken, articulate versions of the same type of theory, presented in a form which makes them available for rational criticism. But if this is so, then the political philosophies of the classical texts must share the crucial characteristic of the theories which are presupposed by the intentions of ordinary agents: they are maps which make it possible to move about in the political landscape with some hope of implementing one's intentions.

The metaphor of 'a map' may be instructive at this point. Maps can guide, indeed they can be the only rational resource available, even when they are and are known to be grossly inaccurate. The adventurous seamen of the late Middle Ages and the early modern age must often have survived on the basis of a map (sometimes in the form of a diagram and sometimes in the form of a description) itself grossly inaccurate, but continuously emended or added to by *ad hoc* corrections in this or that port. What is important to observe here is that the emendations and additions were only able to afford the guidance that they did in fact afford by being ancillary to the original map. Lacking that map, there would have been no focus, no way of organizing, often indeed no way of characterizing the items in the list of emendations and additions. And, that is to say, a false map may under certain conditions provide the rational agent with what is a great deal superior to no map at all. In this respect, I want to suggest, the metaphor of a map is illuminating with respect to political theories.

Consider the example of historians dealing with the English seventeenth century. There are two large-scale bodies of theory dealing with that time and place: the Whig account and the Marxist account. What most professional academic history concerned with this period in the last hundred years and more consists in is the accumulation of factual detail in a way which allows the professional historian to dissent from either or both views. But at once this very remark raises an interesting question: could the significance of the detail have emerged in the way that it has done, if it had been detached from its theory-falsifying context? More than one historian has remarked of Christopher Hill's Marxist treatment of the seventeenth century that it provides a 'model' for understanding the period, but a very inadequate guide in any depth. What this clearly implies is that the Marxist theory embodied in Hill's account is *both* false and illuminating. And it is, I think, a significant feature of political theories, as I have characterized them, that they may possess both these characteristics simultaneously.

It may well be, that is, that in a particular period the political landscape is such and the predicament of political agents within it is such that the honest, rational, and well-informed agent can only locate himself within the political landscape by means of a series of denials. But these denials have the significance for him that they have only because of the context provided by the theory or theories, of which they are denials. It follows that such theories, false even in large part as they may be, are an indispensable means in enabling political agents to locate themselves within their contemporary political landscape.

If this is so, we have some grounds for entertaining the thought that the ostensibly a-theoretical historian who proclaims his freedom from all theory may simply be failing to recognize certain features of his own activity. The historian can certainly do his own proper work without himself explicitly and articulately theorizing or engaging in philosophy; what he cannot, however, contend with any cogency is that philosophical theory has therefore been shown to be dispensable, even in understanding what the empirical historian is doing. Theorizing, and more especially political theorizing, as John Plamenatz saw so clearly, are among those indispensable activities which give to human nature and to human society their distinctive qualities.

Linguistic Philosophy and Political Theory*

David Miller
Nuffield College, Oxford

Any discussion of the nature of political theory, and especially one dedicated to an eminent practitioner of the subject in Oxford, must at some point consider the impact made on political theory by linguistic analysis, the most influential philosophical movement of the post-war period. It is true that the movement's force seems now to be somewhat spent, and that contemporary philosophers are less keen to advertise their allegiance to the linguistic school as marking a break with earlier philosophical practice than to emphasize the continuities between traditional and modern philosophy. But this may signal the movement's triumph rather than its defeat; if we are all linguistic philosophers now, there is no need to trumpet the fact. More plausibly and more modestly, linguistic analysis may have taken its place as one among a number of weapons that a philosopher may use to attack the venerable problems of his subject. Even if this more modest claim is true, it leaves open for discussion the role which linguistic analysis may play in the elucidation of political concepts, and more generally in the construction of political theory.

Debate on this topic has centred on two particular questions. The first is whether linguistic analysis exhausts the scope of political theory or whether it should be seen as a (more or less important) preliminary to theorizing of a different kind. The view that political theory can be reduced to the clarification of political concepts through the study of language was most famously expressed by such philosophers as T. D. Weldon and Margaret Macdonald, though it influenced John Plamenatz's earliest work *Consent, Freedom and Political Obligation*, which, he said, 'is concerned to do nothing more than to attempt definitions of several words often used in political discussions, and to discover in what ways the facts which they mean are related to each other'.[1] Weldon's *The Vocabulary of Politics* was

---

* © David Miller 1983.

[1] J. P. Plamenatz, *Consent, Freedom and Political Obligation* (London, Oxford University Press, 1938), p. x.

largely given over to showing that traditional political theory had mistakenly tried to provide 'foundations' for political standpoints. Political theorists had looked for self-evident axioms—logical or empirical truths—from which political prescriptions could be deduced. But since no such axioms could be found, or if they could be found they were so vague that no concrete conclusions could be deduced from them, the whole enterprise was a waste of time. 'The greater part of classical political philosophy really is concerned with recommending and providing worthless logical grounds for the adoption or perpetuation of axioms or definitions involving political words like "State", "law", and "rights".'[2] Macdonald argued that questions like 'Why should I obey *any* law or support *any* government?' were senseless in the same way as questions like 'Am I always deluded when I see things?'. The philosopher's job was to show that such questions were senseless, not to try to answer them. More limited questions like 'Why should I obey the Conscription Act?' were perfectly sensible, but they did not require philosophical treatment since everyone knew how to answer them anyway. The most that could be said for traditional political philosophies was that they provided striking images of political life which might be psychologically valuable in particular contexts.[3]

This line of argument was elegantly summarized by Wollheim[4] when he pointed out that the thesis of philosophical 'neutrality' followed from two other theses: that philosophy was a second-order activity, and that evaluations could not be derived logically from either factual or necessary premises. The first thesis implies that philosophy cannot establish either empirical or evaluative propositions, but can only examine the logical relations between propositions. Given that political principles are a form of evaluative proposition, the second thesis then implies that political principles cannot be justified philosophically. Like Weldon and Macdonald, Wollheim consequently restricts the role of political philosophy to two tasks: the negative task of showing that other people's attempts to provide logical foundations for their political principles were misguided, and the positive task of clarifying the concepts used in

---

[2]T. D. Weldon, *The Vocabulary of Politics* (Harmondsworth, Penguin, 1953), p. 41.

[3]M. Macdonald, 'The Language of Political Theory' in A. Flew (ed.), *Logic and Language*, First Series (Oxford, Blackwell, 1951).

[4]R. Wollheim, 'Philosophie Analytique et Pensée Politique', *Revue Française de Science Politique*, 11 (1961), 295–308.

political argument. Either of these tasks might of course have political effects. Removing the appearance of logical necessity from a political position might cause some of its adherents to give it up; and conceptual clarification might have an equally corrosive effect if, as Wollheim put it, some political beliefs were so 'totally confused' that they could not be clarified without their irrationality becoming obvious. But these incidental results of philosophical analysis do not show that any political standpoint in particular can be justified philosophically.

The apparent aridity of this programme produced a critical response, not least in Plamenatz himself, who argued later that political philosophy as conceived by Weldon and others was no substitute for political theory as practised by such men as Rousseau and Hegel. Linguistic analysis was important to the extent that conceptual ambiguity caused confusion in men's thinking about politics: but it could not replace an intellectual activity whose aim was primarily practical. Men needed political theory to guide their actions in a changing society, and to perform that function the theory must be prescriptive; 'Its purpose is to help us to decide what to do and how to go about doing it'.[5] In similar vein, critics of the linguistic school such as D. D. Raphael[6] and W. G. Runciman[7] argued that political philosophers ought to take on the job of assessing political principles, which could be done by employing the standards of logical consistency and correspondence to fact. According to Raphael, the clarification of concepts is important, but it is only a preliminary to the still more important task of evaluating beliefs. Runciman stresses the use of sociological evidence in assessing political standpoints, since such standpoints usually rest on broad empirical claims which can be compared with the available evidence. It is not being suggested here that political principles can be conclusively validated; it is supposed rather that arguments can be offered in their support and that these arguments can be shown to be better or worse, even though they are not strictly deductive. The task of assessing such arguments, it is claimed, is

[5]J. P. Plamenatz, 'The Use of Political Theory' in A. Quinton (ed.), *Political Philosophy* (London, Oxford University Press, 1967), p. 29.

[6]D. D. Raphael, *Problems of Political Philosophy* (London, Macmillan, 1970), ch. 1.

[7]W. G. Runciman, 'Sociological Evidence and Political Theory' in P. Laslett and W. G. Runciman (eds.), *Philosophy, Politics and Society*, Second Series (Oxford, Blackwell, 1962); *Social Science and Political Theory* (Cambridge, Cambridge University Press, 1969), ch. 8.

properly regarded as part of political theory, and is moreover as important as or more important than the clarification of concepts.

The first controversy, therefore, has been staged between those who think that the task of political philosophy is conceptual clarification pure and simple (plus the negative task of undermining putative 'foundations' for political standpoints) and those who think that conceptual clarification should be complemented by the evaluation of political principles, giving political philosophy a prescriptive as well as an analytical role. The second major issue raised by the advent of linguistic philosophy is whether linguistic analysis as a method is evaluatively neutral, or whether it biases political theory in a conservative direction. Opponents of linguistic philosophy have argued that to explicate concepts by reference to the use of words in everyday speech is to endorse the value-assumptions contained in that speech. According to Herbert Marcuse, linguistic analysis 'contributes to enclosing thought in the circle of the mutilated universe of ordinary discourse'.[8] He contrasts with this a form of political philosophy which aims to develop concepts critical of existing social and political realities, these concepts somehow transcending the everyday meanings of the terms associated with them.[9] In somewhat similar vein, Ernest Gellner argues that linguistic philosophy is politically conservative, because it forestalls radical criticism of existing forms of thought and language.[10] In reply to such criticism, Alan Wertheimer has insisted that there is a distinction between revealing the values implicit in a society's linguistic practices and endorsing those values; and he further points out that, if the stock of words available in ordinary discourse contains terms which are standardly used to criticize existing arrangements, this critical function will be reproduced in the analysis offered by the linguistic philosopher.[11] In general, linguistic philosophers have held to the view that philosophy is a second-order activity, and as such is incapable of confirming or denying first-order political beliefs—so that any political effects produced by linguistic philosophy would be

---

[8]H. Marcuse, *One-Dimensional Man* (London, Routledge, 1964), p. 199.

[9]Ibid. chs. 7–8.

[10]E. Gellner, *Words and Things* (London, Gollancz, 1959), ch. 8 section 2; *Contemporary Thought and Politics* (London, Routledge, 1974), ch. 4.

[11]A. Wertheimer, 'Is Ordinary Language Analysis Conservative?', *Political Theory*, 4 (1976), 405–22.

accidental, occuring only in cases where someone's political beliefs turned out to rest on muddled conceptual foundations. Anthony Quinton, for example, argues that a linguistic philosopher might in principle hold any set of political views and would be confined only in the reasons he could offer for his standpoint; he could not argue for his views using phrases such as 'the Real will of the Nation' which conceptual analysis would reveal to have no definite sense.[12]

It is not my intention to try to resolve either of these controversies in their own terms. I prefer instead to adopt an oblique strategy which consists in pointing out first that both arguments proceed on the basis of a common underlying assumption, and then challenging that assumption. The assumption is that the programme of linguistic analysis can itself be carried out in a non-partisan fashion. The first argument has to do with whether, once the programme has been carried out, there is anything of a more substantive political kind to be done by the political theorist. The second argument has to do with whether the programme, in itself uncontroversial in so far as it offers a correct account of the ordinary uses of political terms, is at a deeper level biased towards the status quo. Both arguments would be vitiated if it could be shown that political commitments entered into the programme of conceptual analysis itself. The issue which is addressed in the remainder of this essay is whether the methods of linguistic philosophy can be applied to the concepts of political theory without admitting such extraneous elements.

To throw some light on this issue, I shall consider three concepts central to political thought, the notions of justice, freedom, and democracy. What is common to these ideas is, first, that they are used to make political appraisals—to call some arrangement just, free, or democratic is, in our culture, to commend it; second, there is prima facie a good deal of dispute about what arrangements actually satisfy the three concepts. Thus we find people arguing about whether a welfare state system is socially just or not; whether men are in general freer under capitalism or under socialism; whether parliamentary institutions are democratic or not; and so forth. Not all political concepts share these two features, but many

---

[12] In his contribution to 'Philosophy and Beliefs', *The Twentieth Century*, 157 (1955), 495–521.

of them do. What are the implications of this fact for a programme of conceptual analysis?

That people disagree over the things to which a concept is to be applied does not necessarily mean that they disagree about the concept itself. Let us take a case where this is true and compare it with a case where the disagreement is actually about the concept. Consider two people disagreeing about the rightness of a course of action—say about whether abortion is right in specified circumstances. One person argues that abortion is right because the mother is entitled to control her own body; the other that abortion is wrong because the foetus is entitled to live. It would be most misleading here to say that the two people were disagreeing about the meaning of 'right' or about the concept of rightness. Let us suppose that the following account of 'right' is roughly correct: to call something right is to prescribe that it be done by everyone who finds himself in a given situation and to imply that this prescription can be justified by reference to human interests. Both parties to the argument could accept such an account. They are not disagreeing about the meaning of 'right' but about the criteria which make actions right (or perhaps about the relative importance of such criteria); their disagreement is substantive, not conceptual. Because of such cases, the material question 'What is right?' is not equivalent to the conceptual question 'What do we mean by "right"?'. The former question asks for a criterion of right action, the latter for an elucidation of the term 'right'.

Compare now two people disagreeing about whether all actions are either voluntary or involuntary. The first claims that if an action is not voluntary it must be involuntary; the second argues that there are certain actions (like shooting a man in mistake for a deer) which are neither fully voluntary (like shooting a man deliberately) nor involuntary (like killing a man because your gun goes off as you climb over a gate). Here the dispute is obviously about the meaning of 'voluntary' and 'involuntary': the concepts are not particularly clear ones, and so there can be a dispute about whether they mutually exhaust the class of actions or not. We can replace the material question 'What actions are voluntary?' with the conceptual question 'What do we mean by "voluntary action"?' without a change of sense.

If we turn to the political terms mentioned earlier, and consider what is in dispute when people argue about their application, I think we shall see that the dispute is neither clearly about the meaning of a word nor clearly about the application of a word whose meaning is agreed. It seems to fall somewhere between our example of a dispute about rightness and our example of a dispute about 'voluntary' and 'involuntary'. First, when people dispute about whether an arrangement is socially just, free, or democratic, they are not generally arguing about the results of applying a shared standard—as, say, are two people who argue about which of two hills is steeper. It is possible that the dispute is of this kind, but more often it turns out that the parties are applying different criteria of justice, etc., or at least weighting various criteria differently. To take a familiar dispute in each case, it is a matter of controversy whether social justice consists in a distribution of goods according to the deserts of the recipients, or according to their needs. It is equally a matter of controversy whether a person who is not formally prevented from pursuing a course of action, but who lacks the material resources to undertake it, is free to perform that action or not. Finally, it is disputed whether democracy consists in government by the elected representatives of the people, or government by the direct participation of the people themselves. To simplify matters, consider a case where two people are arguing because each adopts a different criterion of justice, etc. Are they disputing about the concept itself (the meaning of 'justice', etc.) or are they arguing about how the concept (which they share) should be applied?

It seems difficult to maintain that the dispute is not in part about the meaning of the word. If two people disagree about whether justice consists in a distribution according to desert or a distribution according to need, it is unlikely that they will be able to agree on a definition beginning ' "justice" means . . .'. In the case of rightness, two people could agree about the meaning of 'right' while disagreeing about what actions were right because of the manner in which 'right' functions. It is used to pass a final verdict on what morally ought to be done in a given situation. Its meaning can largely be explained in terms of this function; people can agree about this and yet disagree about the things to which the concept applies. But 'justice', 'freedom', and 'democracy' do not operate in quite the same way as 'right'. Although they are used to appraise institutions, arrangements, etc., their meaning cannot be explicated wholly in terms of their appraising function. To call something just is also to describe it—it is to indicate a certain feature of an arrangement in virtue of which it is favourably evaluated. Were this not so, we should be able to use 'just', 'free', and 'democratic' interchangeably (to pass favourable evaluations), which we clearly cannot do. The descriptive function must form part of the meaning of each word. But then if two people disagree about the features of an arrangement in virtue of which it is to be called just, they must also be disagreeing about the meaning of 'justice'—and similarly for the other concepts.

At the same time, there must be *some* measure of agreement about the meaning of these political terms, or we should not say that the parties are disputing about a concept at all, but merely about a word.[13] Compare two small boys arguing about 'bank'. One of them says that a bank is a sloping patch of ground; the other that a bank is a building where money is lent and borrowed. Here it would be absurd to say that the boys were arguing about the concept of a bank. They are arguing about the word 'bank', failing to recognize that the word has two distinct meanings.

It seems clear that a dispute about 'justice' is not like this dispute about 'bank'. We ought to recognize, however, that the question 'How many meanings does a word have?' is often much harder to answer than philosophers realize. Let us restrict ourselves for the

---

[13] In dealing with this question I depart from W. B. Gallie whose 'Essentially Contested Concepts', *Proceedings of the Aristotelian Society*, 56 (1955–6), 167–98, is otherwise one of the best discussions of the disputed character of political concepts. Recognizing that we need grounds for saying that two users are contesting the *same* concept, Gallie proposes that two conditions should be satisfied:

(1) 'The derivation of any such concept from an original exemplar whose authority is acknowledged by all contestant users of the concept';

(2) 'The probability or plausibility . . . of the claim that the continuous competition for acknowledgement as between the contestant users of the concept, enables the original exemplar's achievement to be sustained and/or developed in optimum fashion.'

Although the first two examples of essentially contested concepts given by Gallie—'A Christian life' and 'Art'—may meet these conditions (arguably in the latter case—is there a single exemplar of 'art'?), the remaining two cases—'democracy' and 'social justice'—certainly do not. If my argument so far is correct, there is no exemplary democratic state or just society which all users of these concepts would acknowledge as such. Rather, a state which appears perfectly democratic to one person may appear quite undemocratic to another; similarly for the just society. And if the first condition fails, the second must also, since it presupposes that exemplars exist. For further discussion of Gallie's views see E. Gellner, 'The concept of a story' in *Contemporary Thought and Politics*; W. E. Connolly, *The Terms of Political Discourse* (Lexington, Mass., D. C. Heath, 1974); J. N. Gray, 'On the Contestability of Social and Political Concepts', *Political Theory*, 5 (1977), 331–48, and also his contribution to the present volume.

moment to simple descriptive words used for singling out a class of objects. There are some words, like 'daffodil' and 'lapwing', of which we can confidently say that they have just a single meaning. They are used to refer to a class of objects which are all roughly alike, having many features in common. Of other words, like 'bank' and 'corn', we can say with equal confidence that they have two distinct meanings. There is nothing to connect a field of cereal with a callus on one's foot. But many, perhaps most, descriptive words fall somewhere between these extremes. How many meanings has 'table', for instance? Does the word mean the same when applied to a dining-table as when applied to a stratum of rock? Does the latter application constitute a new meaning, or is it merely a 'stretching' of the other meaning? Or again, what about 'trunk'? Does the word mean the same when we apply it to the main part of a tree, a metal box, an elephant's snout? Should we say 'a word with three meanings' or 'a word with a rather broad meaning'? In cases such as this, the question 'How many meanings does a word have?' cannot be answered simply. We need to employ a more sophisticated battery of phrases (like 'extended meaning', 'connected meanings') to capture the truth about these words. (It is instructive to see how dictionary-makers approach the problem in compiling their entries.)

With simple descriptive words, however, it is at least clear how we go about deciding whether a word has a single meaning or not. To the extent that the range of objects to which a word applies have features in common, we are inclined to say that the word has a single meaning. If we decide that rock tables are really quite like dining-tables, we shall be moved to say that 'table' has a single meaning. If we think that boles and metal boxes have actually very little in common, we shall tend to the view that 'trunk' has at least two meanings. But can this criterion be used for political concepts as well? Perhaps to some extent it can. Two people disagree about whether social justice consists in a distribution according to desert or a distribution according to need; but they appear to concur in thinking that 'justice' refers to a manner of distributing goods among persons (and implies a favourable appraisal of that distribution). Similarly, two people may disagree about whether 'democracy' means representative government or government by an assembly of the people, but they agree that it refers to a form of political organization in which the people are given some role (again favourably appraised). This seems enough to show why we call disputes about 'justice', 'freedom', and 'democracy' disputes about concepts rather than (pointless) disputes about words. People who use these words agree to some extent about their meaning. But we do not say that they agree wholly about the meaning. Someone who thinks that justice consists in a distribution according to desert means something different by 'justice' than someone who thinks it consists in a distribution according to need. The common element of meaning does not exhaust the word's meaning for either party.

For this reason the linguistic philosopher cannot deal with these political concepts as he might deal with 'right'. He cannot argue that the *meaning* of 'justice' is simply what is common to all uses of that term, and that the disputes about justice are substantive disputes which he (as a philosopher engaged in conceptual clarification) is not competent to tackle. Nor can he deal with these concepts as he might deal with 'voluntary'. Here the dispute is purely conceptual. There is a range of actions which are clearly correctly described as 'voluntary', others which are clearly 'involuntary', and a group in between whose correct description is uncertain. By paying close attention to established use, it should be possible to find an acceptable classification for these actions. But the disputes about 'justice', 'freedom', and 'democracy' are at once substantive and conceptual. There is no reason to assume the existence of a range of cases which everyone would agree were 'just' or 'free' or 'democratic'. For people using these terms in different ways, any overlap in reference would be accidental rather than necessary (for instance one particular distribution of goods might happen to correspond both to the scale of the recipients' deserts and to the scale of their needs—in which case A and B might both describe the distribution as just, but for different reasons).

Is the linguistic philosopher then obliged simply to record the range of meanings attached to these political terms? This raises directly the question of the relationship between the philosopher and the language in which he conducts his analysis. What is the status of the philosopher's account of linguistic use? Is he describing how certain words are actually used by speakers of the language or is he prescribing how they ought to be used?[14] It seems that neither

---

[14]See B. Mates, 'On the Verification of Statements about Ordinary Language' in V. C. Chappell (ed.), *Ordinary Language* (Englewood Cliffs, Prentice-Hall, 1964).

of these alternatives is correct as it stands. The philosopher is certainly not prescribing the use of words according to his own idiosyncratic tastes; but neither is he describing linguistic use in the way that a scientific philologist might. Ryle draws a distinction between 'use' and 'usage'.[15] To discover the usage of a word, he claims, we should have to investigate scientifically how the word was generally used in a given community at a given time. But knowing the use of a word means simply knowing how to operate with it—a skill we acquire as we pick up language. The use of a word is contrasted with its misuse—when the rules for operating with it are broken. In the same way, knowing the rules of chess is different from a scientific investigation of the behaviour of chess players in a given community (which might reveal a certain percentage of wrong moves, when the players were tired, careless, etc.). In short, the philosopher is not concerned, strictly speaking, with describing linguistic usage but with giving the rules for the correct use of words.

Nevertheless, talking about rules for the use of words presupposes that everyone, or almost everyone, follows the same set of rules. Ryle appears to think that it does not matter how many people use a word in the same way as the philosopher—that is an empirical matter of no philosophical interest.[16] But, far from being an empirical matter, agreement in the use of a word is logically presupposed by talk of '*the* use of a word' as opposed to '*my* use of a word'. The philosopher, after all, might have been brought up to misuse a certain term. In this case his statements about the use of that word will all be false until he corrects his mistake by learning how the word is commonly used. It follows that if two or more competing uses of a given word are prevalent in a particular community, the philosopher has to acknowledge this fact, even if his personal preference is for one of the uses. He cannot say 'The use of this word is . . .' and then give his own use. In the same way, if two interpretations of the castling rule, say, are common among the chess-playing fraternity, someone stating the rules of chess will have to record this fact, even though he always sticks to one interpretation in his own play.

Can we not, however, be a little more normative in our

---

[15]G. Ryle, 'Ordinary Language' in Chappell (ed.), *Ordinary Language*.
[16]Ibid., p. 33.

discussions of linguistic use without falling into personal idio-
syncrasy? We do, after all, sometimes speak of the correct use of
a word even when we recognize that the word is quite commonly
used in another way. We say, for instance, that the proper meaning
of 'to refute' is 'to disprove by argument' even though we know that
many people now use it to mean 'to deny'. Again, we say that the
correct meaning of 'disinterested' is 'unbiased by interest', even
though it is often used as a synonym for 'uninterested'. What is the
force of 'correct' in these cases? In each case we are appealing to a
longer-established meaning against a more recent departure in use.
Is our argument then merely one of linguistic conservatism? Not
quite, because we may reasonably demand agreement in linguistic
use to prevent the confusion which arises when two people
unwittingly employ a word in different ways (someone says 'I shall
refute that claim' and we wait in vain for his argument). But this
condition would be satisfied by dropping the established use as well
as by banishing the new one. To show the superiority of established
use, we should have to show that it provided us with distinctions of
meaning which were of importance, and which were lost when the
word was used in its new sense. In other words, language with the
word used 'correctly' was a better instrument of communication
than language with the word used 'incorrectly'. In the case of
'refute', for instance, we should have to say something like this: if
'refute' is used to mean the same as 'deny' we have two words
performing the same function, but no word left to refer to that
precise kind of disproof we now call 'refutation'. This seems the
most promising way for the philosopher to deal with a problem of
divergence in the use of a term, and in so far as linguistic
philosophers have recognized such problems at all, they seem to
have gravitated towards this solution.[17]

Could this way of discovering the 'correct' use of a word help us
in dealing with political terms whose meaning is disputed? Perhaps
we could persuade people who want to attach one meaning to such a
word that this is not really what the word means, that the term in
question is not correctly used in the way they are using it. Let us see
how such a case might be made for the three concepts we have been
considering. In the case of a dispute about the meaning of 'justice',

---

[17] See, for instance, S. Cavell, 'Must We Mean What We Say?' in Chappell, (ed.),
Ordinary Language.

we might try to argue with those who think that justice consists in a distribution according to need in the following terms. 'Admittedly we often refer to people's needs when trying to show that some policy is socially just. But do we really mean what we say in such instances? Perhaps we are pointing to the existence of unsatisfied needs in order to show that some deserving people have not been given their just rewards. But if no such questions of desert arise, even implicitly, should we really be talking about justice at all? Isn't it better to describe a policy which aims solely to satisfy people's needs as a policy of humanity or benevolence? Wouldn't this be strictly correct, as well as avoiding the current conceptual confusion about "justice"?'[18]

In a similar way, we might argue against someone who thinks that freedom implies the practical ability to do something. 'You say that someone who lacks the resources to buy books, for instance, is unfree to read them. But don't you strictly mean that he is *unable* to read them? Admittedly it may be rather cynical to say that someone is free to perform an action which he is clearly unable to perform— but isn't it nevertheless true? If we use ''unfreedom'' in your way, to mean lack of ability, we shall have no words left to refer to the case where someone is legally prohibited from reading books.[19] Doesn't it make for clearer discussion if we keep to the stricter sense of ''freedom''?'

Finally, we could try to persuade someone who used 'democracy' to refer to government by elected representatives that this was not the literal meaning of the term, that we already had adequate ways of referring to this system of government—'representative government' or even 'representative democracy'—and that he was leaving us with no way of describing a system of direct popular participation.

What force is there in these arguments for giving each term a single, unambiguous meaning? Their persuasive force might not be very great, for in each case we are trying to induce someone to give up a word of great rhetorical power. Arguing against prescription charges, for instance, on the grounds of 'humanity' sounds less compelling than arguing in terms of 'social justice'. A campaign to

[18]An argument of this type is developed by T. D. Campbell in 'Humanity Before Justice', *British Journal of Political Science*, 4 (1974), 1–16.

[19]See W. L. Weinstein, 'The Concept of Liberty in Nineteenth Century British Political Thought', *Political Studies*, 13 (1965), p. 151.

make books more widely available will do better under the banner 'Freedom to read for all' than under the suggested replacement 'Ability to read for all'. 'Fighting for democracy' has a better ring to it than 'fighting for representative government'. But are these rhetorical advantages the only reasons for retaining the uses of 'justice', etc. which the above arguments sought to show were incorrect? I believe that the reasons go rather deeper than this, and that people who use such notions 'incorrectly' may have better grounds than those of rhetoric for persisting in their use.

I have already suggested that disputes about political terms are simultaneously conceptual and substantive disputes. This suggestion perhaps needs qualifying, since hypothetically two people might be in complete political agreement and yet disagree about the meaning of a particular term. But typically, if two people disagree about the meaning of a word in this area, they also disagree over a matter of substance. (It is certainly hard to believe that political concepts would be contested in the way that they are in a society where everyone held the same political attitudes.) Thus if people differ over whether 'justice' means a distribution according to desert or a distribution according to need, they will most probably differ over distributive policy itself—about how far society's goods should be distributed according to desert and how far according to need. Suppose someone favours a distribution according to need. He is most unlikely to be impressed by the claim that, even if he prefers this policy, he ought to use 'social justice' to refer to a distribution according to desert. What, he may say, is so important about a distribution according to desert? Why should we need a special term to refer to it? He may quite possibly be sceptical about the notion of desert itself, or at least think that no society can actually organize itself in such a way that each person gets his deserved reward. In that case the distinction his opponent wants to draw between 'justice' and 'injustice' will be an empty distinction —there is nothing in the world that corresponds (even approximately) to 'justice'. Therefore the term is best used to apply to a policy which *can* be implemented—a distribution according to need. For this person the important distinction is between an allocation˙of goods according to need and all other modes of allocation.[20]

[20]I have explored the character of disputes about social justice more fully in *Social Justice* (Oxford, Clarendon Press, 1976).

In a similar way, a person who thinks that freedom implies the practical ability to do something is likely to believe that the mere absence of legal and physical constraint, without the power to act, is not a condition worth talking about. For him, if someone lacks the financial resources to buy books, it does not make a significant difference whether the reading of books is legally prohibited or not. The distinction which his opponent wants to mark is for him a trivial distinction; and, being trivial, there is no need to reserve a special word, 'freedom', to make it.

We can sum up the argument here with the help of a remark of Austin's, made in defence of linguistic analysis: 'When we examine what we should say when, what words we should use in what situations, we are looking again not *merely* at words (or "meanings", whatever they may be) but also at the realities we use the words to talk about . . . .'.[21] I have argued with reference to political concepts that the 'realities' which they are used to talk about may appear differently to different people. I have in particular suggested two ways in which this may be so: first, two situations may appear importantly different, from a moral or political point of view, to one person, but only trivially different to another person; secondly, one person may regard as possible (and desirable) a range of situations which the other person thinks unrealizable. If they differ in these ways, should we not expect that they will differ in their use of political words, in the meanings they attach to political expressions? What is the point of having two words to refer to situations that are only trivially different, or in having a term which refers solely to impossible states of affairs? Perhaps, to quote Austin again, 'our common stock of words embodies all the distinctions men have found worth drawing, and the connections they have found worth marking', but in political matters it is a subject of controversy what these worthwhile distinctions and connections are. It depends on one's substantive political position, on what one thinks is politically important, and what one thinks is politically possible. So we should expect that the meanings men attach to political terms vary intelligibly and systematically according to the political standpoint of the user.

This places the linguistic philosopher in a considerable dilemma. On the one hand, he wants to maintain the distinction between philosophy and philology. The philosopher explains the use of words, which necessitates distinguishing between correct and incorrect usage, whereas the scientific philologist catalogues the actual usage of a linguistic community. On the other hand, the linguistic philosopher wants to separate conceptual analysis from the justification of principles. In the case of the concepts of political theory, we have found that the two requirements are incompatible. If a philosopher wants to show that one meaning of a term is the 'correct' meaning, he will have to engage in substantive political argument. He will have to justify the general standpoint which corresponds to the interpretation of the concept which he favours. This justification cannot be carried out merely by further appeals to language. Claims like 'There is an important distinction which you're missing here by your use of terms' are in this context political claims—'important' here means 'politically important'. Defending the view that justice consists in a distribution according to desert involves showing that a distribution of this nature is morally valuable and socially feasible: this is a matter of justification, not simply of conceptual analysis.

Faced with this dilemma, the linguistic philosopher may opt for an intermediate position. I have conceded that there must be some common elements of meaning involved in all uses of a political term, which allow us to say that there is one (disputed) concept rather than several. A linguistic philosopher might argue that his first job was to locate these common elements of meaning: beyond this he would list the permissible fuller meanings without, however, seeking to establish that any one of them was 'correct'. In this way his activity would still be distinct from that of the philologist (who reports verbal usage without any regard for standards of propriety) while avoiding any substantive political commitment.

Such a position is not, however, ultimately satisfactory. Let us look more closely at what it involves. The philosopher, let us assume, has his own favoured way of using political terms like 'justice' and 'democracy'. Among the alternative usages found in practice, he distinguishes between simple misuses of these terms and 'permissible uses' which are nevertheless different from his. How is this distinction to be made? Presumably not by counting heads—this would reduce the philosopher to the status of an amateur philologist. The distinction must rely on the extent to which different usages of a term are *justified*. Consider an example: a philosopher may believe that the correct use of 'democracy' is to refer to a system of government by direct popular participation. Among the other usages, he accepts the use of 'democracy' to mean 'representative government' as permissible; on the other hand, he regards it as a simple misuse when 'democracy' is used to mean 'social equality' or 'the capitalist economic system'. On what grounds does he believe this? He must think there are *no* grounds for using 'democracy' in either of the last two senses, while there *are* grounds for using it to mean 'representative government'—though not such good grounds as for using it to mean 'government by direct popular participation'. There is some justification for the permissible use, but no justification for the misuses. But in evaluating usage in this way, the philosopher cannot be sure of remaining politically neutral, for the reasons that we have already given. To show that there is no justification for using 'democracy' to mean 'social equality', for example, he will have to make some political assumptions, even though these may be rather obvious (he will have to assume, for instance, that there is some point in discussing political systems independently of social systems). Having set foot in the political arena to arrive at the list of permissible uses of a term, why is the philosopher reluctant to take the second step and argue for the correct use?

The intermediate position which I have attributed to the linguistic philosopher is therefore curiously half-hearted.[22] One may guess that it is taken up by philosophers who believe that the permissible uses of contested terms can be established without engaging in political argument. This I hold to be an illusion—unless the philosopher is to turn philologist and give 'permissible' a strictly statistical meaning. There may indeed be good reasons for distinguishing permissible uses of a term from misuses; it may be important at the outset of an argument to identify the serious competitors to one's own view in order to give them the detailed refutation that they deserve, while other positions can be dismissed comparatively swiftly. But there is no logically compelling reason for stopping at a list of acceptable meanings when one is analysing a political term. Having begun a political argument, one should carry it through to its conclusion and show which of the term's meanings is the most adequate.

---

[22]There is an element of self-criticism involved here since the position in question is the one I adopted in *Social Justice*. In self-defence may I reiterate that the political assumptions needed to establish the permissible uses of a term are often considerably weaker than those needed to show that a particular use is preferable.

Political Theory and Ideology: the case of the state*

Larry Siedentop
Keble College, Oxford

Academic political theory is sometimes accused of being tainted with ideology. If that charge amounts to a rejection *tout court* of the method which, under the influence of linguistic philosophy, has shaped political theory in recent decades—i.e. rejection of the concern with concepts and definitions apart from any theory of economic and social change—then the charge is not particularly worrying. It can be met by showing that identifying the boundaries of concepts and the more important disputes over them is a necessary but *not* a sufficient condition for adequate political theory. The need to explore connections between different versions of a concept and the major ideologies—which can in turn be related to phases of economic and social development—is a clear and important need. This is so even when it involves moving into areas where normative and empirical arguments intersect, areas which have been shunned by the 'purest' exponents of analytical political theory.

Far more worrying, however, are suggestions that when treating particular concepts political theorists have, through excluding some issues in favour of others, begged important questions. At times, I fear, this charge is valid. A striking example of this can be found in conventional treatments of the concepts 'the state' and 'the individual'. A good deal of argument in recent political theory takes these terms as relatively unproblematic. Indeed, these terms are often presented as neutral or descriptive—as terms of political science rather than of ideology (in the way that 'liberty' or 'justice' or 'democracy' are terms of ideology). Anthony Quinton's widely read introduction to the volume *Political Philosophy*[1] provides but one example. Yet the conceptual hazards, the hazards to clarity, involved in taking these terms as unproblematic are considerable.

Of course, a certain amount of discussion of the terms 'state' and

---

*© L. A. Siedentop 1983
[1] A. Quinton (ed.), *Political Philosophy* (London, Oxford University Press, 1967).

'individual' has taken place. When examining the political ideas of
Rousseau and Hegel, theorists have often identified a moralized
version of each term—a metaphysical theory of the state tied to a
metaphysical theory of the self. But, on the whole, the search for
value implications in these terms has stopped there. The values
which may be implied by (for want of a better expression) less
metaphysical uses of these terms have not been explored. In this
way perhaps the most interesting ideological issue raised by the
basic terms of modern Western political discourse has been
overlooked.

Taking the concepts 'state' and 'individual' for granted has led
to two mistakes which are widespread in recent Anglo-American
political theory. The first is the slipshod use of 'government' and
'state' as if they were synonymous rather than—as I shall argue—
the state being historically specific, a type or species of government.
Properly speaking, the state is to government as species to genus.
The second widespread mistake is to speak of 'society' as if it always
and necessarily consists of individuals—i.e. a failure to make clear
the sense in which the individual is a type of social role, resting on a
set of normative and material pre-conditions. After all, there are
many types of society. There are societies made up of tribes, castes,
or estates. In these social types there are no agents who would or
could identify themselves as individuals in the modern Western
sense. To use 'individual' and 'social agent' as if they were
synonymous is to breed confusion. It is to impose a value in the form
of a method. By assuming that society is composed of individuals,
we may be tacitly endorsing just such a state of affairs.

Besides, if 'state' and 'individual' are presented as
unproblematic terms, political theorists fail to make clear that the
'political' itself is a contested notion. Often the 'political' has simply
been defined by reference to the state and positive law. It is, *ex
hypothesi*, a sphere called into being by the so-called transfer of
sovereign rights—to identify, apply, and enforce rules of
conduct—from 'natural individuals' to a centralized agency. That
model of argument is, of course, only too familiar to students of
Social Contract Theory. What political theorists have done, in fact,
is to take over the framework of Contract Theory in defining their
own activity but have done so in an apparently uncontentious way
by abandoning talk of the 'state of nature'. Quinton's tactics are
again typical.

For it is by the transfer of this executive power from free, natural individuals to a common sovereign that a natural society is turned into a civil, or politically organized, society . . . The executive power of the law of nature can be used to distinguish political societies, as those in which it is formally centralized, from non-political ones, in which it is informally distributed amongst all individuals.[2]

To the extent that this model is presented as an adequate basis for argument in political theory, it is fair to conclude that any ideological baggage carried by the Contract Theorists has been transferred to new porters—porters who aspire, however, to a neutrality in analysis which was not the primary or avowed aim of their predecessors. Through this transfer the 'natural individual' survives, and becomes the social type over which Leviathan is raised. In other words, a *de facto* restriction on the range of social structure takes place. Nor is this an accident; for the two 'mistakes' I have just pointed to are intimately connected.

If, latterly, the concept of the state has received attention, it has occurred indirectly through discussion of the correlative concepts of 'sovereignty' and 'positive law'. Political theorists often assume that analysis of these concepts exhausts interesting questions about the meaning or use of 'state'. Thus, the concept of the state has been resolved into a few interrelated definitions:

What is positive law? Positive law is a set of commands or rules, written and relatively precise, issuing from a sovereign. Positive law stands in contrast to custom and so-called natural law.

What is a sovereign? The supreme power (Hobbes, Austin) or authority (Kelsen, Hart) in a society and, *ex hypothesi*, the source of law.

How is a sovereign identified? By its ability to enforce its commands (Hobbes), by habitual obedience to its commands (Austin), by general acceptance of its right to command (Hart), or by its (logical) role as the supreme norm or source of validity within a legal system (Kelsen).

Clarification of these terms has involved drawing distinctions between 'power' and 'authority' and led to further discussion of

[2]Quinton, *Political Philosophy*, p. 5.

what categories of rights and duties positive law ought to create—
i.e. into discussions of justice. But, for the most part, philosophical
analysis of the concept of the state has stopped there. Any
remaining questions about the state are assigned to historical or
sociological enquiry in general, and to Marxism in particular.
Thus, the relationship between state power and social privilege or
class conflict is characteristically hived off as appropriate to
empirical rather than normative theory.

Even within the confines of normative theory, however, it is
possible to argue that the concept of the state has not been explored
carefully enough. In restricting themselves to questions about the
meaning of 'law' or 'sovereignty', political theorists have neglected
others which are no less important—in particular, the question of
what values may be 'carried', indirectly, by the concept of the state.
I shall argue that political theorists have not made clear the way the
concept of the state rests implicitly on a certain type of social
structure—i.e. that built into the concept is a criterion which *limits*
the range of social structure consistent with a state properly so
called. Or, to put the matter differently, I shall argue that the state
presupposes an individualist model of society. It is important to
notice this if we are to use the terms 'state' and 'individual' critically, and *not* become the unwitting mouthpieces of an ideology.

Austin's account of sovereignty, which stipulates that there must
be a sovereign for there to be a political system, has at times been
used to suggest that 'state' and 'government' coincide. But if the
political is defined in terms of the state, and is also used to describe
government of all kinds, then a highly equivocal use of 'political'
results. That usage involves lending the term 'state' to describe
government in societies as different as ancient Egypt, the Greek
polis, and feudal Europe. That usage obscures the extent to which
the concept of the state restricts, implicitly, the range of social
structure. It helps to foster the view that society always and
necessarily consists of individuals in the modern sense.

Anglo-American political theorists sometimes speak as if society
is *by definition* a collection of individuals. That, they suggest, is what
we mean by 'society'. But it takes only a little reflection to recognize
that such an assertion is untrue. The term society may always imply
normative order, but it does not exclude a priori—as it would have
to do on the above account—normative orders which do not
sustain the role of the individual in the modern sense, but give

instead to membership of family, clan, or caste the crucial role in conferring identity on social agents. In such societies there are no agents who understand themselves or others as 'individuals'. Such a self-description is not available. Thus, to use 'individual' as if it were synonymous with 'social agent' is to impose one type or conception of society on to our notion of society *as such*. If the concept of acting or action implies some normative order, so that action is inconceivable outside a social context, norms or rules may differ radically from one social context to another. Clearly, then, it does not follow that all social agents are, *au fond*, individuals. The practices and ideas which sustain the role of the individual may or may not be present in any society. It is not a question which can be settled a priori.

Yet that is precisely what Quinton's argument does. Nor is his way of arguing at all unusual.[3] Thus, the 'political', when defined in terms of 'state' and 'individual', carries a value commitment which is not explicit. It turns the concept of the state into a carrier of individualist values or ideology. That is so by virtue of the social structure presupposed by such a political institution. The concept of the state may be used to limit the range of social structure a priori. Thus, at one and the same time the state becomes 'unavoidable' and the individual 'natural'. But, of course, neither is really the case. By presenting such terms as descriptive or neutral, political theory as an activity is committed to individualist values without making it clear how and why that is being done. A range of questions about the relationship between social structure and personal identity—questions which bring together problems of fact and value in an especially subtle, complicated way—are simply ruled out. Yet that does the defence of individualist values a disservice.

The crucial individualist value is equality. Without a fundamental (or underlying) equality of status, the social role of the individual—one type of social role—has no basis. It is only by means of such equality of status, and the shared attribute it contri-

[3]See, for example, J. R. Lucas, *The Principles of Politics* (Oxford, Clarendon Press, 1966), p. 10: 'A Community is a body of individuals who have a common method for deciding questions which may arise among or between them'; R. M. Maciver, *Community* (London, Macmillan, 1917), p. 67: 'Society is nothing more than individuals associated and organized'; J. D. Mabbott, *The State and the Citizen* (London, Hutchinson, 1948), p. 84: 'I maintain therefore that there is only one type of social unit and that is the organized association [of individuals]'.

butes to identity, that a person can see himself or herself as *one* among *others*. The recognition of a common or 'human' nature results—a more abstract form of self-description than, say, 'son of Eric', 'untouchable', or 'Lord of Artois'. A purely normative basis for the role 'individual' can be found in the Natural Law tradition, in both its secular and religious forms. But the practical basis is provided by the state through the doctrine of its sovereignty. That is, the state is tied by definition to the value of equality in at least this sense: it entails *equal* subjection to a supreme authority or power, the sovereign. Thus, to speak of a 'state' is to postulate an equality of status antecedent to the definition of specific, enforceable rights and duties. For that reason the concept of state sovereignty, when it develops in a society, introduces a kind of *tabula rasa*, a Hobbesian or normative *tabula rasa* rather than Locke's epistemological *tabula rasa*. *Ex hypothesi*, inherited rules and rights do not have the status of law unless they are recognized by the sovereign. There is no logical limit, therefore, to the degree of innovation in a society with a state (though there may, of course, be severe practical limits) provided only that it does not contradict the criterion of equal submission which defines the sovereign's relations with subjects. In consequence, no subject has, *ab initio*, an obligation to obey another as such—that is, a basic right to command or duty to obey is no longer written into separate hereditary or customary roles. Particular social roles are henceforth circumstanced by the unlimited legal right of the state—by *equal* subjection to the sovereign. For that reason the notion of sovereignty becomes the fulcrum of individual identity. It gives the state, *de facto*, a basic role in the socializing process.

Furthermore, the possibility of endless legal innovation introduced by the postulate of sovereignty helps to create and sustain the idea of individual autonomy, the idea that the individual can free himself or herself from the past (from the causal nexus) and, within limits, start afresh. Again, Hobbes's *tabula rasa*—that break with inherited rules and roles (even if only a logical break) in order to confer unlimited legal right on a sovereign agency—can be seen as the institutional correlative of a change in the self's relationship with its own roles. That is, the right to legislate for everyone entails and helps to create a society in which the self sees itself in a newly abstract way, as distinct from any particular social roles it may in fact assume. That change in the self's relationship with its own roles marks the birth of the will in a peculiarly modern sense—the sense in which the potentialities of the self can never be exhausted in the actual, leaving an abstract 'I' over and above social structure. Here the analogy with the sovereign is very striking. In modern moral philosophy the individual agent is deemed to be 'sovereign' in moral authority. Though not strictly entailed by the idea of state sovereignty, the idea of individual freedom draws plausibility from it. Historical evidence bears that out. 'Freedom' ceased to describe a particular social rank or status and became a general moral principle during the period which saw the emergence of the state. And that is not surprising: freedom would have had little role as a general principle in a society in which status was assigned at birth, a society in which no fundamental equality of status (or human nature) was acknowledged—except perhaps by the Church, custodian of the interests of the other world.[4]

Clearly, the emergence of the state alters social agents' relationship with their own roles. It introduces a point outside themselves by which to judge the particular sets of rights and duties which define their various roles. In a society without a state—in which rights and duties are assigned by custom, by the ways of the group or culture—no such external point of reference exists, *ex hypothesi*. When a special set of rules constituting positive law are (*a*) seen to be made in response to changing conditions and purposes rather than as immutably constituting the identity of the group or culture and (*b*) seen as determined and enforced by a relatively remote or

---

[4]It might be useful to draw a further distinction, with respect to the state and roles, between early modern society in the West and society in the last century. In the earlier period the number of social roles was still very confined. Limited division of labour and the survival of feudal status differences, carried forward into the post-feudal period by property and education, at first restricted the impact of 'equal submission'. Even if people no longer had a legally fixed social status, they none the less occupied, *de facto*, clearly defined positions in a social hierarchy. The range of shared ('human') attributes was still minimal—though the appeal of Protestantism, with its implicit reliance on a principle of equality through emphasis on the right of conscience or private judgement, suggests how important and subversive even that minimal range could be. In any case, since the nineteenth century the rapid multiplication of social roles has, *pari passu*, reinforced the sense of underlying equality of status. Increasing division of labour, itself made possible by the impersonal mechanism of the state and individual rights, has meant that people take on an ever larger number of roles. That, in turn, encourages and indeed requires the individual to see himself or herself as essentially a role-bearer—that is, in the newly abstract way—rather than merely as *being* one specialized role. The ability to take on and shed roles grows apace. Thus, the individual as a type of social role develops from its state basis in 'equal subjection' and becomes the outstanding social fact.

central agency (a person or set of persons) to which *everyone* is
subject, then, and only then, does the individual as a type of social
role come into being.

Two features of Western political thought may help to illustrate
these observations. The sixteenth and seventeenth centuries saw
the elaboration of the concept of sovereignty, with Jean Bodin and
Thomas Hobbes as the leading theorists. The sense in which the
concept of the 'state', by way of the notion of sovereignty, restricts
the range of social structure emerges in the relative importance now
attached to the thought of Bodin and Hobbes. The reason why
Hobbes rather than Bodin is usually given the credit for the
definitive analysis of the concept of sovereignty is, I suggest, that
Hobbes's argument is clearer on the point of equal subjection and, *a
fortiori*, obviously tied to an individualist model of society. Bodin, on
the other hand, wavers between a notion of equal subjection of
individuals to the sovereign and a notion of the subjection of
families before the Crown (with the survival of paternal authority to
a point where the civic status of subordinate members of the family
is in doubt). That Hobbes's analysis of sovereignty is definitive and
that his model of society is clearly individualist are not
unconnected.

A second and familiar illustration has to do with the development
of the idea of justice in modern times. The building of the criterion
of equal subjection into the concept of the state, by way of
'sovereignty', calls into doubt (even if not in a way that can be
described as logical) all inequalities of status and treatment.
Inequality no longer seems 'natural' or inescapable; on the
contrary, equality becomes associated with the term 'natural'.
There is, in other words, a decisive reversal of assumptions. That
reversal emerges in the convention of starting political argument
with 'the state of nature'. Once equality is deemed to be 'natural',
inequalities of status and treatment seem to require justification.
That is the underlying significance of the Contract theorists of the
seventeenth and early eighteenth century, whatever the differences
between their detailed arguments. The linking of justice and
equality, even if only in a presumptive way, has generated a series
of steps in argument about justice which can (at least in retrospect)
be seen as potentially present since the first move.

To sum up the argument so far, there is nothing immutable
about the state, nor is there anything necessary about the individual

as a social role. Just as the state is a species of government, so the individual is only one type of social role. While in purely normative terms the role 'individual' may be (and I think is) superior— because it involves and fosters an autonomy which raises it morally above traditional social roles—it rests *de facto* on beliefs and practices which may or may not be present in any particular society. Thus, to postulate the individual as a universal and necessary, rather than a potential, social role is to confuse fact and value. It is to impose a valuation as a matter of fact. Defining the political in terms of 'state' and 'individual' has precisely that effect. It ties political theory to methodological individualism. Such a tactic weakens the force of normative individualism by making some of its claims ambiguous. Certainly it obscures the intrinsic connection between the concepts 'state' and 'individual'—and the sense in which, *de facto*, development of the 'state' is a necessary condition for the emergence of the individual as a social role.

That this is so, and yet has not been recognized, springs from the residual connection between analytical philosophy and early empiricist philosophy. The atomism which was a feature of empiricist epistemology in the seventeenth and eighteenth centuries had important consequences for Anglo-American social and political thought. It led to what can be seen, in retrospect, as a rather naïve use of the notion 'natural individuals', to the presentation of values in the form of an ontology. That is, the notion of the individual was presented as unproblematic, as not being obviously or necessarily tied to a particular social structure. Individuals—in the sense of a social role, presupposing equal subjection to a superior—were confused with physical bodies. That emerges in the utilitarian formula that 'everyone shall count for one and no one for more than one'. Is this a matter of fact or a valuation? Or merely a tautology? There is nothing self-evident about this principle. Why should not some count for six, others for two? The failure to see a problem, or to separate methodological from normative individualism, is a symptom of the physicalism which empiricist philosophy bequeathed to Anglo-American political theory. Because every person has a body, does it follow that every person conceives of himself or herself as an individual? The answer, surely, is no—unless the term 'individual' is stretched so wide that it covers the roles available in all societies, tribal and hierarchical as well as egalitarian. But the atomic model which underlay empiricist philosophy made it very tempting to assimilate social units to physical units. 'Society' became, *a fortiori*, an aggregation, a collection of individuals.

That empiricist-inspired ontology involved a radical down-grading and misunderstanding of the role of norms or rules in social life. It failed to make clear the sense in which reasons for acting and intentions are only conceivable within a context of social rules. That ontology presupposed that individuals, with identifiable wants and intentions, exist independently of the concepts and rules which constitute particular social orders. Perhaps that is why Anglo-American political theory, influenced by empiricist philosophy, has on the whole preferred want-satisfying models to want-changing models for normative theory. Theories such as Rousseau's, which combine normative and empirical interests in order to explore how social conditions *shape* wants and intentions, have been ruled out both as metaphysical and as morally repugnant. Thus, the defence of negative liberty—of not asking too many questions about why we want what we want—has sometimes served as an indirect defence of methodological individualism.

We have seen that for the emergence of the individual as a social role, the development of the state and the claims of the state embodied in the concept of sovereignty are indispensable. For, by definition, the sovereign is that authority or power to which *everyone* is *equally* subject. By reference to the sovereign, agents can identify themselves as individuals in a society composed of such rather than, say, of apparently immutable castes or clans. For that reason, the emergence of the state and the doctrine of sovereignty have had a profound and lasting effect on the socializing process in the West. Nineteenth-century French liberals such as Guizot and Tocqueville saw this more clearly, perhaps, than any other modern social and political thinkers. In their view, the atomization of society and political centralization are intrinsically or necessarily connected, two aspects of the same process of change. The equal subjection to a sovereign power which enables individuals to identify themselves *as such* is both logically prior to and historically precedes the elaboration of basic civil liberties, the structure of fundamental rights which confirms and extends the 'individual' as a social role.

In that sense the emergence of the state and sovereignty is more important even than the definition of particular civil liberties for the development of the individual as a type of social role. One or two examples should make that clear. The laws of the state may ratify or create forms of inequality—say, unequal treatment of races or sexes—which may seem to run against any connection (even implicit) between the state and the idea of equality. But that break is more apparent than real. For the mere existence of a centralized agency to which *all* are understood as *equally* subject sustains an awareness in subjects that there is at least one level at which they share an attribute, even if it is only equal subjection to the same authority. That shared attribute, and the sense of a common identity as individuals which it sustains, can easily become the basis for insisting on extending the range of shared attributes, in a way that would be inconceivable in a society in which social roles and rights had their only source in custom.

A striking example of this can be found in the erosion of the status of the French *noblesse* before the Revolution. During the last century of the *ancien régime* the noblesse no longer contested the sovereign right of the Crown—in principle, the King was acknowledged as the source of all positive rights and duties. But at the same time the *noblesse* clung to an older notion of their rights, as indefeasible or prescriptive. That notion, after all, helped to constitute them as a caste, and they could hardly abandon it without ceasing to exist as such. But the incompatibility between prescription and the new notion of rights as general was felt even when it was not acknowledged. The result was an ideological erosion during which the *noblesse* began to see their traditional rights as mere privileges—happy accidents rather than something justified by Natural Law or limiting the King's sovereign right. That ideological incoherence—which resulted from the individualist presuppositions of the concept of the state being increasingly felt, I suggest—contributed to the collapse of the *ancien régime* and the final disappearance of a caste society in France. It also contributed to the need felt by spokesmen for the *noblesse* (such as Boulainvilliers and Montesquieu) to find new arguments in defence of their traditional privileges—arguments which, through emphasizing the need to disperse power and authority, were really functionalist or utilitarian rather than prescriptive.

Equal subjection is not the only way in which the state sustains the social role of the individual. There is another, equally important way. That is by means of the distinction between types of social rules which follows *necessarily* from the emergence of a sovereign power, a society with a state. When sovereign right is attributed to some agency in society, it follows that a distinction between laws properly so called—the commands or rules laid down by the sovereign—and other social rules or customs become not only possible but necessary. Those rules which issue from the sovereign and are enforced by its agents are specific and obligatory in a way that other social rules or customs are not. In consequence, it is no longer true that all social rules have the same status. Some are enforced by public power, while others are not (though public opinion or religious belief may commend the latter). Suddenly, there is a class of rules to which the state is, at least formally speaking, indifferent. That contrast is, I think, the source of the distinction which has become so important in social and political thought since the emergence of the state—namely, the distinction between public and private spheres. The notion that there is a private sphere, a sphere in which personal choice, whim, or conscience has its play, would have been inconceivable and would have had no function in a society without a state, where all rules were customary—where all had the same status and were backed by the same kind of sanction. Yet recent political theorists have often relied upon that distinction between public and private as if it were immutable or self-evident. The contrast between Benjamin Constant's *On Ancient and Modern Liberty*, which does *not* take the distinction for granted, and the collection   edited by Stuart Hampshire, *Public and Private Morality* (Cambridge, Cambridge University Press, 1978) is striking in that respect.

In societies without a state, there can be no such separation between public and private spheres, no gap between what the Marxists call the state and civil society. In such societies there can only be one sphere, because there is no basis in institutions or ideas for distinguishing between publicly enforced rules and rules which are discretionary. All rules would then have the same status, whether they were self-enforced (as in some Anarchist models) or enforced by custom, the group. In societies with a state, on the other hand, there is necessarily what might be called an incoherence in life—given the presence of classes of rules having a different source and status. Now it is precisely that incoherence which, I think, is the deeper source of worries about alienation which can be traced back to Rousseau, Adam Ferguson, and Hegel. The response to such worries has been to postulate some new wholeness as a goal, to overcome the 'gap' between the state and civil society. If society with a state necessarily introduces such a gap, then the state must be superseded. But if, on the other hand, the state is a necessary fulcrum of the individual as a social role, is such an enterprise doomed to fail because it is internally incoherent? That is the rub. Noticing this 'state' source (both organizational and conceptual) for the distinction between public and private may thus have important consequences for the use of counterfactuals in political argument.

My argument, then, is that the concept of the state is intrinsically connected to individualist values through the notion of equal subjection and the emergence of a public/private distinction—and in that way the 'state' is necessarily related to the 'atomization' of society. Looked at historically, the state can be seen as the medium through which Stoic and Christian values were secularized and spread. For the Christian assumption that 'men are equal in the sight of God' has an obvious parallel in the sovereign's relation to his subjects. Fundamental equality of status is postulated in each case. Of course, it could also be argued—for those interested in the sociology of knowledge—that it is no accident that Stoic and Christian assumptions about a common 'human' nature arose when the Roman Empire first introduced something like centralized government in the ancient Mediterranean world, and when the concept of sovereignty in the form of the Emperor's *imperium* developed. Thus, we are confronted with a chain of cause and effect in which institutions and ideas each played a part.

That implicit connection between the concept of the state and the idea of equality is important in understanding the reactions against modernism in many non-Western societies. Arguably, the concept of the state is now by far the most potent means of transmitting individualist values outside the West. For what is involved in building a 'state'? The mere taking-over of the 'state' as a political form carries with it values which traditionalists in other countries may sense (even if they cannot articulate their misgivings) are deeply subversive of their customary social order and religion. But the problem facing them is how to express their objections without falling back on the very terms or concepts which are, in fact, carriers of the values they seek to oppose. Thus, it might be argued that terms like 'Islamic state' or 'Islamic democracy' are essentially confused in so far as they mix incompatible ideas.

On the one hand, 'Islamic' may stand for a rejection of the distinction between law and custom, and an appeal for a return to a customary society, in other words a rejection of the state *as such*.

On the other hand, reliance on terms like 'state' or 'democracy' carries into their own rhetoric egalitarian or individualist values which they ostensibly deplore, and probably do in fact deplore as Western or Christian.

Thus, the dilemma facing such traditionalists is that they themselves can no longer conceive of government on any model other than the state. Yet that model carries with it the very individualist values which they wish to oppose. The state thus becomes a sort of Trojan Horse, bringing with it egalitarian or individualist implications which need not be explicit in the policy it pursues.

I want to turn to a number of problems in modern political thought which look different in the light of a more critical approach to the concepts 'individual' and 'state'. The first has to do with arguments put by Montesquieu, the second with Traditionalism as expounded from Burke to Oakeshott, while a third arises from Marx's theory of alienation and the 'withering away' of the state. Finally, I shall look at a recent account of the problems of political obligation.

It has often been observed that Montesquieu's classification of regimes differs from the classical schema of monarchy (one), aristocracy (few), and democracy (many). For Montesquieu, the number of people wielding power ceases to be the only basis of classification. He introduces another criterion which he calls 'moderation'. Relying on the latter he distinguishes Oriental depotism from European monarchy. He also reclassifies democracy and aristocracy as two forms of a single type of government, termed republican—which, like monarchy, is an essentially moderate type. Now, I suggest that what Montesquieu sought to identify with the help of this 'moderate' criterion is precisely the state, the rule of law. That is, equal subjection is built by definition into his category of 'moderate' regimes. By contrast, Oriental despotism is the type of unadulterated power, not exercised through law or restrained by law. It is untainted, Montesquieu says, 'by the idea of Natural Law'. By that he means, I suggest, that the equality of fundamental status implied by the concept of sovereignty is absent—so that government is not necessarily the government of individuals. To that extent, one might say that Montesquieu's criterion of moderation is essentially post-Stoic and Christian.

That criterion, however, creates problems for his theory. 'Moderation' is so closely tied to the rule of law that it is debatable whether the ancient *polis*, which he considers a moderate form, can properly be so described. For positive law was not a feature of the Greek communities, which had not developed the conception of law as essentially man-made, made by a common superior. The concept of law, when it was used at all, was embedded in a concept of reason, attached to an ontology rather than a postulate of sovereignty. For that reason, there was no practical basis for distinguishing between law and custom, between the state and civil society, or, for that matter, public and private life. The individual did not have any status *as such*, nor any rights against the group. In that sense it is open to doubt whether the Greek *polis*, whether democratic or aristocratic, satisfies Montesquieu's criterion of moderation. He seems to have read back into the Greek world meanings and practices where were essentially Stoic and Roman. For notions of sovereignty and positive law must be traced back to Hellenic ideas of kingship, and in particular, to the Roman idea of *imperium*, suggesting the subjection of individuals to a single centralized authority.

Grasping the connection between the concept of the state and an individualist model of society raises an interesting question, too, about the Traditionalist point of view, as set out from Burke to Oakeshott. Can the state and the form of social control identified with the state—i.e. positive law—be reconciled with so strong an emphasis on inherited social roles and a prescriptive notion of rights? Undoubtedly the Traditionalists' preferred instrument of social control is custom or assigned status (though they may, like Burke, extol a *limited* amount of social mobility). Their conception of society as an integrated and harmonious set of roles, necessarily unequal, does not strictly require a sovereign or state. Historically, the emergence of a sovereign or state may be understood as the symptom of the failure of custom as a sufficient instrument of social control. In turn, the monopoly of legal power or right which is by definition the sovereign's threatens custom. It introduces, as we have seen, a kind of normative *tabula rasa*. Rights, in order to be legal rights properly so called, must now at least be confirmed by the sovereign. There is good reason for believing that the normative *tabula rasa* implied by the concept of sovereignty contributed to the steady weakening of the notion of prescriptive right since the seventeenth century. To that extent, Traditionalists might plausibly view the state with suspicion if not downright hostility. Yet, on the other hand, the considerable *de facto* overlap between positive law and custom—and perhaps even more the possibility of using the state machine to shore up customs under threat—makes it difficult for the Traditionalists to reject the state *in principle*. That ambiguity in Traditionalists' attitude to the state opens the way to a radical reliance on state power, and suggests why Fascism may be seen as an extreme or pathological form of Traditionalism. If customary roles have been radically eroded, then the temptation to use state power to reinforce them may be irresistible. The political theory of Joseph de Maistre, who brings a starkly Hobbesian doctrine of sovereignty to the aid of an aristocratic society and the Church, stands at the border between Traditionalism and proto-Fascism.

A third problem in political thought which benefits from applying this analysis is the Marxist argument about the 'withering away' of the state in a post-revolutionary society. That hypothesis has, of course, been criticized on many counts. It is extremely difficult even to conceive of a society with an advanced division of labour—that is, a society with the sort of industrial machine which could eliminate scarcity and not be held back by outmoded relations of production—which would not involve forms of planning requiring a centralized administrative machine, whether it be called a state or not. The use of this counterfactual in Marxist theory is problematic, to say the least. But it is not the only, and perhaps in the long run not the most serious, issue arising from Marx's hypothesis. Even more serious, I think, is the goal of 'liberating' the individual, or encouraging self-fulfilment, assuming that the state has withered away.

The problem becomes apparent if one assumes that the state has a role, indeed a crucial role, in the socializing process that creates and sustains 'individuals'. The contrary view, that the individual is a self-sustaining role more or less independent of social organization, is the view usually attributed to classical liberalism by its critics, both conservative and socialist. The former tend to make this criticism by insisting on the social sources of identity—in particular, by insisting that society 'properly so-called' entails hierarchy; while socialists or radicals have characteristically pointed to economic changes, especially the development of a market economy, which are necessary pre-conditions of the development of bourgeois or individualist society. In that sense, both the right and left have criticized liberal thought as sociologically naïve. And, of course, there is much truth in that criticism in the case of the Contract theorists of the seventeenth and eighteenth centuries and of economic liberals, from Ricardo to Marshall. But it is by no means true of all liberal thought or necessarily true of liberal thought—and, in particular, it is certainly not true of nineteenth-century French liberal thought (as I have argued elsewhere[5]). Indeed, the criticism of sociological *naïveté* can be turned against those who have usually made it. Conservatives such as Burke and Maistre can be shown to limit the possibilities of social change a priori, by stipulating that society *means* a hierarchical or aristocratic order. Any departure from that model is then defined as decay or degeneration, an invitation to anarchy and despotism.

The same charge of sociological *naïveté* would, if it were levelled against Marx, take a different form. If equal subjection to a common authority or power is a crucial fulcrum for personal identity—if, that is, it is indispensable in the socializing of an 'individual'—then it is far from clear what the consequences of the withering-away of the state might be. To destroy the much lamented 'gap' between the state and civil society (in ideas and practices) can only mean that there is no longer any point or means of distinguishing between law and custom or, indeed, between law and morality. What exactly is the role of the individual when such distinctions, together with areas of free choice and scope for individual will which they sustain, are obliterated? Whether the goal is anarchical or a form of community, harmony can then only be *guaranteed* by stipulation—by postulating a moralized agent.

Marx assumes that once a class society has been destroyed, so-called natural individuals will be liberated from the roles and rules which previously imposed strait-jackets on them and prevented them from satisfying the diverse needs and impulses harboured in their breasts. Here Marx's argument for a society beyond roles

[5]L. Siedentop, 'Two Liberal Traditions' in A. Ryan (ed.), *The Idea of Freedom* (Oxford, Oxford University Press, 1979).

seems to me to ignore the sense in which the natural individual is itself a social role—i.e. the extent to which the so-called natural individual's role or identity is itself the product of, and depends upon, a particular form of social and political organization *and* the extent to which the individual's concept of himself as such, as a free and equal agent, rests on the doctrine of sovereignty. In that sense, the state may be said to be intrinsic to personal identity in an individualist or atomized society. Ironically, then, it could be argued that there is more *bourgeois individualism* in Marx than in French liberals such as Tocqueville.

So far I have argued that the treatment of a number of issues in modern political thought needs revision when the connection between the concept of the state and one type of social structure is made explicit. Of course, *de facto* restriction on the range of social structure is at the same time a restriction on the range of beliefs and motives typical of social agents. That becomes important when we consider general accounts of the problem of political obligation itself, the problem which preoccupied political thinkers during the period which saw both the emergence of the state and what French liberals called the 'atomization' of society (i.e. the emergence of the individual as a type of social role).

Why should I, or anyone, obey the state? Put thus, the problem of political obligation only makes sense on individualist presuppositions—i.e. given an individualist model of society or individualist criteria for morally right action. Does a theorist like Quinton make that clear? Alas, he does not. Quinton's use of 'state' and 'government' as if they were synonymous blurs the issue. In fact, Quinton presents several 'answers' to the problem of political obligation in a way that is seriously misleading. He presents as 'answers' or accounts of political obligation a number of theories which, strictly, do not allow the problem itself to arise. That is, he presents as theories of political obligation what are really conceptions of society which rule out any such question *ab initio.*

Quinton distinguishes three sorts of answer to the question of political obligation.[6] They are what he calls intrinsic, extrinsic, and organic theories. As an example of intrinsic theories Quinton cites the Burkean defence of aristocracy, while he assigns the organic position to Rousseau and Hegel; what he calls extrinsic theories, on

[6]Quinton, *Political Philosophy*, pp. 10–13.

the other hand, are contractarian or utilitarian—justifying obedience to the state by pointing, indirectly or directly, to the desirable consequences *for the individual* which follow from it. The trouble with these distinctions is that they misrepresent two out of the three types of theory. Two of the three types do not even seek to answer the 'question'. Rather, they eliminate the problem of political obligation a priori. What Quinton calls intrinsic theories of political obligation are really pre-individualist conceptions of social order, in which status is customary and society by definition consists of a set of interlocking, unequal roles. Hence the importance of prescriptive right for such theories. On the other hand, what Quinton calls organic theories of political obligation can more accurately be understood as post-individualist conceptions of society, in so far as they postulate an individual who is also, by definition, a fully moralized agent. Hence the frequent charge that they involve a metaphysical theory of the self tied to a metaphysical theory of the state. Thus, intrinsic theories do not recognize a problem of political obligation at all, while organic theories supersede it. *Neither accepts the conventions of the individualist model of society.* Each attacks the convention whereby a 'natural' individual is postulated, either as disruptive of social hierarchy or as sociologically naïve and morally repugnant. Hence too—and this is no accident—each is obliged to tinker with the concept of the state. The intrinsic theories suffer from radical ambiguity over the relationship between prescriptive right and state sovereignty, while organic theories involve assumptions which give positive law a higher status as embodying the real or rational or higher will of the citizens and thus blur the distinction between law and morality.

I have taken Quinton's introduction to *Political Philosophy* as an example of a type of argument fairly widespread in recent Anglo-American political theory. A more refined political theory would define itself in relation to 'government' rather than 'the state' and would, in turn, explore the social sources of identity to make clear that 'individual' implies a certain range of social structures rather than being the element out of which every society is necessarily composed. A more systematic and explicit defence of individualist values would then become both necessary and possible. It would be a defence which made clear the sense in which the 'state' is, indirectly, a carrier of individualist ideology or values. By taking that step, political theory would protect itself from the charge of being an instrument of bourgeois ideology. Nor is that all: such a step would also sharpen and clarify views about the 'political'. The term—and the subject which it helps to constitute—would no longer be taken for granted. Indeed, any sharp distinction between political theory and social theory would begin to look dubious.

*   *   *

There is another way in which my point may be made. A society composed of individuals is a society in which primary and secondary roles can be distinguished. The primary or meta-role, that of being an individual, follows necessarily from 'equal subjection' in any society with a state. To this primary role an indefinite number of other roles may or may not be added, as the attributes of a subject. But they do not define the subject. Thus, being a father, a Roman Catholic, a doctor, or a debtor may be added to (or subtracted from) an individual's identity, but the individual remains. In a society without a state that is not true. *Ex hypothesi*, there is no primary or meta-role conferred by a sovereign agency, and so the descriptions conferred by particular roles are not mediated by a role shared *equally by all.* Even the identity conferred by a common language or tribal bond is different from that conferred by equal subjection to a sovereign. A language or tribal bond enables social agents to distinguish themselves from *outsiders,* but it does not necessarily confer any fundamental or under-lying equality of status *within* the group—so that being a Hausa or speaking Hindi does not entail that an agent is an individual, whereas (in the late twentieth century world of nation-states) being a Nigerian or an Indian does. It is this separation of a primary role from secondary roles which the doctrine of state sovereignty brings about. The history of English usage bears that out. The first recorded use of 'individual', 'as opposed to Society, the Family, etc.' is recorded by the Oxford English Dictionary as 1626. This is no coincidence. Linguistic change reflects changes in institutions and beliefs—in this case, the emergence of the state and of the doctrine of sovereignty. Through the idea of the state and the process of political centralization the Natural Law tradition's stipulation of equal fundamental status acquired a practical embodiment. A process of social transformation began which has by no means ended.

The argument I have made will probably strike some as alarmingly relativist. But that objection seems to me misplaced. By understanding the individual not as a natural fact, but as a social construct—a cultural achievement, so to speak—the strategy for a more satisfactory defence of individualist values is suggested. By taking account of the social conditions of our own knowledge, the individual as a social role is better understood and revealed to be a more fragile and precious achievement than either defenders or critics of individualism have often implied. Clearly, the individual can no longer be taken for granted as a brute fact always available for constructing social orders. But why should that weaken the normative appeal of the individual as a social role? It seems a confusion of fact and value to suppose that the social role legitimated by individualist values should also be 'natural' in the sense of brute, uncreated, or timeless. That supposition strikes me as the last refuge of seventeenth century philosophical materialism.

Political Power, Social Theory, and Essential Contestability* †

John Gray
Jesus College, Oxford

The starting-point of my enquiry is an observation. In recent years social theorists have been much occupied in controversy about power. Theorists have argued as to whether power is to be attributed to social actors or to social structures, about how the possession of power may be distinguished from a disposition to exercise power on specified occasions, and so on. I begin my enquiry with the commonplace observation that these controversies in the theory of power express divergencies in the philosophy of the social studies. Often, these controversies are interpreted as expressing divergent views about the merits of positivism as a stance in the philosophy of social science. Differences between positivists and the critics of positivism are posed differently in different traditions, but here 'positivism' seems to stand for the claim that in its methods and goals the study of society ought to replicate a received model of the study of nature. The practice of natural science is understood to be insulated from the value-commitments and from the philosophical bias of its practitioners and (at least in its normal periods) to display agreement on rules of method and convergence on a common body of theory. For positivists, there can be no reason why the dispassionate study of society should not in due course yield a like body of common theory, or why such theory should not serve as a common resource for partisans of opposed policies and competing interests. According to positivism's critics, the subject-matter of the social studies disqualifies any natural-scientific model for their investigation. The observational basis of the social studies (they insist) is not neutrally accessible to rival theoretical frameworks, it is captured differently by each of them. Social theories in turn are not dissociable from the moral and political commitments of their

*© John Gray 1983.

† For their comments on early drafts of the paper, I am indebted to W. E. Connolly, John Dunn, Steven Lukes, Mark Philp, Quentin Skinner, and W. L. Weinstein. I am also grateful to David Miller for his many helpful suggestions as to how to make my meaning clearer.

exponents. Often, critics of positivism maintain that the theory-dependency of social facts along with the value-dependency of social theories introduces a dimension of relativity or contestability into social thought. It is in virtue of this character of relativity that social theory can never replicate natural science. Social theory remains an area of intractable and inherent controversy for these critics of positivism, primarily because it is unavoidably informed by value-commitments between which reason cannot arbitrate.

This common story about controversy in the philosophy of social science may be illustrated by reference to controversy in the theory of power. Here the writings of Steven Lukes and W. E. Connolly[1] are particularly illuminating for, despite several differences of emphasis in their writings, they share three beliefs which go far to support the conventional view of controversy in this area as expressive of debate for and against positivism. First, they hold that the concept of power, along with many other concepts in social theory, is essentially contestable. This is to say that its proper range of uses is inherently a matter of irresolvable dispute. For Lukes and Connolly, the essential contestability of the concept of power derives from the fact that rival applications of it embody conflicting value-commitments. So, inasmuch as it cannot help invoking some notion of power, social theory (in Lukes's and Connolly's account of it) cannot avoid being a normative exercise. Second, Lukes and Connolly agree that the point of locating power in society is to fix responsibility. They insist that responsibility, like power, is an essentially contested concept, and they acknowledge that fixing responsibility involves making a moral appraisal. Further, they wish to contrast exercises of power with the structural determination of social happenings: they assert that, though opportunities for action are structurally constrained, the subject-matter of the theory of power is human agency rather than the workings of social or historical necessity. Power is an interstitial phenomenon, arising in the gaps in the structural determination of social events. Understanding the exercise of power inescapably involves the application of moral notions connected with responsibility and with the nature of persons. Thirdly, Lukes and Connolly argue for the dependency of rival views of power on competing

---

[1] I refer especially to Steven Lukes, *Power: a radical view* (London, Macmillan, 1974) and Lukes's *Essays in Social Theory* (London, Macmillan, 1977); and to W. E. Connolly, *The Terms of Political Discourse* (Lexington, D. C. Heath, 1974).

conceptions of human interests. These are normative notions inasmuch as they have ratifying and validating as well as descriptive and explanatory uses, but Lukes and Connolly insist that judgements about interests remain none the less partly empirical in content. They are to be spelled out in terms of the preferences that are displayed by autonomous agents who have a clear apprehension of the relevant alternatives open to them. For Lukes and Connolly, then, power is an essentially contestable concept depending on opposed conceptions of human interests, where it is the preferences of an autonomous man that finally determine his real interests.

At the meta-theoretical level, the central thesis advanced by Lukes and Connolly is that, in virtue of the essential contestability of its constitutive concepts, any kind of social theory is a form of moral and political practice. I shall have much to say in criticism of the nuts and bolts of their accounts, but at this point I want to observe only that there seem to be two entirely distinct theses in their writings about power. One is the thesis that the theory of power, like the rest of social theory, is beset by an ineradicable conceptual relativism such that no account of power can compel rational assent. The other is the thesis that social theorizing cannot avoid being a normative activity, that theory-making about the social world is informed by the theorist's values, so that making such theory is (whether self-consciously or not) an aspect of its practitioner's moral and political life. My comment here is that, whereas Lukes and Connolly cite the latter thesis in support of the former, the supportive connection between the two remains unspecified. Nothing that Lukes and Connolly argue about power goes any distance towards linking the theory-dependence of social facts with the value-dependence of social theories. The upshot of my argument at this meta-theoretical level will be that relativism or scepticism in social theory may have sources other than the claim that social theories are value-laden. One reason that arguments about the value-neutrality of social theories have been run together promiscuously with arguments about the theory-neutrality of social facts is to be found in the vogue for a jargon of essential contestability. I shall argue that, whereas claims about essential contestability may once have had utility in a campaign against certain obsolete positivisms in social science, the idiom of essential contestability constitutes an impediment to further advance in social theory. Talk of essential contestability conflates a range of distinct problems and insights in social theory whose careful disaggregation is a condition of progress in understanding its prospects and limitations.

My programmatic conclusion will be that there are many reasons for scepticism and humility in social theory, but none of them imply or presuppose that theorizing about society is necessarily informed (or corrupted) by the theorist's values. Before I can reach this conclusion, I must consider in detail the account given by Lukes and Connolly of the relations between power, human interests, and autonomy and their claim that judgements about the exercise of power embrace judgements about responsibility. I shall argue that there are not the logical links between the concepts of power, interests, and autonomy postulated by these writers and that they are mistaken in their belief that discourse about the distribution of power in society need be connected with the moral assessment of responsibility. A further result of my examination will be the claim that in both Lukes's account and that of Connolly liberal and socialist positions in political theory, and sceptical and realist positions in moral theory, coexist and compete with each other. The account of power offered by these writers is a theory divided against itself at more than one point, and I shall in conclusion suggest how this self-division may best be resolved.

POWER, AUTONOMY, AND INTERESTS

According to Lukes, the common core of all conceptions of power is found in the notion of one agent affecting another. Further, when the notion of power is invoked to capture the import of a social exchange, it always comprehends the idea of significant, non-trivial affecting, Using John Rawls's distinction[2] between a generic concept and the many specific conceptions a concept may spawn, Lukes goes on to distinguish three views of power as 'alternative interpretations and applications of one and the same underlying concept of power, according to which A exercises power over B when A affects B in a manner contrary to B's interests'.[3] Each of

---

[2] The distinction between a concept and its conceptions is made in John Rawls, *A Theory of Justice* (Oxford, Oxford University Press, 1972), pp. 5–6, and cited by Lukes in *Power*, p. 27.

[3] Lukes, *Power*, p. 27.

these three views of power emerges from and operates within a definite moral and political perspective and carries with it a definite conception of human interests. The first, 'one-dimensional' or 'pluralist' view, defended by such writers as Dahl, Polsby, Wolfinger, and Merelman, for whom power is exercised in observable conflict over policy issues, presupposes a 'liberal' understanding of interests in terms of policy preferences expressed in political participation. The second, 'two-dimensional' view expounded by Bachrach and Baratz holds that power is exercised, not only when there is victory in a conflict over policies, but also when potential issues are organized out of the political arena, and this second view embodies a 'reformist' conception of interests which allows that they may be submerged or concealed, distorted or deflected from full expression by a series of non-decisions. According to the 'three-dimensional' view which (like Connolly) Lukes himself defends, each of the conceptions of interests presupposed by the first two views is defective. Power may be exercised over men even when their wants have been fully satisfied, and, in Lukes's 'radical' conception of power and interests, a man's real interests are not in what he happens to want, but in whatever it is that he would want if he were to become a fully autonomous agent.

As far as Lukes and Connolly are concerned, a power relation exists whenever one agent affects another significantly and does so detrimentally to the latter's interests. Before I try to probe the links they postulate between power, interests, and autonomy, it may be worth making a few preliminary observations about the conceptual analysis of power contained in Lukes's and Connolly's writings. To start with, it is not clear to me why significant affecting should be placed at the core of the concept of power. Significant affecting is a feature of many sorts of social interaction —it characterizes love and trade, among many other involvements—and it is not plausibly represented as especially or distinctively characteristic of power relations. Again, it is wholly unclear why the exercise of power should always involve a significant impact on human interests, or, most crucially, why power relations are defined as social relations involving conflicts of interest. It seems clear—and this is a point to which I will return—that power relations may involve a conflict of goals or of preferences without thereby turning on a conflict of interests. As a corollary of this last point, I cannot see why the attribute of power should be restricted to social interactions where one agent affects *detrimentally* the interests of another. No such restriction is found in ordinary thought and language, and imposing one by stipulation has counter-intuitive results.

The conceptual analysis of power advanced by Lukes and Connolly is unduly restrictive in focusing attention on the significant affecting of interests and in insisting that power has to do, only or centrally, with conflicts of interest. It introduces into the concept of power the requirement that the exercise of power occurs always in a circumstance of (manifest or latent) social conflict. This is to sanction a conflictual conception of power of the sort repudiated by those theorists (Arendt and Parsons are examples[4]) who conceive of it as a collective resource, possessed in greater or lesser magnitudes by different societies. Further, it writes into the notion of power a presumption of its maleficence, a presumption commonly made in liberal and socialist intellectual traditions, but hard to sustain for all that. The concentration on 'power over' to the exclusion of 'power to' cannot be justified by the claim that such power is especially salient to political contexts, since the claim already carries with it the indefensibly restrictive (and distinctively liberal) conception of political life as somehow inherently a domain of conflicts.

It is not hard to show that the requirement of any exercise of power that it injures the interests of the agent over whom it is exercised yields counter-intuitive results. At a microsocial level, I may apply force or coercion to another individual, not in order to protect or promote any interest of mine, but with the aim of benefiting him. If I succeed in attaining my aim, the exchange between us may be neutral, adverse, or favourable to my interests while it benefits those of the other. At a macrosocial level, Stalinist policies in which working-class liberties and current living standards are repressed have been defended, coherently if not plausibly, by invoking the long-term and on-balance interests of the working class itself. What reason could there be for denying the character of power to these relationships?

In citing these examples, I do not seek to rebut the contention that a man always loses something when power is exercised over

---

[4]For his discussion of the contributions of Parsons and Arendt, see Lukes, *Power*, pp. 27–31. For Connolly's discussion, see Connolly, *Terms of Political Discourse*, pp. 114–15.

him, but only to remark on its triviality. Presumably, everyone has an interest in acting on his current wants, even where his so acting prejudices his interests taken on balance. Presumably, also, the interest that is damaged when anyone is prevented by another from acting on his current wants is the interest in autonomy. Still, it remains a commonplace that we all have interests other than the interests we have in our autonomy: no one can plausibly deny that these other interests might be promoted at the expense of our interest in autonomy. This is only to utter the truism that the damage done to an agent's interest in autonomy may well be compensated for by gains to his other interests and by an improvement in his interests as a whole. All this begs a natural question about how someone's interest in autonomy is to be weighted against his other interests when their claims compete, but nothing important hinges here on this omission. A competition between the interest in autonomy and a man's other interests can be circumvented altogether only by the fraudulent expedient of attaching an infinite weight to the human interest in autonomy (relative to other human interests). I take it that, whatever the interest in autonomy comprehends, no one could sensibly allow it to overwhelm or engross all other human interests. This point is not met by the response that, when a man's interest in his autonomy conflicts with his other interests, it is up to the man himself to trade them off against each other. Even making the heroic assumption that he decides always to promote his interest in autonomy against all his other interests, the possibility remains that weakness of will or poor calculation on his part will thwart this policy. This possibility opens up the prospect of an *autonomy-maximizing paternalism* in which a man's autonomy in one area is restricted so as to promote his chances of autonomy on balance. In the case I am considering, the hypothesis is that this paternalist intervention promotes the agent's interests. Whether or not it does so, I cannot see why an intervention of this sort should be refused the character of an exercise of power.

So far in my discussion, the term 'autonomy' has been used almost as a cipher. Its content has gone unspecified. We may take it for granted that its provenance is in Kantian ideas about moral personality, though as my argument proceeds it will become clear that, in Lukes's and Connolly's use of the notion, matters are not so simple. At this point I want to observe that, however the ideal of autonomy is in the end filled out, it must on any account of it be a complex achievement, having a variety of elements and capable of being realized in differing degrees. If this is so, and (as both Lukes and Connolly are at pains to insist) autonomy should be regarded as a variable magnitude rather than a threshold phenomenon, then it should be obvious that autonomy may be promoted (and even maximized) by an intervention that restricts it. A policy of restricting a man's autonomy might, then, be licensed solely by reference to the value of autonomy. It might be so justified if, as in the case of autonomy-regarding paternalism to which I alluded earlier, the autonomy promoted is that of the agent whose autonomy is restricted. Alternatively, it might be justified in this way if an intervention reducing someone's autonomy on balance at the same time increases the autonomy of all the others affected by it and maximizes the value of autonomy in the circumstances under consideration. There are, admittedly, questions that go unanswered in the sketch I have offered of such a policy and its justification. We do not know how weighty is the interest each man has in his own autonomy: is it weighty enough to support a side-constraint against policies which promote autonomy (now or in the long term) at the expense of his (current or lifetime) prospects of autonomy? Nor do we know how, when once it is acknowledged that autonomy is a complex achievement having various elements, we are to weight these elements when a policy having regard only to the value of autonomy promotes its constitutive elements in differing degrees: we have no guidance as to how we are to make on-balance judgements even of one man's autonomy. But neither of these questions is answered in Lukes's or Connolly's accounts, and I do not see that they impeach the drift of my argument at all.

The observations I have made so far have all been about the conceptual analysis of power held in common by Lukes and Connolly. I have questioned its special connection with significant affecting and argued that the general link with interests is undefended. More controversially, I have maintained that the requirement that exercises of power be always in circumstances of social conflict, latent or manifest, disqualifies conceptions of power as a collective resource. One general point illustrated by these observations is that Lukes's and Connolly's account of the generic concept of power is itself non-neutral in its implications for debate about the appropriate conception of power. It establishes boundaries for any bona fide conception of power, and such boundaries are certain to be intensely controversial. It is hard to see how matters could be otherwise, if power is indeed an essentially contestable concept. There is no more reason to expect agreement on the formal features or conceptual analysis of power than there is to expect it on the merits of its various conceptions. The fact that neither Lukes nor Connolly has anywhere satisfactorily defended their conceptual analysis has led one commentator to observe that Lukes's argument makes sense only if it is seen as reposing on a real definition of power.[5] Given the conventionalist and relativist aspects of essential contestability theses, this is an ironical and paradoxical result.

A crucial claim made in both the accounts I am considering is that judgements about a man's real interests, and so about his power situation, retain an empirical dimension inasmuch as they are spelled out in terms of the preferences of an autonomous agent. This is a crucial claim, for on it depends the belief that the view of power it supports is a part of empirical social theory and not merely an ideological assertion. If a power relation always involves a conflict of interests, and these interests may be latent rather than manifest, then whether a judgement about a power relation is true will depend wholly on claims about the (hypothetical and counter-factual) preferences of an autonomous agent. Everything then turns on whether the conception of autonomy at work here can be satisfactorily elucidated, defended, and given operational value.

An initial uncertainty concerns the nature of the link postulated in Lukes and Connolly between the preferences or choices of an autonomous man and his real interests. It is obvious that a man's preferences when he is (relatively highly) autonomous cannot be *identified* with his interests for there can be no presumption that an autonomous man will have prudence as his dominant motive: he may, after all, choose autonomously to sacrifice his interests to some ideal he cherishes. The link must be between a man's real interests and his autonomous judgement of his interests, not between his real interests and whatever it is that he prefers when he is autonomous. This has the important implication that there may be occasions for conflict among highly autonomous men, even if (implausibly) the interests of such men cannot conflict. There seems no reason why

---

[5]This suggestion is advanced in Martin Hollis, *Models of Man* (Cambridge, Cambridge University Press, 1977), pp. 173–80.

the social conflicts engendered among autonomous men whose interests harmonize but whose goals or ideals do not should not express themselves in power relations.

A deeper uncertainty concerns the nature of the link postulated in Lukes's and Connolly's accounts between interests and autonomous choice. What a man chooses autonomously as to his own welfare might merely be useful *evidence* as to where his interests lie, or else it might serve as the *criterion* of his interests: in the latter case, a man's interests are necessarily constituted by his autonomous preferences about his own welfare. In general, though in both writers there are occasional equivocations, Lukes and Connolly go for the view that autonomous choice is the criterion of interests, not just good evidence about them.

But, if the necessary link is not between autonomous choice or preference and real interests, but between what an autonomous man takes his interests to be and what they are, it begins to look again as if human interests constitute a subject-matter independent of anyone's choices or preferences. On the one hand, if the link between autonomy and interests is criterial, then a man's judgement of his interests will be incorrigible, while on the other hand there must be room for the notion of a mistake being possible in this kind of judgement if indeed it is a judgement with a determinate subject-matter. How is this difficulty to be resolved? It might be suggested that this is not a deep problem. The distinction needed might simply be that between a man's preferences for his own welfare and those he has for the welfare of others: his interests are constituted by the former. Whereas some such commonsensical distinction is in place and will be presupposed by much of what I myself later argue, it does not seem to me to meet the difficulty I have in mind. This is that there seem to be two views of the relations between autonomy and interests at issue here. One view is that a man's preferences about his own prospects just are his interests: his only reason for action is that he has goals, and his interests are those of his goals or preferences that concern himself. The other view is that a man's interests are a matter of fact for him: they give him reasons for action whether or not he knows about or assents to them.

At this point in their theory of interests Lukes and Connolly confront an unavoidable parting of the ways between subjectivist and objectivist accounts. In one perspective, argued for by Brian

Barry,[6] the concept of having an interest may be analysed wholly in terms of opportunities for the satisfaction of wants. In this view, the only relevant authority to which appeal may be made to settle questions about a man's interests is the judgement of the man himself. To be sure, inasmuch as legal or financial expertise enters into a man's deliberations about his interests, others may advise him as to where his interests lie and even, in special circumstances, act as guardians of his interests. Except in cases of this latter sort, where a man's judgement is rendered corrigible by his lack of special knowledge, the fact that a man's wants are his own entails that his own assessments of his interests, spelled out in terms of his basic preferences for his own welfare, are indefeasible. Apart from cases where technical expertise or suchlike is involved, this view of interests implies that, whenever a man's basic preferences about his own welfare change, his interests change too: a man's basic preferences cannot be the subject of a criticism in terms of his interests. It is true enough that a man's current wants and his interests are never the same thing even on a subjective view; a man's interests even on that view of them must encompass all the wants he is reasonably likely to conceive in a lifetime. Indeed, if (as I have assumed) it is a man's preferences and not his mental states which go to make up his interests, then his interests may be protected or damaged even after he is dead. In this subjectivist view, then, a man's current preferences may be overridden so as to protect his prospects of satisfying all his preferences, taken over a lifetime, and his interests may thereby be promoted; but it cannot be the case that his wants or preferences, when they are taken as a whole, could be thwarted for the sake of his interests. In an objective view, on the contrary, the criterial link between wants and interests is severed, and a man's interests are explicated in terms of some notion of the conditions appropriate to his flourishing. On this objectivist view, a man may well be in error as to what his interests are, for though his wants remain his own, his wants no longer decide his interests.

How does this, admittedly rather crude, distinction bear on the arguments of Lukes and Connolly? I think it impales them on a fork. Lukes, at any rate, cannot endorse the objectivist view of

---

[6]For this see B. M. Barry, *Political Argument* (London, Routledge and Kegan Paul, 1965), ch. 10. Also, Barry's contribution to the present volume is relevant here.

interests without abandoning the value-relativism he has elsewhere avowed[7] and without elaborating upon the theory of moral knowledge and the philosophical anthropology which links interests with conditions of human flourishing. Again, adopting an objectivist view of interests creates problems for the claim that judgements about men's interests are liable to a straightforward empirical and behavioural test—a claim to which Lukes wishes to hold.[8] If a subjectivist view is adopted, on the other hand, problems about testability of a different sort surface. Discussing Crenson's analysis of air pollution in American cities, Lukes tells us that it is impressive because '. . . there is good reason to expect that, other things being equal, people would rather not be poisoned (assuming, in particular, that pollution control does not necessarily mean unemployment)—even where they may not even articulate this preference'.[9] On a subjective view, this 'good reason' of which Lukes speaks can only be an inductive wager grounded in exception-ridden generalizations about human behaviour. Where other things are not equal, where people must make trade-offs and the influence on their choices of culture, circumstance, and temperament cannot be discounted, such inductive wagers are fraught with uncertainty. Where an inductive wager of this kind is invoked counterfactually to explain a historical development, it is hard to see how it can be the subject of any sort of test.

Underlying this disjunction between objective and subjective views of interests lies a divergence in the concept of autonomy itself. On one view, which has perhaps a genuine Kantian ancestry, autonomy is primarily a formal, procedural, and open concept: it desiderates the general conditions of any respectworthy choice. Such a choice, if it is to be autonomous, must be rational—it must, let us say, satisfy criteria of means-end efficiency, embody a precept to which the agent can give a relevantly universal assent, and so on. If autonomy is construed in this way as an open notion, then it should be evident to us (even if it was not clear to Kant) that it will not specify any very determinate range of ways of life as being in

[7] See Steven Lukes, 'Relativism: Cognitive and Moral' in *Essays in Social Theory*, ch. 8.

[8] Lukes, *Essays in Social Theory*, pp. 24–6, asserts that disputes about power and responsibility may in some cases be resolvable empirically. He makes the same claim in his 'On the Relativity of Power' in S. C. Brown (ed.), *Philosophical Disputes in the Social Sciences* (Brighton, Harvester, 1979), pp. 261–74.

[9] Lukes, *Power*, p. 45.

conformity with human interests. It will in fact be pretty destitute of prescriptive content. If autonomy is construed in a more Aristotelian way as a relatively closed concept, autonomous choice will be compatible only with a fairly narrowly defined range of ways of life. In this conception, the relation between autonomous choices and real interests intimated in Lukes's account will actually have been reversed: the conditions of human flourishing will now serve as providing *criteria for the identification of autonomous choice itself.* It should be clear that, whatever else it might be, this is an account in which the requirement that identification of real interests have an 'empirical basis' has been abandoned.

In Connolly's more extended treatment[10] of the concept of autonomy, an attempt is made to resist criticisms of this sort. 'The idea of real interests', he says, 'is bounded by a set of core ideas we share, if often imperfectly and to a large extent tacitly, about those characteristics particularly distinctive of persons.'[11] This reference to certain defining features of persons acts as a restriction on the use of the choice criterion. Notwithstanding this restriction, Connolly's account of real interests remains within the subjectivist view; it differs from the standard 'liberal' account only by virtue of the stringent conditions it comprehends for the specification of the privileged choice situation in which the relevant preferences (which express a man's real interests) are to be displayed. Specifically, Connolly's account goes beyond the liberal account, and deviates from the standards of ordinary thought and practice, in allowing for the possibility of internal constraints on action. Like David Riesman, Connolly suggests that a man fails to be autonomous if he is swayed by peer-group pressure or social convention or guided by imprintings of socialization which he has not himself critically sifted.

Connolly's account fails to meet the criticisms I have advanced and breaks down in much the same way that Mill's theory of the higher pleasures does: it underestimates the variety of human nature. This is to say that reference to the powers of deliberation and capacities for emotional involvement which make persons what they are will not allow agents' preferences to be overridden in the name of their interests in a variety of dilemmas of the sort that

[10]Connolly, *The Terms of Political Discourse*, chs. 2 and 4.
[11]Ibid., p. 68.

concern Connolly. The contented lifelong heroin addict, and the man who lives and dies in willing slavery,[12] will sometimes be able plausibly to defend their life-styles as most efficacious in the promotion of their interests. Certainly, invoking in an aprioristic fashion the idea of the person cannot defeat this possibility. There is nothing to support the presumption that an autonomous agent cannot autonomously and reasonably act to abridge his future prospects of autonomy.

The variety of human nature creates difficulties for the supposition, entertained by both Lukes and Connolly,[13] that there may be a power-free mode of consensual authority resting on autonomous choices and involving a harmony of real interests. Given the variety of human nature, and the fact that autonomous choice is a necessary ingredient of some but not of all ideals of life and is incompatible with some valuable involvements and ways of life, we have no reason to suppose that the choices of autonomous men will converge on any single way of life, or even that they will converge on an extended family of life-styles, all of whose members have autonomy as a necessary ingredient. It may be that Lukes and Connolly, like Mill, imagine that, whereas there is no one way of life which all autonomous men will elect to live, yet there is for each autonomous man one sort of life that is appropriate to him. Here the idea of a real interest or real will is affirmed but predicated in Romantic (and late Scholastic) fashion of the essence of the individual rather than of his species. Apart from the point that the choice criterion has fallen away, this construal of real interests abandons the assumption that they cannot conflict with one another. Once this assumption has been abandoned or relaxed, however, we have no reason to suppose that a community of autonomous agents will lack power relations, or even that these latter will be less prominent than they would be if men were more heteronomous. Nor can the idea of a power-free community be saved by arguing that judgements about interests cannot have a purely subjective character.[14] It might well be the case that men's

---

[12]I have myself considered (very inadequately as I now think) the question of the lifelong contented slave in D. Robertson and M. Freeman (eds.), *The Frontiers of Political Theory* (Brighton, Harvester, 1980).

[13]Lukes, *Power*, pp. 32–3, and Connolly, *Terms of Political Discourse*, pp. 107–16.

[14]Such Wittgensteinian arguments are invoked in an otherwise very forceful critique of Connolly by Grenville Wall, 'The Concept of Interest in Politics', *Politics and Society*, 5 (1975), 487–510. See also John Plamenatz's earlier treatment in 'Interests', *Political Studies*, 2 (1954), 1–8.

judgements about their interests always appeal to shared standards of a worthwhile life, and it is sometimes the case that the want-regarding and the ideal-regarding elements in interest-judgements are inseparable. This norm-dependency of judgements about interests does not support the possibility of a general will, if only because of the manifest diversity of moral practices in the societies with which Connolly is concerned. That there are some common elements in all judgements about interests, which go some way to make them publicly defeasible, in no sense supports a Marxian (or classical liberal) thesis of the universality or non-conflictability or real interests. And finally, as I have already intimated, power relations might emerge from conflicts of goals, even in a society of autonomous men whose interests harmonized.

Two comments emerge from this critical survey of Lukes and Connolly on power, interests, and autonomy. There is in the first place a deep obscurity in the concept of autonomy itself. Different conceptions of autonomy and of human interests seem to be embedded in different views of human nature whose status is only partly empirical. If the choice between rival views of human nature is not empirically severely constrained, the possibility arises that autonomy may itself be an essentially contestable concept. If it is, then so will be the concept of power, but the empirical usefulness of Lukes's theory of power will be impeached. If autonomy is not an essentially contestable concept, and rationally consensual judgements about autonomy and interests are feasible, then it is hard (on the other hand) to see how power can be characterized as essentially contestable. The possibility arises that the conception of autonomy implicit in Lukes's and Connolly's accounts may even be incoherent. Both Lukes and Connolly hold to a view of the self as a social construct: human individuality is not for them a natural datum but a cultural achievement. Further, Lukes explicitly and Connolly tacitly endorse a value-relativist stance in which the possibility of cross-cultural, pan-human standards of flourishing is excluded. It seems at least plausible that a substantive ideal of autonomy can be combined with the view of the self as socially constructed only if a strong conception of human flourishing together with a tough realism in ethics is incorporated into the theory of autonomy; but this is a move neither writer seems willing to make.

My second comment is in the nature of a summary of the foregoing examination. Neither in Lukes's nor in Connolly's accounts are the criterial links between the concepts of power, autonomy, and interests postulated in their theory satisfactorily upheld. There seems no reason to regard conflicts of interest as especially salient to power relations, or to treat interests as analysable into the preferences of autonomous agents for their own welfare. The natural relation to be expected between autonomy and interests is rather the reverse: different construals of autonomous choice are likely to be embedded in different conceptions of human interests. In part, the differences between rival conceptions of power will be found to derive from the different views of human nature by which they are sponsored. It is most unlikely that any purely empirical test will enable us to select one from among the available range of such conceptions of human nature. I will turn to the question of how such conceptions of human nature, which lie at the root of different conceptions of power, may yet be criticizable in the third and last section of this essay.

POWER, RESPONSIBILITY, AND SOCIAL STRUCTURE

Against the one-dimensional view, Lukes insists[15] that power may be exercised by institutions, collectivities, and social forces as well as by natural persons. He preserves the link between attributions of power and the ascription of responsibility by making the claim that power is definitionally exercised by agents, whose omissions as well as actions may figure as exercises of power. He goes so far as to claim that structuralist social theory, in excluding all possibility of ascribing responsibility for social events, actually eliminates the concept of power from social theory. It is hard to see how this latter claim can be maintained. A structuralist perspective in which the exercise of power loses its connection with agency and so its interstitial character and instead is identified with the operation of social structures is a perspective in which the primitive notion of power singled out by Lukes—that of significant affecting—is preserved. In Marxist structuralist theory, the requirement that exercises of power occur in a social situation of conflict of interests is also preserved. What we have in structuralist social theory is unfairly characterized as the elimination of the concept of power.

The nub of the three-dimensional conception advocated by Lukes and shared with Connolly is in the thesis that the exercise of

---

[15]Lukes, *Power*, pp. 52–3.

power includes the determination of preferences by socialization. Note that this is a far stronger claim than the claim that, because overwhelming power pre-empts any challenge to it, overt conflict cannot be a pre-condition of the exercise of power or of the existence of power relations. Rather, it is the claim that power relations may be most pervasive and most efficacious when they are invisible to their victims. This is a claim easily recognizable in theories of ideology for which the propagation of beliefs, the maintenance of social norms and so on may all count as exercises of power. A difficulty here is that the production of ideology is rarely effective when it is a matter of conscious fabrication. If experience is any guide, moreover, those who are recognized as exercising power in ordinary thought and practice are typically no more autonomous than those over whom it is exercised: typically, that is to say, the exercisers of power are imbued with values that they have absorbed from their early social environment and which they have never submitted to a critical assessment. Since those who exercise power, no less than those upon whom power is exercised, have their preferences determined by the culture in which they are immersed and the institutions by which they are surrounded, how can it be justified to impute responsibility to the former but not to the latter? I take it that the latter are excused responsibility for their actions and for their omissions because manipulation and socialization may be represented as the application of force to men's minds and as constituting an excusing condition. It should be obvious, though, that those we ordinarily think of as exercising power (or as being in the upper levels of a power structure) are invariably also at the receiving end of a three-dimensional power relationship. So invariably is this the case that the analogy of a chain of command, which is irresistibly suggested by Lukes's insistence that the conditions of responsibility are conterminous with those of the exercise of power, tends to break down. In the real social world, what we tend to find are feedback loops rather than causal chains which begin in a determinate agent. If this is so, what reason can there be for insisting that judgements about power always involve fixing responsibility? This insistence seems part of an individualist, residually voluntarist aspect of the theory for which no real justification has been given.

I have pointed out already that, since the primitive notion of power is retained in structuralist social theory, it cannot be a conceptual truth within Lukes's argument that power has no place in structuralist thought. Further, I have observed that Lukes's combination of the claim that power may be exercised by collectivities and social forces as well as by individuals with the claim that its exercise always presupposes a responsible agent comes under great pressure when we recognize the ubiquitousness of heteronomy. I want now to suggest some positive reasons for dissociating the notions of power and responsibility.[16] Such an association yields highly counter-intuitive results. Consider the mad dictator, who throws his weight about, does great damage to others' interests, but is not responsible (morally or in law) for his actions. Are we to deny that power is being exercised in a case of this sort? This example illuminates important areas of obscurity in the accounts of Lukes and Connolly. It is not wholly clear whether the responsibility always presupposed by the exercise of power is merely causal or properly moral. Again, are we to accept that power waxes and wanes as the conditions of responsibility are more or less satisfied?

Above all, treating power as an interstitial phenomenon always manifested by responsible agents imposes an arbitrary terminus in the regress of explanation. In a structuralist approach, by contrast, a circumstance of social change is incompletely understood unless the deliberations of the agents it includes are incorporated (at a higher level of abstraction) into a theoretical framework in which are elucidated the mechanisms of ideological production whereby social systems reproduce themselves. In this structuralist account, revolutions occur not because men unaccountably take advantage of opportunities history offers them, but in virtue of crises within the mechanisms of ideological reproduction which are in principle fully intelligible and whose necessity might conceivably be demonstrated. The voluntarist perspective intimated in Lukes and Connolly has as much difficulty in accommodating the idea of a systemic social contradiction as it does that of a power structure.[17]

The rigorous determinism of the structuralist approach may

---

[16]Some difficulties in the attempt to combine these claims are explored by Alan Bradshaw, 'A Critique of Lukes's *Power: a radical view*', *Sociology*, 10 (1976) 121–37. I am indebted for some of the points I make against the association of power with responsibility to a paper criticizing Lukes and Connolly's views written by Andy Reeve and forthcoming in *Political Studies*.

[17]The problems generated for their account by the notion of a power structure are discussed, but not resolved, by Lukes, *Essays in Social Theory*, pp. 9–10, and Connolly, *Terms of Political Discourse*, pp. 116–26.

usefully be contrasted with the uncompromising voluntarism or actionism espoused by ethnomethodologists and by writers in the tradition of Schutz. For these theorists, social structures can never be more than the precipitates or crystallizations of the actions of individuals. This is a stance that is also displayed in Popperian writings and in the theories of interactionist sociologists for whom agents' identities are themselves supervenient upon their social activities. In this perspective, the terminal explanatory level in any social theory is provided by the intentions, beliefs, decisions, and activities of individuals. I do not want here to comment on the large issues of methodological individualism and determinism suggested by the contrast I have sketched, except to say that the explanatory frameworks yielded by the two approaches may not easily be subject to comparative critical assessment. Indeed, the explanatory terminus imposed within Lukes's and Connolly's account by the requirement that power relations be initiated by responsible agents seems arbitrary given the fact that power exercisers are ordinarily themselves the recipients of three-dimensional power.

If these are truly incommensurable frameworks of explanation, the attempt made explicitly by Lukes to adopt a commonsensical or dialectical middle way between them approaches the brink of incoherence. For the structuralist, after all, the realm of agency—of teleological and intersubjective modes of understanding and explanation—must finally disappear into a system of objective social co-ordinates. Any methodology which retains a decisive explanatory role for men's hopes, regrets, intentions, and decisions remains wedded to an obscure, moralistic, and reactionary humanist anthropology. For the actionist, on the other hand, it amounts to an error of reification, a mystifying and animistic superstition, to regard social structures as more than the residues of the practical and intellectual activities of human subjects. It is acknowledged in the actionist account that social situations may acquire a logic (though not a necessity) of their own, but this is always accounted for by reference to the unintended consequences of human actions.

Thus, whereas structuralists seek to subsume discussions about human agency into an explanatory framework in which it is altogether replaced by reference to objective social co-ordinates, actionists try to account for the constraints operative upon human agents in terms which always make decisive reference to the acts of agents. Whereas structuralists want to eliminate discourse about agency from the discursive practices of social science, actionists aim to collapse social structures into the momentarily uncontested products of the practice of individual subjects. Whereas the actionist perspective incorporates a strong conception of the autonomy of the individual subject, for the structuralists 'autonomy' refers rather to modes of theoretical discourse or of social practice whose independence must, in the last analysis, be undermined in a comprehensive social theory.

We can now see, then, that, since judgements about power and structure are theory-dependent operations, actionists and structuralists will approach their common subject-matter—what goes on in society—using divergent paradigms in such a fashion that incompatible explanations (and descriptions) will be produced. This much is indisputable: but are we to go one step further, and say that each of these divergent perspectives generates its own corroborating evidence? If we adopt this relativist position, then we will be committed to the view that we have here incommensurable views of man and society between which a rational choice is impossible. This radically relativist position depends on the claim that as between such views of man and society what we have is meaning-variance rather than theory-incompatibility. Is what we have here, then, an instance of competition between incommensurable paradigms? And, if so, must we accept that the choice between them is rationally unconstrained? Are we here at last in an area of genuine essential contestability?

SOCIAL THEORY, ESSENTIAL CONTESTABILITY, AND COMPETING PARADIGMS OF POWER

Before I try to answer this question, it may be worth looking briefly at the history of the idiom of essential contestability. The epithet 'essentially contestable' was coined and first applied to concepts by W. B. Gallie in a paper presented to the Aristotelian Society in 1956,[18] but a closely similar idiom was adopted by Stuart Hampshire when in his *Thought and Action* (1959) he referred to 'essentially questionable and corrigible concepts'.[19] As a crude

---

[18] See W. B. Gallie, *Philosophy and the Historical Understanding* (London, Chatto and Windus, 1964), ch. 8, for a slightly revised version of this article.

[19] Stuart Hampshire, *Thought and Action* (New York, Viking, 1959), pp. 230–1.

approximation, it may be hazarded that, however these writers conceived the *sources* of a concept's essential contestability, its contestability *consisted* in its being somehow inherently liable to rival interpretations. Nor could this simply be passed off as a matter of the open texture of many or most, perhaps all, of our concepts: what distinguished essential contestability from ordinary open texture was precisely that rivalry and dispute tended to break out, not at the edges of a consensus of agreed uses, but in what each side regarded as the heart of the concept's subject-matter.[20] Naturally, these claims tended to spawn a considerable interpretive literature, which does not seem to have done much to clear up their many obscurities. One very obvious area of obscurity is expressed in the question whether the disputes mentioned by these early writers—disputes about art, Christianity, democracy, and morality, for example—are really disputes about concepts at all. Might they not be just quarrels about the use of words? How, in any case, was an essentially contestable concept to be distinguished from a pseudo-concept hidden in an expression that is ambiguous, confused, or incoherent? For that matter, how are concepts whose uses just happen to be a matter of continuing dispute to be distinguished from those that are essentially contestable? (Might not the identification of essentially contestable concepts as such take us into areas of essential contestability?) Further, if some concepts or terms are inherently liable to generate intractable dispute while others are merely ambiguous or confused or just happen contingently to be matters of dispute, what is it that accounts for this difference?

It is this last question that is particularly germane to my enquiry. It has already been suggested that there are no very forceful reasons for tracing the disputability of the terms of social thought back to their uses in promoting rival moral and political commitments. The result of my analysis of the Lukes–Connolly perspective on power, however, has been that two incommensurable perspectives on power are left in the field, each (the voluntarist and the structuralist) carrying with it a specific framework of explanation. Given that it seems extremely implausible that any purely empirical deliberation might settle the issue between these two perspectives, what kind of considerations could be decisive? The situation seems even worse

[20] On this see Alasdair MacIntyre, 'The Essential Contestability of Some Social Concepts', *Ethics*, 8 (1973–4), 1–9, and David Miller's crucially relevant contribution to the present volume.

on further reflection. If these perspectives really are incommensurable, it seems odd to say that they have any common subject-matter: perhaps what we have is indeed meaning-variance rather than competition in the use of a shared vocabulary. Perhaps, it has been suggested,[21] an incoherence in the idea of essential contestability reveals itself at this point. For, apart from the fact that realist discourse about essences seems at variance with the conventionalist implications of essential contestability, there seems to be a radical fault in the very notion of a contest which cannot by its nature be won or lost. If the essential contestability of a concept or of a term flows inexorably from some aspects of its subject-matter, how can useful argument proceed about the use of the term in contention that is on balance to be adopted?

I do not see any of *these* obscurities as erecting insuperable obstacles to criticizing the two perspectives on power, or as detracting from what the writers on power I have discussed call the essential contestability of ideas and judgements about power. Whether these disputes are linguistic or conceptual in character, they involve a pragmatic competition in which conflicting demands are made on ordinary thought and practice and on the disposition of resources for research. Further, the point at which my analysis of the Lukes–Connolly approach was broken off itself suggests how commitments standing at a terminal level of justification within the theory of power may yet be criticizable at another level. Each of the perspectives I have distinguished intimates a philosophical anthropology—a moral psychology and a philosophy of mind and action—in terms of which it may be criticized. Social theories invariably repose on some such philosophical standpoints, and it is this dependency which accounts for one aspect of their permanent vulnerability to contestation and openness to questioning.

Consider in this connection one variant of the structuralist approach to power—that elaborated in structural-Marxist writings. The central area of difficulty in all such accounts has been indicated obliquely by Hindess and Hirst in their comment that

---

[21]On this see my 'On Liberty, Liberalism and Essential Contestability', *British Journal of Political Science*, 8 (1978), 385–402, where I depart from some of the formulations of an earlier and less satisfactory paper of mine, 'On the Essential Contestability of Some Social and Political Concepts', *Political Theory*, 5 (1977), 331–48. A highly relevant and useful contribution to this area of debate is made by Quentin Skinner in his 'The Idea of a Cultural Lexicon' in *Essays in Criticism*, 29. 3 (July 1979), 205–24, especially in footnote 10 on p. 224.

'. . . there is as yet no systematically elaborated theory of the political level to compare with the Marxist analysis of the economic level of the capitalist mode of production'.[22] The difficulty hinted at here is that, in developing a systematic account of ideology and of superstructural phenomena such as the capitalist state, the structuralist cannot avoid invoking some of the assumptions of a 'humanist' anthropology which the terms of his account of social structure compel him to reject. These anthropological assumptions, officially suppressed by structuralist thought but presupposed by some of its main theses, are to do chiefly with the complex capacities and attitudes necessarily possessed by role-bearers in post-traditional (and, perhaps, also in traditional) societies. A worker who enters into a wage contract, for example, must be capable of understanding a whole set of internally complex background notions, the possession of which gives him the capacity to form alternative concepts and beliefs about his circumstance in society. If a worker understands his situation well enough to discharge the roles assigned to him in a capitalist (or a socialist) society, he has the capacity to imagine himself situated in a very different social landscape.[23]

It will immediately be objected that it is precisely the function of ideology so to constrain the political reflection of workers (and others) that it remains at the level of ideology and false consciousness. To say this, however, is entirely to miss the point. For it is precisely the human capacity of critically transcending one's immediate social circumstances that generates the necessity —which, according to Althusser, will remain a feature even of communist society—for ideological beliefs which restrict the scope of such reflection. What I am claiming is that the myopically deterministic account of human reflection encapsulated in structural-Marxist thought disables its advocates from developing any remotely plausible theory of social consciousness. Nor do I forget the self-criticisms of Althusser's more recent writings, or the revisions made to structural Marxism by his disciples Étienne Balibar and Jacques Rancière. None of these saves the structuralist-Marxist project from failure. To acknowledge that human

[22] B. Hindess and P. Hirst, *Pre-Capitalist Modes of Production* (London, Routledge and Kegan Paul, 1975), p. 33.

[23] I am indebted here to W. E. Connolly, *Appearance and Reality in Politics* (Cambridge, Cambridge University Press, 1981).

thought and social relations are reflexive, that is to say, that reflection on the conditions of our thought changes those conditions in that it modifies the beliefs and attitudes by which they are constituted, imposes upon us the task of elaborating a philosophical anthroplogy in which these distinctively human powers are explored. The metaphysical reasonings by which such an anthropology will be supported are bound to have an inherently controversial character, but this is not to say that criticism is altogether out of place here. In this instance, it is to note the latent positivism of those Marxists in the structuralist tradition who are committed to the self-defeating project of elaborating a rationalist science of society which is supposed to be able to do without a metaphysic of human nature.

My argument is that structural-Marxist theory about power and social structure incorporates a philosophical anthropology at odds with official structuralist commitments. These latter commitments, in turn, I suspect, could be shown to be at odds with the anthropological postulates of our ordinary thought and practice. At no point is my argument intended to be conclusive or coercive. It is taken for granted that in discussing questions in the philosophy of mind and action we are in an area of metaphysical uncertainty where what are at stake are only more or less well-defended statements of opinion. As Stuart Hampshire has put it: 'No critical philosopher can now believe that an inquiry into the concept of man, and therefore into that which constitutes a good man, is the search for an immutable essence. He will rather think of any definition or elucidation of the concept as a reasoned proposal that different types of appraisal should be distinguished from each other in accordance with disputable principles derived from a disputable philosophy of mind. He will admit that this is the domain of philosophical opinion, and not of demonstration.'[24] One major source of intractable dispute in social theory (and in moral theory) is its connection with areas of metaphysical uncertainty explored in questions in the philosophy of mind and action. Dispute is interminable in social theory, in part because it slides irresistibly into dispute in philosophy, and there we have the defence of opinion and not demonstration. At any moment in discussion, one stand in social theory may well be better supported, better defended than others in the field: others (such as

[24]Hampshire, *Thought and Action*, p. 233.

the structural-Marxist view I have criticized) may do badly. This characterization of criticism in social theory shows that acknowledging the inherently controversial aspects of social concepts may be combined with affirming the criticizability of social theories.

I have not suggested that intractable dispute in social theory is always an expression of conflicts in philosophy. It has another source in the under-determination of social theory by evidence. That this is so ought to be clear from my discussion of the methodological difficulties faced by the Lukes–Connolly account. The decision procedure proposed for the identification of power relations is not just counterfactual in method, but doubly so: power relations exist if men's interests would conflict under certain circumstances, and their interests are a sub-class of the preferences they would display in a condition of relative autonomy. This approach commits Lukes and Connolly to an extraordinarily arduous testing procedure. Apart from all the difficulties involved in assessing degrees of autonomy where this is regarded as a complex achievement having distinct and diverse elements, the method seems to have an aspect of circularity: we test for power by hypothesizing what an autonomous agent would do, but we know that an agent is autonomous only if we first know his power situation. Lukes's suggestion[25] that we study circumstances of social breakdown and disorder for evidence of men's latent interests is no help here: such social conditions, typically conditions where demagogy and crowd psychology are important factors, seem peculiarly ill-suited for the purpose. The Lukes–Connolly approach seems wanting if its empirical usefulness and testability are seen as including its capacity to yield falsifiable predictions and retrodictions.

These difficulties are plainly only one instance of a greater problem in any project for a science of society. Many of the evidences going into any such science will be matters of historical interpretation, and large-scale social experiments will rarely, if ever, be conclusive, owing to the impossibility of isolating distorting variables. Most crucially, however, a science of society comes up against a problem having to do with its public character. Evidence tends to elude the social-scientific investigator, if only because his

---

[25]Lukes, *Power*, pp. 47–9.

subjects tend to react to the categorial framework of interpretation which his investigations impose on their activities. There is this contrast of social science with natural science, thắt its subject-matter is men's notions and beliefs, and these are worked over reflexively, both by the investigator and by his subjects in response to him. I am far from attempting to dismiss in aprioristic Winchian fashion any project for a scientific study of society: at microsocial level, as Milgram's study of authority and obedience and Laing's studies of the family suggest,[26] studies satisfying fairly rigorous standards may be deeply instructive. But the reflexive relations between social-scientific investigation, human beliefs, and the objects of the social world should confine the prospects of such study within very narrow limits. In the natural sciences, as in the social studies, available evidence may be compatible with a range of theories whose implications are themselves incompatible; but the social studies have the extra disability that crucial experiments are rarely, if ever, practically possible.

It may be time to try and tie together the loose ends of my enquiry and to assess the bearing of its results on the prospects of social theory. I began by making the observation that disputes in the theory of power have been widely and not unreasonably interpreted as expressive of deeper differences over the merits of a positivist philosophy of social science. We can now see that this interpretation has validity only with important qualifications. If the ideal of value-freedom in social thought is one test of positivism, our conclusion must be that nothing in Lukes's or Connolly's writings on power impeaches this tenet of positivism: so far as we have been able to discern, this Weberian standard of scientific rigour in the social studies remains uncompromised. Persisting relativity in social science has two sources in the under-determination of theory by evidence and the dependency of theory on metaphysical commitment. These aspects of the limitation of social thought should incline us to a Pyrrhonian humility about our own social theorizing and encourage us in scepticism about any large claim for social thought. I cannot see that these insights into the limitation of social thought warrant description in the inflated idiom of essential contestability.

---

[26] See S. Milgram, *Obedience to Authority* (London, Tavistock, 1974) and R. D. Laing and A. Esterson, *Sanity, Madness and the Family* (2nd edn., London, Tavistock, 1971).

The writings of Lukes and Connolly retain the greatest heuristic (and pedagogic) interest in disclosing two radically divergent paths of development for social thought. One, associated with an open conception of autonomy, a non-cognitivist moral epistemology and a fallibilist and conventionalist methodology, supports a recognizably Weberian conception of social theory. It has no direct bearing on conduct, but in its commendation of impartiality as an intellectual virtue and its frank recognition of the diversity and internal conflicts of human values it may have some affinity with a tradition of justifying argument in liberalism. The other, bound up with a closed view of autonomy, a form of moral objectivism and a method of real definition, is familiar from Marxist projects for a social science. Here the scientific study of society, because it is supposed to reveal necessary laws of social development, has a directly practical motive. It is such a conception which is supported by the constant emphasis in both Lukes and Connolly on the supposed fraudulence of the distinction between fact and value in social theory and by their attribution to social theory of an ineradicable political dimension. Nothing in recent writing *justifies* the attribution to social theory of this political or practical character, and even the thesis of the essential contestability of social concepts may be impoverished by it.

The current of writings on power and related concepts in which theses about essential contestability or conceptual relativism are deployed has had the virtue of strengthening the sceptical spirit in social thought and of undermining dogmatic and absolutist claims. But, if social thought is not to be lost in a no-man's-land of political controversy, its practical character needs to be denied and its direct links with moral and political life severed. We need to be able once again to assert with confidence that, however meagre its result in increased insight, social theory has no warrant for existence save in the pursuit of understanding.

Can the Base be distinguished from the Superstructure* †

Steven Lukes
Balliol College, Oxford

In the social production of their life, men enter into definite relations that are indispensable and independent of their will, relations of production which correspond to a definite stage of development of their material productive forces. The sum total of these relations of production constitutes the economic structure of society, the real basis, on which rises a legal and political superstructure, and to which correspond definite forms of social consciousness.[1]

I suppose that this must be the most well-known and argued-over pair of sentences in the entire Marxist canon. Ever since Engels tried to sort out some of the problems they raise, they have been returned to again and again, both by Marxists, orthodox, 'critical', and 'neo', and by critics and opponents of Marxism. Some have suggested that they, and the text from which they come (the Preface to *A Contribution to the Critique of Political Economy*), should be seen as over-simplified and even unimportant, when set against the great mass of Marx's and Engels's writings about political economy and history. But Marx clearly saw the 'general conclusion' he reports here as having 'continued to serve as the guiding thread' of his studies; and the thoughts distilled in these two sentences are as distinctive of Marxism as is the continuing dispute over what it is that they really mean.

They raise at least five issues: the theory of developmental stages, the relation between structure and agency, that between material productive forces and social production relations, that between the base, or economic structure, and the legal and political superstructure, and that between the superstructure and its

*© Steven Lukes 1983.

† I am grateful to G. A. Cohen, David Miller, and Joseph Raz for their very helpful comments on an earlier draft of this paper.

[1] K. Marx, 'Preface to *A Contribution to the Critique of Political Economy*' in Marx and Engels, *Selected Works* (Moscow, Foreign Languages Publishing House, 1962), vol. 1, pp. 362–3 (slightly amended translation, S. L.).

corresponding forms of consciousness. I shall here focus exclusively on the fourth of these issues (leaving largely aside the relations between the third and the fourth and between the fourth and the fifth) by asking the narrow but deep question: Can the economic structure, or base, be distinguished from the superstructure? This is a basic question, for unless it can, the explanations promised by historical materialism, at least as set out in the Preface, will fail. I shall consider the question by presenting the negative answer to it advanced by John Plamenatz and the positive answer advanced by G. A. Cohen.[2] Plamenatz's carefully stated doubts constituted a major foil for Cohen's recent attempt to make sense of Marx's historical materialism, in the most coherent and analytically refined defence it has yet received. It should therefore be peculiarly instructive to examine the grounds for Plamenatz's scepticism and see whether Cohen's ingenious arguments succeed in showing it to be misplaced.

Plamenatz makes two claims. One looks empirical, the other conceptual, and each is expressed in both a particular and a general form.

(1)(a)   The first claim, in its particular form, is that the economic structure 'is to a considerable extent independent of production, that there are other things besides production making it what it is'; and, furthermore, 'the relations of production or property . . . in turn can profoundly affect production'. Thus,

If we identify relations of production with relations of property (as I think we must if they are to have any identity at all), it becomes easy to see that they are not determined by what is produced and how it is produced.

Moreover, the system of property, both by putting fetters on the development of productive forces and by creating opportunities, 'has a great influence on what is produced and how it is produced'. Since the so-called, but misdescribed, relations of production 'owe

---

[2]Plamenatz's arguments are most fully set out in *Man and Society* (London, Longman, 1963), vol. 2, pp. 274–92. Cohen challenges them in three places: 'On Some Criticisms of Historical Materialism, 1', *Proceedings of the Aristotelian Society*, Supp. vol. 44 (1970), 121–42; 'Being, Consciousness and Roles: on the Foundations of Historical Materialism' in C. Abramsky and B. Williams (eds.), *Essays in Honour of E. H. Carr* (London, Macmillan, 1974); and *Karl Marx's Theory of History: A Defence* (Oxford, Clarendon Press, 1978), esp. Chs. III and VIII.

their character only in part to the form of production, may they not owe it equally to the other sides of social life? In what sense, then, are they the real foundation of these other sides?'[3]

(1)(*b*) This question leads us to the general form of Plamenatz's first claim, which concerns 'every attempt to distinguish, among the larger aspects of social life, between a fundamental causal factor and what is derivative from it'. 'No doubt', he writes,

if we take a small enough part of social life, we can easily show that it is derivative, in the sense that it is much more affected by the rest of social life, or even by some other part of it, than it affects it. If we take something like fashion in dress, we can show that it greatly depends on certain other things which it hardly influences. But if we take larger sides of social life, like religion or science or government, it is no longer plausible to treat any of them as fundamental or derivative in relation to the others.[4]

(2)(*a*) The second claim, in its particular form, is that the relations of production 'cannot be defined without using moral or normative concepts':

Unfortunately, it is quite impossible to define these relations except in terms of the claims which men make upon one another and recognize— except in terms of admitted rights and obligations.[5]

(2)(*b*) The general form of this second claim is that 'all properly social relations are moral and customary; they cannot be adequately defined unless we bring normative concepts into the definitions, unless we refer to rules of conduct which the persons who stand in those relations recognize and are required to conform to'. For,

Since claims and duties and mental attitudes are involved in all social relations, in every side of social life, no matter how primitive, since they are part of what we mean when we call a human activity social, we cannot take any side of social life and say that it determines, even *in the last resort,* whatever that may mean, men's moral and customary relations and their attitudes towards one another.[6]

---

[3]*Man and Society*, vol. 2, pp. 275–83.
[4]Ibid., p. 283.
[5]Ibid., pp. 283, 281.
[6]Ibid., pp. 283–4, 284–5.

How does Cohen rebut these claims and what alternative does he offer? In the first place, he largely *agrees* with Plamenatz as to the identity of the relations of production. For both writers, the relations of production are social relations and should be understood, in the context of historical materialism, to *include* what Plamenatz calls property relations and Cohen ownership relations (though Cohen, unlike Plamenatz, takes these not to be legal relationships but relations of *effective control*) and to *exclude* what Cohen calls purely material work relations and Plamenatz 'relations involved in production'[7] (though Plamenatz, unlike Cohen, also includes what Acton calls 'paratechnological' relations, which are needed to make production go smoothly[8]).

Against Plamenatz's first (general) claim, Cohen maintains that *whether* or not it is plausible to treat 'larger sides of social life' as fundamental or derivative in relation to others cannot be decided in advance of a clarification of what constitutes a 'side of social life' and of what it is for A to affect B more than B affects A, and of a careful study of the historical record, in the light of such clarifications. In particular, Cohen suggests that Plamenatz's observation about fashion, as obviously more influenced than influencing, though intuitively plausible, must rely on an implicit principle of interpretation which, when made explicit, might show whether or not a 'larger side of social life' may influence another more than it is influenced by it.[9]

Against Plamenatz's second (general) claim, Cohen argues that, on Plamenatz's view of 'determination', A determines B if variations in A explain variations in B. On this view of 'determination', Cohen writes, 'it is conceptually in order to assert that the character of men's ideas and customs is determined by the stock of instruments of production available to them and/or by their level of economic development. Each of the latter can be described without referring to customs or ideas.' Indeed, Cohen argues, Plamenatz is wrong even in his general claim about sides of social life, for

[7]Ibid., p. 279. Cohen originally included these (in 'On Some Criticisms . . .') but excludes them in *Karl Marx's Theory of History* (see p. 35 fn.).

[8]See *Man and Society*, vol. 2, p. 280 and H. B. Acton, *The Illusion of the Epoch* (London, Cohen and West, 1955). Acton's arguments on the general topic of this paper parallel those of Plamenatz, and Cohen's arguments are developed in response to both authors.

[9]'Being, Consciousness and Roles', p. 87.

it is not clear that a side of social life, as he conceives it, is incapable of determining the ideas associated with it, as he understands determination. The ideas associated with a side of social life may vary as and *because* the side as a whole varies, and this will meet his sense of 'determine'.[10]

But the key issue, so far as historical materialism is concerned, is raised by 2(*a*): whether as Cohen claims, the economic structure 'may be so conceived that it is free of all such superstructural encumbrances'. In facing this issue, Cohen takes up the challenge of the second claim by submitting 'a method of *conceiving* the economic structure which excludes from it the legal, moral, and political relationships of men'. He does this in response to what he calls 'the problem of legality': 'if the economic structure is constituted of *property* (or *ownership*) relations, how can it be distinct from the *legal* superstructures which it is supposed to explain?' His proffered solution is to propose '*rechtsfrei* descriptions of production relations' and then 'show how production relations, so described, may be said to explain property relations'.[11] I shall not here discuss Cohen's account of that explanation as functional explanation, but focus rather on his attempt to conceive the economic structure independently of the superstructure, that is, non-normatively.

That attempt consists in displaying ownership as a matter of enjoying rights, formulating for every ownership right a 'matching power' and then describing production relations in terms of such powers, which 'match' property relations. Thus the pertinent ownership rights (such as the rights to use or to withhold the means of production [or labour power], to prevent other persons using them, or to alienate them) are said to 'match' corresponding powers, where 'power' is defined as follows:

a man has power to ϕ if and only if he is able to ϕ, where 'able' is non-normative. 'Able' is used normatively when 'He is not able to ϕ' may be true even though he is ϕ-ing, a logical feature of legal and moral uses of 'able'. Where 'able' is non-normative, 'He is ϕ-ing' entails 'He is able to ϕ'.

The relationship of 'matching' is explicated as fully determined by replacing the word 'right' by the word 'power' in the phrase

---

[10] Ibid., p. 88.
[11] *Karl Marx's Theory of History*, pp. 235, 217–18, 225.

'right to ϕ. Cohen adds that the possession of powers does not entail possession of the rights they match, or vice versa: 'Only possession of a *legitimate* power entails possession of the right it matches, and only possession of an *effective* right entails possession of its matching power.'[12]

Rights, Cohen further maintains, not only match (non-normative) powers. On the (unargued) ground that 'a power is always a power to do something', he argues that some rights (e.g. my right that no one else use my land) are equivalent to the duties of others to forbear, and these will match others' lack of power, or inability. So, an adequate *rechtsfrei* account of the economic framework of production relations which allegedly 'matches' the legal framework must incorporate 'not only powers or abilities, but also inabilities or constraints'. But here again, 'just as a power is distinct from the effective right ensuring it, so a constraint is distinct from the enforced duty imposing it. It is not trivial to say that the serf is constrained to work because he is legally obliged to.'[13]

Cohen gives two illustrations of how this programme might be put to work: ideal-typical and descriptive. The first is a contrast between the ideal-typical proletarian (who owns his labour power) and the ideal-typical slave (who does not). Applying his method, Cohen concludes that the slave does not have the power to withhold his labour power, while the proletarian does have this power, but only with respect to a given capitalist, not the capitalist class as a whole. The second comes 'closer to reality' by considering the 'rights and powers of contemporary workers, in countries where bourgeois legality prevails'. Applying his method again, Cohen concludes that, with the development of workers' collective power, through unions, workers do now, though in a qualified sense, have the power to withhold their labour power, and indeed the further power individually to escape their proletarian situation: they are, therefore, 'not *de facto* "owned" by the capitalist class'. On the other hand, their power to overthrow capitalism and their power to build socialism are, in various ways, obscured from their consciousness, and limited by all kinds of costs and difficulties.[14]

[12] Ibid., pp. 220, 219.
[13] Ibid., p. 237
[14] Ibid., pp. 222–3, 240–5.

If Cohen's programme were to be carried through, it would, he claims, enable one to *explain* property relations, that is show how 'the property relations change in the service of changes in production relations (which in turn reflect development of the productive forces)' So, for example, following Mantoux, one can explain the collapse of the law of settlement in terms of, first, the law's violation, as production relations allowing mobility were formed illegally, and second, the scrapping of the law, thereby re-establishing conformity between 'rights and powers, the *de jure* situation and the *de facto,* property relations and production relations'. Other examples are the eventual legal recognition of escaped serfs as freemen in cities, the repeal of the law restricting entry into the clothing industry (allowing 'a proletariat of textile workers to exist *de jure* as well as *de facto*'), the repeal of the Combination Acts and the development of early trade union legislation, the abolition of feudal tenure of land at the Restoration, the development of factory legislation and the use of Roman law in capitalist society to facilitate the development of certain production relations.[15]

More generally, Cohen argues, property relations are thus

functionally explained by production relations: legal structures rise and fall according as they promote or frustrate forms of economy favoured by the productive forces. Property relations have the character they do because production relations require that they have it.

In human society might frequently requires right in order to operate or even to be constituted. Might without right may be impossible, inefficient, or unstable.

In general, production relations are given stability by their legal expression. Historical materialism asserts that that legal expression is to be explained by its function, which is to help sustain an economy of a particular kind: 'right *r* is enjoyed because it belongs to a structure of rights, which obtains *because* it secures a matching structure of powers'.[16]

I have characterized Cohen's programme of purging the base of normative elements, or seeking to identify 'a *rechtsfrei,* (*moralitätsfrei,* etc.) economic structure to explain law (morals, etc.)'. It is now time to ask: can it be carried through?

[15]Ibid., pp. 226–9.
[16]Ibid., pp. 231, 232.

In the first place, Cohen's own account of his programme is insufficiently radical. For he speaks of the 'proletarian' and the 'slave', 'landowners' and 'capitalists' as having or lacking (non-normative) powers. But in speaking thus, he is not speaking non-normatively, since the actors in question are not identified in a non-normative fashion. A slave, for example, is a slave just because he lacks certain rights, just as a landowner by definition possesses certain rights. Statements attributing powers to occupants of roles such as these are plainly not *rechtsfrei,* at least where they have or lack these powers in virtue of their roles. So, to carry out Cohen's programme systematically, one must eliminate all reference to features of the actors and their roles that refer to or presuppose rights and, more generally, ownership relations. Unless this is done, one will not have excluded from the economic structure 'the legal, moral and political relationships of men'. The principle of a *rechtsfrei* conception of the economic structure must be applied rigorously.

In reply to this, it might be claimed, as Cohen does, that the economic structure consists in production relations which relate terms that do not belong to the structure itself (though they do belong to the economy). On this account, one could describe the structure as relating variables, just like the structure of a bridge or an argument: the economic structure is a form whose proper description makes no reference to the persons or productive forces related together by it, and indeed necessary for it to exist. But the relations in question hold by virtue of the rights and obligations attaching to the roles occupied by persons so related: as Cohen himself says, 'The structure may be seen not only as a set of relations but also as a set of roles.' Therefore, a proper description of the structure will not, as Cohen rightly says, make specific reference to the specific role-*occupants,* but it can scarcely avoid reference to their normatively-defined roles. To this, of course, Cohen will reply that such roles *can* be identified non-normatively: as he puts it, 'economic roles in the required technical sense will be determined not by what persons are *de jure* entitled and obliged to do, but by what they are *de facto* able and constrained (= not able not) to do'.[17] We shall come to this claim shortly. Only if it can be sustained, will Cohen's programme have been carried out rigorously.

[17]'Being, Consciousness and Roles', p. 95.

But, in the second place, we must ask: can it be carried out at all? Recall that the aim is to identify an economic structure of production relations, as a set of *de facto* powers, which will in turn explain the superstructure of law, morality, etc., as a set of rights and obligations. Let us, then, look more closely at this purged or purified 'matching' economic framework of 'powers or abilities' and 'inabilities or constraints'.

I propose here to offer three arguments. The first two attack Cohen's project indirectly; only the third meets it head on. The former, if accepted, put in question the idea that the economic structure, conceived as a set of 'powers and constraints', could be described in a single, determinate, objective and rationally incontestable manner. If this is doubted, then the 'hardness' of the economic structure (and thus of historical materialism itself) is no longer easy to believe in: how it is conceived will be relative to perspectives that are, in turn, not normatively neutral. The latter puts in question Cohen's claim that norms can be seen as bringing about and sustaining relations of production while remaining no part of their content.

First, then, what count as an agent's abilities and inabilities will be closely dependent upon how that agent is conceived (which only strengthens the first point made above). If the agent (whether individual or collective) is conceived in a sufficiently 'substantial' way, then that agent's abilities will appear to be very narrowly circumscribed; if conceived sufficiently abstractly, they may appear to be very wide indeed. Consider the question: did Bukharin have the power, or ability, to resist Stalin? If you incorporate into your conception of Bukharin enough about his history, his personality traits, his loyalties, commitments, beliefs, and attitudes, then your answer may very well be no. If, however, you conceive him as an abstract, choosing self, capable, within limits (which limits?), of changing course, modifying his traits, abandoning commitments and beliefs, then you may well answer yes. Or consider the question: did the British Labour Government in 1929 have the power, or ability, to avert (or at least better manage) the economic crisis? Here again, the answer depends upon how that Government is conceived—as irremediably constituted by given traditions of thought and action, or as capable of alternative strategies in a time of crisis. Or, to take Cohen's own example, different conceptions of contemporary British workers yield different answers to the question of what powers they have (to withhold labour collectively, to escape individually, to overthrow capitalism, to build socialism) and how much of such powers they have. Moreover, if the agents in question are defined in terms of their *roles,* that is *eo ipso* to define their abilities and inabilities, assuming of course that they act in accordance with their roles. But in terms of *which* roles should they be defined, and how role-determined should they be taken to be?

Second, what counts as enabling or constraining is never a simple matter of fact but it is always relative to background assumptions and judgements, some of them normative. To attribute abilities to agents is to accept as possibly true a set of conditionals, most of them counterfactual, of the form 'under conditions C, agent A will do or be x', and to attribute an inability is to rule some such conditionals out. But a deep question is: what are to be included in the conditions specified in the antecedent? Until that is answered, attributions of abilities and inabilities remain indeterminate. But it cannot be answered in a definitive and rationally incontestable manner.

Consider Cohen's own example of the slave's alleged inability to withhold his labour power. Under certain interpretations of C, this is plainly false, even on pain of death, of some, even perhaps of most slaves (as the history of slave rebellions demonstrates). If, however, one includes in C the condition that the slave behaves 'reasonably' or 'normally' (that is, that he conforms to yet-to-be-specified norms of reasonableness), then Cohen's claim may well be true. Here I merely wish to draw attention to the fact that not merely is the latter interpretation not normatively neutral, but the choice between them is not so either. Accordingly, no Cohenite description of the economic structure of slavery could be normatively neutral. So, to sum up these two arguments, I have suggested that if it is sought to describe the base in terms of abilities and inabilities, powers and constraints, then (1) which description is appropriate will always be contestable and (2) this will be so partly on normative, that is moral and political, grounds.

Third, it is worth focusing directly on one type of enabling and constraining condition, namely *norms.*

In general, enabling and constraining conditions may be external or internal to agents. Thus some physical factors are plainly external and some psychological factors plainly internal. Within a certain range, however, whether they are external or internal will itself depend on how the agent is conceived, where the boundaries of the self or the collectivity in question are drawn.

Norms are distinctive in being both external and internal, and in a particular way. They confront individuals as externally given but they can only be generally effective in enabling and constraining them in so far as they are (in H. L. A. Hart's phrase) 'internally accepted'. Of course, I may be induced to comply with a custom or convention or moral principle or legal rule by the fear of the sanction that would be brought to bear in the case of my non-compliance, but no set of norms stably regulating the behaviour of adults could rely on this mechanism alone. For such regulation to be generally effective, there must exist a high degree of intersubjective acceptance of rules, and of the purposes the rules are taken to serve (though an individual need not believe, in any given case, that his compliance will lead to the fulfilment of that purpose). In short, a stable system of enablements and constraints, to be effective, requires that I and relevant others are generally motivated by certain kinds of shared (teleological) reasons for acting and not acting.[18] These give such enablements and constraints their distinctively normative character.

Now, it is essential to Cohen's programme that such enablements and constraints be identifiable in non-normative terms, that is in abstraction from what gives them their distinctively normative character. The programme, he claims, 'says what production relations are, not what maintains them'. He cites the case of an illegal squatter who secures his dominion over a tract of land by having retainers who use force illegally on his behalf, or by perpetrating a myth that anyone who disturbs his tenure of the land will be damned to eternal hell-fire. What that squatter has *in common with* a legal owner of similar land, whose tenure is protected by law, is that both have the *power to use their land*. This, so the argument runs, is the content of the production relation in question, in the one case sustained by force and myth, in the other by the law. So the relations embodying normative enablements and constraints are, on Cohen's argument, abstractable from the norms that may have brought them about and maintain them in being. Is this so?

[18] See G. H. von Wright, *Explanation and Understanding* (London, Routledge and Kegan Paul, 1971), pp. 145 ff.

Consider the basic economic relationship of contract. If any relation of production is central to the economic structure of capitalism, this must be it. Can it be described in the manner proposed?

Interestingly, Durkheim took Herbert Spencer to be asserting just this—that economic life consisted in 'the spontaneous accord of individual interests, an accord of which contracts are the natural expression', society being 'merely the stage where individuals exchanged the products of their labour, without any properly social influence coming to regulate this exchange'. To this Durkheim replied that 'in the play of these relations themselves . . . social influence makes itself felt. For not everything in the contract is contractual.' By this he meant that 'a contract is not sufficient unto itself, but is possible only thanks to a regulation of the contract which is originally social'. Recall that Durkheim defined the social in terms of externality, constraint, and generality (throughout society), plus independence (of individual circumstances); and that he saw the law, in particular, and norms, in general, as paradigmatically social phenomena. Contract law 'determines legal consequences of our acts that we have not determined . . . We co-operate because we wish to, but our voluntary co-operation creates duties for us that we did not desire.' Contract law is not 'simply a useful complement of individual agreements; it is their fundamental norm'.[19] Durkheim is here making two points (which he did not distinguish from one another): that contract law, together with a whole network of customary and conventional norms, combine to define the social practice of contracting; and that other such laws and norms regulate contractual behaviour, rendering certain actions possible and proscribing others on pain of sanctions. In short, the relation of contract is, in this double sense, essentially norm-governed. Does not this fundamental objection apply to both Marx and Spencer—or at least to Cohen's Marx and Durkheim's Spencer?

But, it may be asked, is there not a *rechtsfrei* relationship here, abstractable from the norms that govern it, in either sense?

How would we go about describing it? Cohen's answer is: in terms of the abilities and inabilities of the contracting partners. But abilities and inabilities to do . . . what? The performance of

---

[19] E. Durkheim, *The Division of Labour in Society* (London, The Free Press of Glencoe and Collier–Macmillan, 1933), pp. 203, 211, 215, 214 (amended translation: S. L.).

contractual obligations is normally described in a vocabulary (paying wages, supplying services, buying and selling, honouring debts) which *already presupposes* the institution of contract and its regulating norms, as well as a whole network of supporting informal norms. In this sense, the norms that define the practice of contracting enter into the description of the activities involved in that practice. To this, it may be replied that a thin 'behavioural' description of such activities (e.g. handing over money of a certain value, performing certain tasks, etc.) could suffice in the description of the abilities and inabilities. But the trouble is here that such thin 'behavioural' descriptions would underdetermine the appropriate thick, normatively-loaded descriptions: only some payments of money by certain persons in certain ways would count as 'payment of wages', only certain kinds of task performance as the supplying of a contracted service. Recall that Cohen's non-normative relations of production are intended to be 'matching'. But how could the 'thin' non-normative description of transactions and dependencies between agents succeed in identifying *just those* transactions and dependencies which the normative relations involve unless the normative description were already, implicitly or explicitly, presupposed?

Suppose, however, that we overlook this difficulty, arising from the first sense in which contracts are norm-governed. What about the second sense: that is, the sense in which laws and conventions supply agents with certain kinds of *reasons* for acting and not acting, thereby enabling people to do what they otherwise would not, and preventing them from doing what they otherwise would? Can one describe contractual relationships in terms of abilities and inabilities in a way that abstracts from the operation of such reasons?

An ability and an inability, as we have already seen, are explicable as sets of conditionals, most of them counterfactual. In a pure, non-normative relationship of power—say, of simple coercion—my ability to secure an outcome may be stated as a set of conditionals of the following type: 'If I order my slave to sweep the floor, making threat t, he will do so' or 'If I threaten workers with redundancy, they will come into line'. But what of normative power-relationships? Here a whole new range of counterfactual conditionals enters the story, of the following type: 'If I offer employment at the going rate for the job, the workers will accept the offer' or 'If I break the agreement thus made, they will come out on strike'. In these cases the enablements and constraints *consist in* internally accepted norms and would not exist if attitudes changed. The normative beliefs in question enter irreducibly into the description of the powers and constraints linking the contracting parties. In other words, the norms, both informal and formal (the pay norm and the legal obligation to pay it once agreed), *are* what enables and constrains the parties—enabling the employers to secure the work on the terms agreed, but not if the terms are broken, by giving the parties certain reasons for acting as they do.

Let us return to the illegal squatter and the legal landholder. I can sum up the two points just made concerning norm-governed economic relationships by observing that (1) both squatter and proprietor can, it is true, keep people off their land; (2) the proprietor, unlike the squatter, can in addition secure the respect of people for his title to the land (e.g. should he wish to bequeath it); and (3) he can do so only by virtue of the reason-giving prevalent legal norms governing ownership of property and informal norms governing what landholders may legitimately lay claim to. From all of which I conclude that one cannot identify the powers and constraints embodied in norm-governed economic relationships independently of the norms which, in both senses, govern them.

Is there any interpretation of Cohen's purportedly purified economic structure, allegedly purged of all normative, superstructural encumbrances, that escapes the foregoing objections?

So far as I can see, there are only two possibilities. On the one hand, Cohen's proposal may be a purely linguistic one—a proposed translation manual converting all statements about rights and obligations into statements couched in a purged vocabulary of 'matching' powers and constraints.

There are, however, two decisive objections to this interpretation. First, it will not serve Cohen's purpose, since the objectionable normative elements would all survive, albeit covertly, in the identified economic structure: the purging would be solely at the linguistic level. But second, this is plainly not Cohen's intention anyway. His aim, after all, is coherently to 'represent property relations as distinct from, and explained by, production relations'.[20] He believes that his proposed *rechtsfrei* characterizations refer to a set of relations distinct from and explanatory of those referred to by talk

[20] *Karl Marx's Theory of History*, p. 219.

of rights and duties in the normal sense. Thus, he explains away Marx's own continued adherence to legal terminology when speaking of the relations of production by remarking that

> there was no attractive alternative. Ordinary language lacks a developed apparatus for describing production relations in a *rechtsfrei* manner. It does have a rich conceptual system for describing property relations, strictly so called. Given the poverty of the vocabulary of power, and the structural analogies between powers and rights, it is convenient to use rights-denoting terms with a special sense, for the sake of describing powers.[21]

In short, Cohen clearly believes that his proposed *rechtsfrei* terms (and Marx's allegedly special use of *rechtsvoll* terms) identify relations distinct from, if structurally analogous to, those that rights-denoting terms normally identify.

The only alternative possibility I can see is that Cohen's economic structure, composed of powers and constraints, is intended to *exclude* all those that are norm-governed. But to this interpretation too there are two decisive objections. The first is that this would result in a hopelessly impoverished, indeed scarcely coherent, conception of the economic structure. The second objection is that, in any case, it is doubtful that this *is* Cohen's Marx: that is, that Cohen's programme of identifying a non-normative economic structure is to be understood in this way. For, in answering the possible objection that he is merely expounding the so-called 'force theory', condemned by Engels, Cohen remarks, as we have seen, that 'our definition of production relations does not stipulate how the powers they unfold are obtained or sustained. The answer to that question does involve force, but also ideology and the law. The programme says what production relations are, not what maintains them.'[22]

I have argued that these two are the only remaining interpretations of Cohen's general programme of purging the economic structure of superstructural encumbrances, that neither does the job; and that neither squares with Cohen's intentions. There is, however, a third and final possibility: to reduce the generality of the programme. That is, one could read it as an attempt to purge the economic structure only of specifically legal elements, narrowly

[21] Ibid., p. 224.
[22] Ibid., p. 223.

defined, as distinct from those pertaining to custom, convention, and morality. (It is, after all, formulated in response to the so-called 'problem of legality'.) Interestingly enough, this interpretation fits rather well the historical cases that Cohen cites to illustrate how his programme enables one to explain changes in property relations—the free circulation of labour in violation of the law of settlement which was eventually scrapped, the admitting of those of low status to the clothing industry in violation of a law eventually repealed, the formation of illegal unions leading to their eventual legal recognition, and the process leading to the early factory legislation: 'the struggle led to fairly well recognized practices, and then the law broke its silence and gave the facts legal form'.[23] In all these cases, informal norm-governed practices (responding, it is true, to developing productive forces, which they in turn facilitate) eventually acquire legal form.

But this, less general, interpretation of Cohen's programme once more encounters two decisive objections. It does not square with Cohen's general objective of finding 'a method of conceiving of the economic structure which excludes from it the legal, moral and political relationships of men'. And second, therefore, it does not succeed in distinguishing the base from the superstructure, in the manner required. At the most, it distinguishes an expanded (norm-governed) 'base' from a diminished (narrowly legal) 'superstructure'.

What, then, are we to conclude from this dispute between Plamenatz and Cohen with respect to the question with which I began?

First, that Cohen makes of Plamenatz some perfectly proper demands for clarification. Second, that he rightly points to the need to specify more clearly what kind of 'determining' is involved in historical materialism; and in his book he has contributed greatly to this task. But third, that he has failed to solve the (misleadingly) so-called 'problem of legality' or, more generally, to purge the economic structure of normative elements and thus to distinguish the base from the superstructure.

What follows from this last conclusion? Nothing directly about the explanatory power of Marxist ideas, to the extent that what we may now call this non-distinction is neither assumed nor implied by

---

[23] Ibid., p. 229.

them. And indeed it is not obvious that even the 'technological' reading of historical materialism that Cohen favours, or Marxian-type class analysis, or, in general, a Marxist approach to the explanation of social processes, whether in primitive or early or modern societies, do require it. It is irrelevant to the distinctions between material and social factors, between class position and class consciousness, and between economic as against legal, political, and ideological factors (provided that these terms are taken to identify spheres of social life that are not required to be conceivable independently of one another). It is, moreover, a dead, static, architectural metaphor, whose potential for illumination was never very great and which has for too long cast nothing but shadows over Marxist theory and Marxist practice. Is it not now time to consign it to the scrap-heap?

Self-Government Revisited*

Brian Barry

University of Chicago and California Institute of Technology

The least-known of any of John Plamenatz's books is, it seems safe to say, *On Alien Rule and Self-Government*.[1] This may, indeed, be its first citation in a scholarly article. There are, I suspect, two reasons for this lack of influence or (probably) readers. The first is that it must have jarred the expectations of any of its three natural audiences. Those who came to it from Plamenatz's mature work hoping for more of the same must have found that it contained little, at any rate explicitly, on the history of political thought. Devotees of 'conceptual analysis', looking for something on the lines of *Consent, Freedom and Political Obligation*,[2] must have been disappointed by its relative lack of concern for definitions and distinctions. And political scientists, who would in other respects have found its substantive concerns with such topics as nationality congenial, must have been put off by its total indifference to any modern empirical literature and its substitution of 'conversations with Margery Perham' for more conventional source citations. The second reason is that it was overtaken by events. The argument was primarily focused on the case for self-government among peoples who were still under colonial rule, and within a few years of publication the argument had been settled, as far as Britain was concerned (and to a large extent altogether), by history, in the person of Harold Macmillan.

In spite of these disadvantages, I would like to suggest that *On Alien Rule and Self-Government* is worth resuscitating. Indeed, I would go so far as to say that the present intellectual climate ought to be more propitious than the one existing when the book was originally published. Nobody can now read the political science of the period without squirming, so Plamenatz's disregard of it means that the book is free of what would otherwise have turned out to be an

*© Brian Barry 1983.

[1] John Plamenatz, *On Alien Rule and Self-Government* (London, Longman, 1960).

[2] Oxford, Oxford University Press, 2nd edn., 1968.

incubus. Nobody now thinks that conceptual analysis pursued in the absence of some definite theoretical problem is worth doing. And the rise of the contextualists, such as John Pocock and Quentin Skinner, has cast into a (perhaps temporary) eclipse the approach typified by John Plamenatz, which was essentially that of a very intelligent and serious man sitting down with a text and trying to make sense of it. But for an intelligent and serious man to sit down with a substantive problem can never, on any change of fashion, be anything but a good thing. As far as subject-matter is concerned, the question of topicality has by now entirely faded away and what is left is a contribution to an enduring question: that of the basis of the claims that are persistently made by the people in some area to be associated together in an independent state.

Plamenatz took the view, which one might think on the face of it rather commonplace, that there was quite a lot to be said for the principle of self-determination, and that national feeling was a force that should as far as possible be accommodated. In fact, however, such a line was rather heretical for a political theorist in Plamenatz's age-group. Native Englishmen tended not to regard the problem as salient. From the supposed end of the Irish Question in 1922 until its revival in the 1960s, problems of boundary-making and nationalism had little personal significance. This is not, of course, to say that Englishmen are not chock-full of nationalism, but it takes the form of that unconscious assumption of superiority that so infuriates foreigners: Shakespeare is not easily mistaken for Fichte. So, Michael Oakeshott, the leading native English theorist of that generation, takes the existence of a 'society'—with all that that entails—for granted and focuses on the question of the appropriate 'arrangements' for managing such a society.

It becomes more and more striking, as the main outlines of our century begin to emerge, that an extraordinary amount of what makes it intellectually distinctive is the achievement of members of two groups: assimilated German-speaking Jews and Viennese—and, indeed, that an amazingly high proportion is owed to those in the intersection of the two sets. This is true in social and political theory as in other basic subjects. And it is hardly to be wondered at if, in the circumstances, the doctrines of nationalism and self-determination have been treated as inimical to civilized values. Self-determination reduced Vienna from the status of the cosmopolitan capital of an empire to something closer to that of a provincial town. And for assimilated Jews the rise of nationalism obviously threatened at best remarginalization after the emergence from the ghetto and at worst, under Hitler, physical destruction.

One way of meeting the situation was, of course, to embrace Zionism. The rise of nationalism in others is then countered by Jewish nationalism. (This is, of course, another twentieth-century theme that can be chalked up to Vienna.) Michael Walzer, in the next generation, illustrates the way in which dedication to the cause of Israel can give rise to a general protectiveness to the claims of the nation state to autonomous development. This, however, was not the route followed by the distinguished central European refugees who dominated English-speaking political theory during the quarter century following the Second World War. Karl Popper's attack on what he tendentiously called 'tribalism' (actually nationalism) in *The Open Society and Its Enemies*[3] is the most comprehensive example, but I think that one could find the same basic antipathy to the use of political means for any collective ends—the same repugnance to the idea of a society as anything except the result of individual actions in pursuit of individually-defined ends—in Hayek, Talmon, Kohn, and (with more shading) Berlin.

Cold War Liberalism was a response not only to the post-war situation but also to the pre-war one. The popularity of the dubious concept of 'totalitarianism' to cover not only Stalinism, Nazism, and Fascism, but also (in terms such as 'totalitarian tendencies') any kind of collectivistic thinking is perhaps the best indicator. In the lexicon of, say, *Encounter* in its heyday, charges of 'totalitarian tendencies' could be deployed against a wide variety of targets with remarkable rhetorical effectiveness.

As far as I can tell, Plamenatz adhered to the tenets of what I have here called Cold War Liberalism except in one respect: he did not share the antipathy to nationalism or more generally to the idea that people might properly use political means to determine the conditions of their common life. As he wrote in *On Alien Rule and Self-Government*, he 'belong[ed] by birth and affection to a "backward" nation'[4] and his sympathy with the aspirations of colonial peoples in the rest of the world is evident. In this paper I want to undertake

---

[3] K. R. Popper, *The Open Society and Its Enemies* (London, Routledge and Kegan Paul, 1962).

[4] Plamenatz, *On Alien Rule and Self-Government*, p. viii.

an enquiry of a rather abstract kind that I think relates to the concerns that separated Plamenatz from his contemporaries. I want to ask how far, starting from individualist premises, we can hope to say anything definite about the appropriate criteria for political boundaries. In particular, I want to ask if there is any way of fitting in the characteristic doctrines of nationalism that can be reconciled with individualist ideas.

For the purpose of this paper, I understand the individualist principle to be that the only way of justifying any social practice is by reference to the interests of those people who are affected by it. By a 'social practice' I mean to include social institutions like marriage, organizations like schools or businesses, or methods of reaching collectively binding decisions like elections, rules of legislative assemblies, etc. The concept of interests is, of course, notoriously controversial and the individualist principle takes on a rather different coloration depending on the interpretation adopted. Conceptions of interest fall into three categories: those that identify it with the satisfaction of preferences (perhaps only of certain kinds, e.g. for states of oneself, or only under certain conditions, e.g. perfect information about alternatives); those that identify interest with pleasure, happiness etc., as in Bentham's statement that 'a thing is said to promote the interest, or to be *for* the interest, of an individual, when it tends to add to the total sum of his pleasures: or, what comes to the same thing, to diminish the sum total of his pains';[5] and, finally, those that identify interests with opportunities to act and with access to material advantages (Rawlsian primary goods are this kind of thing). I intend my definition of individualism to cover all three ways of understanding 'interest'. (Indeed, it is apparent that there are potentially close connections, conceptual and/or empirical, between them.) The individualist principle, understood in this way, may seem so hospitable as to exclude very little, but that appearance simply illustrates its contemporary predominance. It rules out appeals on behalf of God, Nature, History, Culture, the Glorious Dead, the Spirit of the Nation or any other entity unless that claim can somehow be reduced to terms in which only individual human interests appear.

From the present broad perspective, all three of the doctrines which are currently regarded in mainstream Anglo-American

[5] Jeremy Bentham, *An Introduction to the Principles of Morals and Legislation* (New York, Hafner Publishing Co., 1948), p. 3.

philosophy as the primary contenders—utilitarianism, rights theories, and contractarian theories—are to be seen as variants on the principle of individualism, as set out above. Utilitarianism in its classical Benthamite form is the most straightforward. It starts from the basic idea of individualism—that interests are what matter— and, indeed, Bentham's most general statement of the principle of utility simply is what I am calling the individualist principle: 'By the principle of utility is meant that principle which approves or disapproves of every action whatsoever, according to the tendency which it appears to have to augment or diminish the happiness of the party whose interest is in question. . . .'[6] Bentham then provides the simplest possible rule for bringing the interests of different people into relation with one another, namely that we sum the total interest-satisfaction over all the people concerned and adopt the criterion that one arrangement is better than another if it produces a larger total.

On the surface, rights theories stand in opposition to utilitarianism, for rights, whatever their foundation (or lack thereof), are supposed to trump claims that might be made on behalf of the general welfare. The point here is, however, that the whole notion of rights is simply a variation on utilitarianism in that it accepts the definition of the ethical problem as conterminous with the problem of conflicting interests, and replaces the felicific calculus (in which the interests are simply added) with one which does not permit certain interests to be traded off against others.

Contractarian thinking is a further twist on the basic individualist principle. We arrive at it by starting again from the general formulation and stipulating that a social arrangement may be justified only by showing that it operates in the interests of each and every participant in it. This contractarian version of individualism may take a variety of forms, depending on the way in which certain key questions are answered. Is the contract taken to be actual or hypothetical? Is weight attached to the contract itself or is the contract significant only as an indication of mutual gain? Must the mutual gain be realised or is it enough for it to be anticipated? If anticipated, what are the circumstances in which the *ex ante* estimation is to be made? And, either way, what is the standard against which 'mutual gain' is to be counted? My object in

[6]Ibid., p. 2.

mentioning these puzzles within contractarian thinking is not to pose them as subjects for present discussion but once again to observe that common to all strands of contractarian thought is the individualist principle that interests are what matter, and that the content of political theorizing is exhausted by the question how potential or actual conflicts of interests are to be resolved.

Each of the three varieties of individualism—utilitarian, rights, and contract—may be (and has been) advanced as an all-embracing theory. Alternatively, a contract framework may be used to derive one (or some mix) of the other two; or it may be claimed that one can derive (some version of) rights from (some version of) utilitarianism. It is beside my present purpose to follow up these possible lines of analysis. But I think it is worth pointing out that the enduring appeal of the three versions of the individualist principle can readily be explained if we appreciate that each of them speaks to a moral consideration of undeniable power. However we want to put them together, it seems awfully hard to deny that (in some circumstances at least) the greater aggregate gain should be preferred to the less, that the pursuit of that aggregate gain should be qualified by certain limitations on the way in which people can permissibly be treated, and that one test for the legitimacy of an arrangement is reciprocity of benefit from it.

I myself find it implausible that, even taking all three together, we exhaust the sphere of morally relevant considerations. But it is important to notice that those who share my scepticism are certainly not committed to the rejection of the individualist principle. It is perfectly reasonable to take the position that moral issues should always be conceived of in terms of individual interests, while at the same time denying that the relevant criteria for adjudicating between interests are adequately reflected in any one of the three theories just discussed or in any combination of them.

Having said something about the meaning to be attached, for the purpose of this essay, to the term 'individualist,' let me now ask what illumination theorists within the individualist tradition have provided in their treatment of one question: the criteria appropriate for determining membership within a common state. I think that we can pick out three standard responses, all of which are, I must confess, so weak as to be a serious embarrassment to anyone sympathetic to the general individualist enterprise.

The first, which is simply a refusal to take the question seriously, is Locke's contract of association: people somehow got together to form a political society and this society then set up a particular form of government. There was, of course, a certain truth obscurely embodied in this idea of a contract to set up a society, namely that in some circumstances there may be general agreement on the boundaries of the polity, so that disagreement about the form it should take does not always have to entail reopening the question of boundaries. The notion of a contract of association thus functioned in Locke's theory to legitimate the assumption that any change of regime in England would leave the same boundaries. But as a theory about the way to set about determining on the basis of some principle the boundaries of a state where there is in fact disagreement, some wanting one boundary and others some other, Locke's piece of fiction is obviously quite useless.

A second approach is to assert a right to self-determination. However, if this is put forward as a right of each individual, it hardly makes any sense, except as an alternative way of expressing the Lockean consent theory; and it breaks down in just the same way wherever there is a lack of agreement because some people want one boundary and others want another—which is, of course, the only context in which there is any problem in the first place.

It is tempting, and the temptation has not always been resisted, to reformulate the individual right as a right to take part in a plebiscite to determine the boundaries of the state that is to include one's current place of residence. But what moral significance could such a right have? Suppose that a majority of the people in an area want the boundaries of that area to be the boundaries of a state, and a minority do not—whether they want to carve a separate state out of that area, attach the whole area or some part of it to another state, or whatever—the question is what claim the majority has in that case. The issue is in effect decided by the choice of the area of the plebiscite, and the minority would presumably begin by dissenting from that. Locke's contract of association, however absurd, did at least correspond to the logic of constructing states out of individual rights. What we have here is in effect an attempt to bypass the step from individuals to a collectivity.[7] We can of course avoid the *impasse* by saying that the right is to be attributed not to individuals

[7] See Henry Sidgwick, *The Elements of Politics* (London, Macmillan and Co., 1891), pp. 621–2.

but to nations. Thus, Article 1 and Article 55 of the United Nations Charter make reference to 'the principle of equal rights and self-determination of peoples'.[8] And the Draft Covenant on Civil and Political Rights shares with the Draft Covenant on Economic, Social and Cultural Rights a common Article 1, whose first clause runs: 'All peoples have the right of self-determination. By virtue of this right they freely determine their political status and freely pursue their economic, social and cultural development.'[9] But attributing rights to collectivities is incompatible with the individualist principle. As Cobban wrote,

it is one thing to recognize rights, and another to attribute them to a collective body such as a nation. Before allowing that there is a right of national self-determination, we should have to admit that the nation is a self, capable of determining itself. . . . Further, even if we accept the idea of a nation as a single self with a single will, can it have rights as such?[10]

The third position is that it is possible to specify in universal terms the interests that states exist to protect, and that we can deduce their appropriate boundaries from that. There are several variants. One is that, since all states ought to do the same things, it shouldn't matter what the boundaries are. Thus, from a Lockean perspective, we can say that states exist to maintain property rights (which are not created by the state, of course, hence the prohibition on conquerors appropriating the property of their new subjects) so the laws should be the same everywhere and it ought not to matter to anyone what state his property happens to be in. Naturally, if you happen to live in a country whose government is violating the laws of nature and (say) taxing your property without your consent, you may wish that you lived in some other state, and I suppose that, if you despaired of any improvement from within, you might wish for your state to be absorbed by a better-run state. But the point is that you would be concerned with boundaries purely as a means to getting the same laws honestly administered, not because you cared who else was in the same state or because you expected differently-composed states to have different policies.

[8]Robert E. Asher *et al.*, *The United Nations and the Promotion of the General Welfare* (Washington, D.C., Brookings, 1957), pp. 1084, 1092. The term 'nations' is already pre-empted as an equivalent to 'states'.

[9]Ibid., pp. 1112, 1123.

[10]Alfred Cobban, *The Nation State and National Self-Determination* (London, Collins, Fontana Library, 1969 (first published 1945)), p. 106.

Elie Kedourie's *Nationalism* argues this kind of case. He claims that, until the French Revolution declared that 'the principle of sovereignty resides essentially in the Nation', nobody believed in nationality as a basis for statehood.

The philosophy of the Enlightenment prevalent in Europe in the eighteenth century held that the universe was governed by a uniform, unvarying law of Nature. With reason man could discover and comprehend this law, and if society were ordered according to its provisions, it would attain ease and happiness. The law was universal, but this did not mean that there were no differences between men; it meant rather that there was something common to them all which was more important than any differences. It might be said that all men are born equal, that they have a right to life, liberty, and the pursuit of happiness, or, alternatively, that men are under two sovereign masters, Pain and Pleasure, and that the best social arrangements are those which maximize pleasure and minimize pain: whichever way the doctrine is phrased, certain consequences can be drawn from it. The state, on this philosophical view, is a collection of individuals who live together the better to secure their own welfare, and it is the duty of rulers so to rule as to bring about—by means which can be ascertained by reason—the greatest welfare for the inhabitants of their territory. This is the social pact which unites men together, and defines the rights and duties of rulers and subjects. Such is not only the view of the *philosophes*, for which they claimed universal validity, but also the official doctrine of Enlightened Absolutism.[11]

Kedourie affirms (without ever offering any supporting arguments) these ideas, and thus finds it incomprehensible that 'a young man of good family' like Mazzini should conspire against 'a government which, as governments go, was not really intolerable: it did not levy ruinous taxation, it did not conscript soldiers, it did not maintain concentration camps, and it left its subjects pretty much to their own devices'.[12] The only explanation he can offer is a psychological one: 'restlessness'. This kind of psychological reduction is indeed inevitable if there is no rational basis for favouring one set of boundaries over another. 'Frontiers are established by power, and maintained by the constant and known readiness to defend them by arms. It is absurd to think that

---

[11] Elie Kedourie, *Nationalism* (London, Frederick A. Praeger, 1960), p. 10.
[12] Ibid., p. 97.

professors of linguistics and collectors of folklore can do the work of
statesmen and soldiers.'[13]

If we say that the task of the state is not only to enforce property
rights but also to cope with externalities (or what are sometimes
called spillovers) we can come up with a criterion for boundaries,
namely that a state should cover an area such that (*a*) most of the
externalities generated within that area impinge on the area and
(*b*) most of the externalities impinging on the area are generated
within it. Thus, if a lake is potentially subject to pollution, there is,
on this criterion, an a priori case in favour of all the shore of the lake
being contained within a single jurisdiction. The basic idea is still
that states are in the business of protecting a standard set of
interests. Boundaries, on this view, are to be determined on a
technical basis, and not with any reference to the desires of the
inhabitants to be associated politically with some people and not
others. Such ideas are characteristic of market-oriented economists,
whose only use for the state is as a remedy for 'market failure', but
we can find their influence in political science too, as in this passage:

> If, because of its boundaries, a political system lacks authority to secure
> compliance from certain actors whose behavior results in significant costs
> (or loss of potential benefits) to members of the system, then the
> boundaries of the system are smaller than the boundaries of the
> problem.[14]

The central image in the book, by Robert Dahl and Edward Tufte,
from which this quotation is drawn, is of an individual with a set of
fixed desires for his personal security and prosperity, looking
around for political units that will deliver them and favouring
boundaries on the basis of the 'capacities' of alternative units to do
so. There is a glancing reference to the 'problem of loyalty in a
complex polity that begins to transcend the nation-state',[15] but this is
presented as a complication in the creation of political units based
on technical criteria, although in other works Dahl has shown a
good deal of understanding of the importance of communal identi-
fications in politics.[16]

[13] Ibid., p. 125.

[14] Robert A. Dahl and Edward R. Tufte, *Size and Democracy* (Stanford, Stanford
University Press, 1974), p. 129.

[15] Ibid., 'Epilogue', p. 141.

[16] For example, Robert A. Dahl (ed.), *Political Oppositions in Western Democracies* (New
Haven and London, Yale University Press, 1966); and *Polyarchy: Participation and Opposition* (New Haven and London, Yale University Press, 1971).

Starting from the same idea, that states should administer a common set of basic services and no more, Lord Acton, in his famous essay on 'Nationality',[17] drew the singular conclusion that it didn't matter how states were composed—so long as they were heterogeneous.

Private rights, which are sacrificed to the unity, are preserved by the union of nations. . . . Liberty provoked diversity, and diversity preserves liberty by supplying the means of organization. . . . This diversity in the same State is a firm barrier against the intrusion of the government beyond the political sphere which is common to all into the social department which escapes regulation and is ruled by spontaneous laws.[18]

Hence,

If we take the establishment of liberty for the realisation of moral duties to be the end of civil society, we must conclude that those states are substantially the most perfect which, like the British and Austrian Empires, include various distinct nationalities without oppressing them.[19]

This 'if' is, of course, crucial: what Acton is pointing out here is that the best way of confining a state to the pursuit of negative liberty is to ensure that its citizens cannot put together a majority for anything more positive. As Madison said in the tenth *Federalist*, the greater the area and diversity of a political authority, the more difficult it is for it to pursue 'an improper or wicked project' such as redistribution of wealth. This principle has clearly worked pretty effectively in the USA and, indeed, Acton's principle came to the support of Madison's in that the ethnic diversity of later immigrants frustrated class-based organization. Today it has potential applications in Western Europe. The attraction of the EEC to some of the more clear-sighted supporters of British entry was that it would hamper the attempts of British governments to manage the economy by using selective import controls or subsidies to industries while at the same time being too divided for there to be any risk of positive community-level intervention. If you are opposed to positive state action, accept that legitimacy must in

[17]John E. E. Dalberg-Acton, *The History of Freedom and Other Essays* (London, Macmillan, 1909), pp. 270–300.

[18]Ibid., pp. 289, 290.

[19]Ibid., p. 298.

contemporary societies rest ultimately on universal suffrage, and fear that majorities cannot be persuaded to share your anti-statism, the best bet is to go for a weak and heterogeneous confederation.

Unlike the contract and rights theories, this third attempt at an individualist theory of citizenship cannot simply be dismissed out of hand. Admittedly, there are objections to each formulation of it: the Lockean theory of property (recently warmed over by Nozick) is palpable nonsense; Kedourie's idea that until the French Revolution everybody believed in Enlightened Despotism is grotesque;[20] it is a fallacy to suppose, as Dahl does, that the only way of assuming that externalities can be taken care of is to have a single authoritative body covering all the producers and all the consumers of the externality;[21] and Acton's idea that the Austrian and British

[20] 'Mayor Bilandic showed us a new and surprising side of his personality last week—he is a keen student of world history.

'In an emotional lecture to a gathering of precinct captains, he demonstrated his scholarship by comparing criticism of his administration [much criticized for its inactivity in the face of a record snowfall] with the crucifixion of Christ, the Jewish Holocaust, the enslavement of American blacks, the frequent occupation of Poland, the oppression of Latin Americans and the revolution in Iran. . . . The fact is, history bears out what Bilandic has said. The parallels between history's most famous persecutions and the attacks on his leadership are amazingly appropriate. . . .

'As for Poland, Bilandic was incredibly perceptive when he compared criticism of himself with the foreign oppression of Poland, which has been going on for more than 300 years.

'As most historians have pointed out, when Russia seized part of Poland in 1772, the Russian czar said: "Now we will plow your alleys."

'In 1914, when the Russian were driven out of Poland, Gen. Pilsudski proclaimed: "Now we will plow our own alleys."

'But in 1947, when the Russians took over again, they said: "We have come here because you have not plowed your alleys. We will plow them. We will also clear the cross walks. Rock salt for everyone!"' Mike Royko, 'Plowing into history', *Chicago Sun-Times*, 18 Feb., 1979, p. 2. If Kedourie were correct, it would be impossible to explain why this is funny.

[21] If there are, say, two or three states around the lake, and pollution of the lake is bad for all of them, they have a common interest in agreeing to control pollution, and there is a built-in sanction (assuming compliance can be monitored) in that any state violating the agreement can expect the others to abandon it too. (See Michael Taylor, *Anarchy and Cooperation* (London, John Wiley & Sons, 1976) for a sophisticated treatment.) The solution will not work where the states are not symmetrically situated, as when several states border a great international river such as the Rhine or the Danube. Here an upstream state that pollutes cannot be threatened in kind by a downstream state. However, if we are concerned only with efficiency, the well-known 'Coase theorem' reminds us that the downstream state can always pay the upstream state not to pollute the water. This is objectionable from the point of view of equity, but the downstream state may instead be able to threaten to withhold some benefit from the upstream state in some other matter unless it refrains from polluting the river. In any case, the question is whether considerations such as these, even where they have a certain substance, should determine the boundaries of a state.

empires were not oppressive is pretty quaint. But, leaving all that on one side, there is nothing demonstrably wrong with the claim that the role of states should be confined to protecting the property and physical security of their citizens against invasions by one another or by others outside.

It may be objected, of course, that many important human desires that require the state for their fulfilment are going to be frustrated by such a narrow conception of the state's mission. But that does not make it incompatible with the individualist principle, which, it may be worth recalling, I defined as the principle 'that the only way of justifying any social practice is by reference to the interests of those people who are affected by it'. For the interpretation of interests that identifies them with all desires is only one conception. (Note, incidentally, that 'Nothing is to count except desires' doesn't entail 'All desires are to count'. A strong and widespread wish to (say) burn heretics at the stake does not have to be accepted as an interest by someone who endorses the individualist principle.)

Anyone who is content with the view of the state that flows from conceiving of interests as being confined to protection against loss and harm may stop here. It is no part of the present project to consider what kinds of moves might be made in arguing for or against alternative conceptions of interest. For those who are still with me, however, what I propose to do in the remainder of the paper is to ask how more full-bodied conceptions of the state articulate with individualist premisses. I shall divide up the additional criteria for common citizenship that are to be considered into three kinds: first, those that are so totally at variance with the spirit of the individualist principle as to be clearly ruled out of court by it; second, those that are equally clearly compatible with the individualist principle (given an appropriate conception of interest); and, third, those that present an interesting problem and challenge us to think again about the principle of individualism itself.

First, then, what I shall call ethnicity seems to me clearly excluded by individualist premisses as a basis for political association in a state. In the several years in which I have been reading around in this area I have reached the conclusion that many apparent disagreements of substance actually reflect differences in the meaning given to words such as 'ethnicity' and 'nationality'.

Let me therefore try to say as precisely as possible here what I intend to have understood by the term 'ethnicity'.

The narrowest (and etymologically primitive) definition of an ethnic group would make it equivalent to a tribe, in the sense of 'the largest social group defined primarily in terms of kinship'.[22] I shall extend it to include (as the Greeks came to do) a group defined by descent without requiring (even the myth of) common descent from a single ancestor. Ethnicity is thus to be understood as a sort of extended analogue of kinship (e.g. the references in the British Press to Rhodesian whites as 'our kith and kin' at the time of UDI). The essence is the conception of oneself as belonging to a common 'stock' or 'race' (either in the contemporary sense or the older sense in which people spoke of French and English 'races' in Canada). Needless to say, conceptions of ethnicity have usually been tied up with phoney biology, sociology, and history, but (unless one wants to load the dice—which it appears many scholars do) there is no need to include any of these notions in the specification.

The significant point about ethnicity is negative: that it is not (generally speaking) possible to join an ethnic group by an act of will. 'Men may change their clothes, their politics, their wives, their religions, their philosophies, they cannot change their grandfathers. Jews or Poles or Anglo-Saxons, in order to cease being Jews or Poles or Anglo-Saxons, would have to cease to be.'[23] This definition of ethnicity in terms of descent is quite compatible with the emphasis of much recent scholarship on the mutability of ethnicity: that ethnic identities can be created, can merge into more inclusive ones, or can be differentiated. The plasticity of ethnic identities that we find in eastern Europe in the nineteenth century and in post-Second World War Africa is not a chance for the *individual* to choose his ethnicity (or only very exceptionally).[24] Nor am I intending to deny that ethnic groups are often identified

---

[22] Anthony D. Smith, *Theories of Nationalism* (London, Duckworth, 1971), p. 180.

[23] Quoted by Carlton J. H. Hayes, *Essays on Nationalism* (New York, The Macmillan Company, 1933), pp. 249–50.

[24] For nineteenth-century Europe, see Eugene Kamenka (ed.), *Nationalism* (New York, St. Martin's Press, 1976), pp. 13–14. For the post-Second World War phenomenon of ethnic transformation, especially in sub-Saharan Africa, see Crawford Young, *The Politics of Cultural Pluralism* (Madison, Wisc., University of Wisconsin Press, 1976).

by traits such as language; but the point is that the language in question is not the one the person actually speaks but (as it is revealingly called) the 'mother tongue'.[25]

The reason why ethnicity cannot *in itself* be a basis for the composition of a state on individualist premisses is quite simply that there is no necessary connection between descent, which is a matter of biology, and interest, which is a matter of the fulfilment of human needs and purposes. To this extent Acton was correct: 'our connection with the race is merely natural and physical, whilst our duties to the political nation are ethical.'[26] Saying 'You're a member of the X ethnic group' cannot in itself constitute a ground for saying you should be in a state with (all of and/or nothing but) other members of the X ethnic group if, as the individualist principle holds, an arrangement can be justified only in terms of the interests of those affected by it. We can invoke God, Nature, or History if we choose but that clearly takes us outside the realm of individualism. Thus, Herder (although there is more to his ideas than this, and I shall return to him later) wrote that 'a nationality is as much of a plant of nature as a family, only with more branches' and that 'a kingdom consisting of a single nationality is a family, a well-regulated household; it reposes on itself, for it is founded by nature, and stands and falls by time alone.'[27] This appeal to what is 'natural' and the tell-tale analogy to the family is clearly in contradiction to the idea that any form of association must be referred to the test of human interests. 'Individualism, political conventionalism, and rational justification were the counterpart to the family/state distinction,' Gordon Schochet wrote in his study of patriarchalism,[28] and all that has to be added is that, as individualism (which in my sense includes conventionalism and rational justification) has strengthened its

[25]Cf. Kedourie, *Nationalism*, pp. 71–2: 'a nation's language was peculiar to that nation only because such a nation constituted a racial stock distinct from other nations.' (Kedourie rather characteristically equates the 'racial' theory with Nazism.)

[26]Acton, *History of Freedom*, p. 292.

[27]R. R. Ergang, *Herder and German Nationalism* (New York, Columbia University Press, 1931), pp. 243, 244–5.

[28]Gordon J. Schochet, *Patriarchalism in Political Thought* (New York, Basic Books, 1975), p. 76.

grip, the family has been assimilated to a voluntary association.[29] James I, in *The Trew Law of Free Monarchies,* 'insisted that as children could not rise up against their fathers even when their acts were wicked or foolish, so subjects could not resist their rulers'.[30] Clearly, the antecedent no longer holds, and the Swedes have, quite consistently, begun to think of giving children the right to shop around for alternative parents if they don't get on with their biological parents.

I went to some trouble to give a precise definition of ethnicity because I wanted to ensure that in my usage ethnicity would be distinguished from nationality. For the next stage in my argument is that nationality is a basis for the composition of states that is unambiguously compatible with the individualist principle. However, to anticipate the third stage of the argument for a moment, I shall go on to qualify this by drawing attention to some manifestations of nationalism that pose problems for the individualist principle.

The question is, then: 'What is a nation?' and the answer I wish to employ is the subjective one that Renan gave in his famous lecture with that title.

A nation is a grand solidarity constituted by the sentiment of sacrifices which one has made and those one is disposed to make again. It supposes a past, it renews itself especially in the present by a tangible deed: the approval, the desire, clearly expressed, to continue the communal life. The existence of a nation (pardon this metaphor!) is an everyday plebiscite; it is, like the very existence of the individual, a perpetual affirmation of life.[31]

More austerely, we may take Max Weber's definition of nationalism as 'a common bond of sentiment whose adequate expression would be a state of its own, and which therefore normally tends to give birth to such a state'.[32] My only reservation about calling this subjective is that subjectivity is often confused with arbitrariness.

---

[29]See David Gauthier, 'The Social Contract as Ideology', *Philosophy and Public Affairs*, 6 (1977), 130–64. Although contractarian thinking is only one form of individualism, much of Gauthier's analysis applies to individualism in general rather than the contractarian variant in particular.

[30]Schochet, *Patriarchalism.*, p. 87.

[31]Ernest Renan, 'Qu'est-ce qu'une Nation?' in Louis L. Snyder, *The Dynamics of Nationalism* (New York, Van Nostrand, 1964), pp. 9–10.

[32]Hans Kohn, *The Idea of Nationalism* (New York, Macmillan, 1946), p. 583, n. 16.

But a sentiment of common nationality is not something people just happen to have. Loyalty to a nation—a wish for it to have a state if it doesn't have one, a wish for it to continue to have one if it does have one, and a willingness to make sacrifices to those ends—tends to grow out of a habit of co-operation between different groups within the nation, which gives rise to stable expectations about their future behaviour, and especially to some degree of trust that a concession made today without a precise quid pro quo being specified will be reciprocated at some future time when the occasion arises.

Scholars who have packed into the concept of the 'nation-state' such things as an integrated economy, common social institutions, and a single status of citizen have often been motivated by suspect ideas about 'political development', but I think we can say simply that the lack of such factors—feudal relations, an estates system, or a Furnivall-type 'plural society', for example[33]—must inhibit the development of habits of co-operation, mutual trust, or fellow-feeling. The same goes for such matters as common language or common culture: they are predisposing conditions but not necessary conditions. It is a commonplace that trust and co-operation are facilitated by communication—which is not only a question of language but of shared outlook. (Thus, it has been found that letting people talk together—about anything—before playing an n-person prisoners' dilemma game increases co-operation.[34]) We can also understand how it is that the sheer survival of a state over a long period tends to bring about a sense of common nationality among those within its territory. The experience of co-operation tends to create a preparedness to co-operate in the future. As Weber observed, nations without states often formed political units—or more precisely were formed by political units—at some time in the past.

[33] For Furnivall, see Leo Kuper and M. G. Smith (eds.), *Pluralism in Africa* (Berkeley, University of California Press, 1971); and M. G. Smith, *The Plural Society in the British West Indies* (Berkeley, University of California Press, 1974).

[34] Robyn Dawes, 'Experimental Analysis of Commitment to Group Benefit in a Commons Dilemma Situation' (Paper presented to The American Political Science Association meetings, September 1976 at Chicago). See also Anatol Rapoport, 'Prisoner's Dilemma: Recollections and Observations' in Anatol Rapoport (ed.), *Game Theory as a Theory of Conflict Resolution* (Dordrecht, D. Reidel, 1974), pp. 17–34, esp. pp. 22–3.

There is a tendency in the literature, I find, to assimilate the nation to either the state or the ethnic group.[35] Reducing the number of elements to two in either way leads to strange consequences. Thus, Reinhard Bendix, in *Nation-Building and Citizenship,* appears (although I can find no explicit definitions) to regard a nation-state as a state that successfully claims sovereignty in the Bodin/Hobbes sense (see especially Chapter 4). A nation-state is, it seems, one with 'a minimum of long-run stability, that is, minimal agreement concerning the rules that are to govern the resolution of conflicts'; but it should be noted that this 'agreement' is hardly equivalent to what I am calling a sense of nationality, for Bendix also writes just before that:

Only the total disloyalty or ostracism of a section of the population is a genuine hazard to the underlying agreement of such a community, though coercion can make a nation-state endure even in the presence of that hazard to its foundations, as South Africa demonstrates.[36]

If South Africa constitutes a 'nation-state' then indeed the idea of a 'nation' has no independent content. A nation-state is simply a state in which the government is able to make its writ run within its territory. (This identification of 'nation' with 'state' is, of course, quite common, as in the name of the United Nations Organization, which is neither united nor made up of nations.)

Going in the other direction, Karl Popper's hysterical attacks on nationalism in *The Open Society and Its Enemies* (especially Chapters 9 and 12) presuppose that the only basis of nationality is some kind of bogus claim that nations are natural:

The attempt to find some 'natural' boundaries for states, and accordingly, to look upon the state as a 'natural' unit, leads to the *principle of the national state* and to the romantic fictions of nationalism, racialism, and tribalism. But this principle is not 'natural', and the idea that there exist natural units like nations, or linguistic or racial groups, is entirely fictitious.[37]

The assimilation of nationality to ethnicity is also illustrated by Orlando Patterson's book, *Ethnic Chauvinism,* though he confuses the issue even further by treating ethnicity as a matter of descent

[35]Smith, *Theories of Nationalism,* p. 176.

[36]Reinhard Bendix, *Nation-Building and Citizenship: Studies of our Changing Social Order* (London, John Wiley & Sons, 1964), p. 22.

[37]Popper, *Open Society*, vol. I, p. 288, n. 7.

group but then identifying it with common cultural characteristics, thus finishing up with the assertion that 'the idea of the nation-state is the view that a state ought to consist of a group of people who consciously share a common culture'. Therefore, in terms of this definition, 'Britain, the United States, Canada, and Switzerland are not nation-states. Ireland, France, and most of the other European states are nation-states; so is Japan.'[38] Again, 'Britain was never a unified tribal or cultural entity';[39] but this is not equivalent to denying that Britain has been a nation, except on the basis of Patterson's peculiar conception of nationality. Similarly, if America and Switzerland aren't nations, what are they? They are, of course, states, and that would apparently be Patterson's answer; but surely that isn't all we can say about them. To share a state with someone is after all merely to recognize a legal fact. Surely Swiss or Americans share more than that: what they share is precisely nationality.

Patterson's list of 'nation-states' is also dubious. Presumably even he couldn't face the paradox of denying that France is a nation; but it hardly is a state inhabited by a single (even mythical) descent-group, and even on the criterion of common culture it was a nation before it could seriously be described as culturally unified:

In 1876, a student at a Teacher's College in Limoges couldn't say more than two words about Joan of Arc; as late as 1906, only one military conscript in four could explain why July 14 was a national holiday. When the Marseillaise was written, most Marseillais barely spoke French. At the time of the Third Republic's founding, French was a foreign language for over one-quarter of the population. . . .[40]

For the reasons already set out, one would indeed expect an increase in cultural unity to bring about a higher level of identification with all one's fellow countrymen, and a tendency to weaken loyalties to smaller units. The only point to make is that cultural unity is not *identical* with nationhood. As far as Ireland is concerned it is important to recall that Irish nationalism in the eighteenth and nineteenth centuries was focused on all the people of Ireland,

---

[38] Orlando Patterson, *Ethnic Chauvinism: The Reactionary Impulse* (New York, Stein and Day, 1977), p. 80.

[39] Ibid., p. 75.

[40] Peter Gourevitch, Review of Eugene Weber, *Peasants into Frenchmen: The Modernization of Rural France, 1870–1914, The American Political Science Review*, 72 (1978), 1140.

and there were Protestant as well as Catholic Irish nationalists (including Parnell and Yeats), though the mass of votes came from Catholics.[41] The effort to create an Irish nationality failed, of course, and politics in Ireland developed along ethnic lines, producing the Ulster problem. But it is, in my view, too easy to say that it was bound to fail. Again, we need, in order to talk about the phenomena, to be able to distinguish between nationality and ethnicity.

We can see how both the statist and the ethnic definition of nationality bedevil analysis by considering the new states in sub-Saharan Africa that inherited the boundaries originally imposed by the colonialist powers by drawing lines on a map. What would be involved in making these into nations? According to the statist conception all that is needed is that the successor regime should succeed in filling the shoes of the colonial administrators by maintaining 'law and order' and suppressing separatist movements. According to the ethnic conception, on the other hand, creating a nation, so far from being relatively easy, is impossible: the whole idea is an absurdity. According to Patterson, 'the idea of the nation-state was . . . an astonishingly stupid one in these states'.[42] Obviously, if nationality is the same as ethnicity, this is undeniable. But rather than lunge around in this way, I suggest that it would have been better to ask whether the stupidity does not lie in Patterson's interpretation.

Patterson's alternative to the nation-state is what he calls the juridical state. This is rather ironic in someone who regards 'reactionary' as a term of abuse, since he is in effect calling for a return to the *ancien régime,* under which 'the state was a juristic and territorial concept', defined in terms of a ruler and the land over which he ruled, rather than as the embodiment of a political community.[43] Patterson claims that such a state could have 'referential symbols': 'A state's flag is such a symbol. So are symbols such as a monarch, or titular head of state, or such ritual symbols as independence day celebrations.'[44] But a symbol presumably must be a symbol *of* something. Why should anybody form an attach-

---

[41] See Kohn, *Idea of Nationalism,* pp. 467–74, for the United Irishmen.

[42] Patterson, *Ethnic Chauvinism*, p. 82.

[43] Cobban, *Nation State*, p. 35.

[44] Patterson, *Ethnic Chauvinism*, pp. 83–4.

ment to an administrative apparatus with a monopoly of legitimate force within a certain territory? Symbols like this would be infused with life only if they became symbols of the nation rather than symbols of the state: what is important is not the machinery of government but that the people should have a sense of shared political destiny with others, a preference for being united with them politically in an independent state, and preparedness to be committed to common political action.[45]

I hope that once nationality has been distinguished from ethnicity and statehood, it is not necessary to take a lot of time to belabour the advantages, from an individualist perspective, of nation states over states that do not satisfy the principle of nationality. First, given the definition of nationality with which I am working, it is an analytic truth that a nation state fulfils the aspirations of those who belong to the nation embodied in the state. Second, the presence of fellow-feeling obviously facilitates co-operation on common projects and makes redistribution within the polity more acceptable. (This is in effect the obverse of the Acton/Madison case in favour of heterogeneity.) Both of these points were taken account of by Bentham, who defined national patriotism as 'sympathy for the feelings of a country's inhabitants, present, future, or both, taken in the aggregate', and insisted that 'as devotion to the commonweal, and especially, to its improvement and reform, national patriotism can be of great service in promoting the greatest good of the greatest number'.[46]

Moreover, as I have already remarked, if trust and understanding have developed between the members of a state, this makes it more possible to carry out policies that apply universalistic criteria and have the result of helping certain regions or groups more than others, because there is some expectation that other policies another time will have the effect of benefiting other groups. Trust might be defined as the willingness to wait: hence the impossibility, according to Hobbes, of covenants in a state of nature. In all kinds of different cultures, paying back gifts or services too quickly is regarded as a refusal of social relations, and in traditional Irish

---

[45]See, for a sensitive discussion of what is really entailed in 'nation-building' (as distinct from state-building), W. T. Bluhm, *Building an Austrian Nation: The Political Integration of a Western State* (New Haven and London, Yale University Press, 1973).

[46]Carlton J. H. Hayes, *The Historical Evolution of Modern Nationalism* (New York, Macmillan, 1950), p. 128.

peasant society, where loans among neighbours were common, the first thing one did upon falling out with somebody was to pay off any outstanding loan.

If we put together the lack of sympathetic attachment to the interests of all those within the polity and the lack of trust in the willingness of others to reciprocate benefits when the need arises, we can see why policies such as those designed to help big cities get diluted in the US Congress until they are so non-selective as to be virtually useless. We can also understand how rational decision-making in countries such as Belgium or (pre-civil war) Lebanon is bedevilled by the political necessity of matching each benefit for one group by an exactly equal one for the other(s)— whether it makes sense as an efficient use of resources or not.

What can be said on the other side, from a similarly broad utilitarian standpoint? Sidgwick, who laboured under the moral and intellectual handicap of being a Liberal Unionist, offered several considerations in *The Elements of Politics* in favour of the 'forcible suppression' of any attempt of a national group to secede 'merely on the ground that the interests of the seceders would be promoted or their sentiments of nationality gratified by the change'. There would have to be 'some serious oppression or misgovernment of the seceders by the rest of the community,—i.e. some unjust sacrifice or grossly incompetent management of their interests, or some persistent and harsh opposition to their legitimate desires' (where presumably suppressing their national aspirations doesn't count).[47]

Sidgwick's arguments boil down to four. First, the state may be concerned for its security 'either through increased danger of war from the addition of the seceding community to the number of possible foes, or from the mere loss of strength and prestige'.[48] Second, there may be a minority within the territory that is opposed to the secession. Third, the loss of the seceding district might be specially serious, from its containing mines or other natural resources, in which the rest of the state's territory was deficient.[49] Finally, 'over and above these calculations of expediency, justifying resistance to disruption, we must recognise

[47] Sidgwick, *Elements of Politics*, p.217.
[48] Ibid., p. 218.
[49] Ibid., pp. 218–19.

as a powerful motive the dislike of the community from which the secession is opposed to lose territory that has once belonged to it, and to which it has a claim recognised by foreigners.'[50]

The last of these points raises in an acute form the question whether we wish to employ a version of the individualist principle that counts all desires equally, if they are of equal strength—the desire to speak and the desire to suppress another's speech, the desire to be free and the desire to oppress, and so on. In any version of the individualist principle that I should be prepared to take seriously, there would have to be some discrimination according to the worth of different desires, and I should therefore regard the desire to hold territory for no reason other than that one has a strong desire to do so as morally irrelevant.

The other three have some force but would presumably be just as strong in defending the annexing of territories against the wishes of a majority of their inhabitants so long as it would increase military security, accord with the wishes of a minority, or make available raw materials. Just about every international atrocity of the past two centuries could be justified on one or other of those grounds—and usually was. Rather than accept Sidgwick's arguments, therefore, I think that we should advocate changes in the international regime that would reduce the importance of ownership of territory for military security and access to natural resources. The problem of minorities is, of course, an intractable one; but if one accepts Sidgwick's claim that a minority loyal to the larger state should have its wishes respected even if this entails overriding the wishes of the local majority, how is one to condemn Mussolini's claims on Dalmatia or Hitler's on Czechoslovakia? Only, it would seem, by sanctifying the status quo; but I can see no reason why, if every other relevant factor is the same, force used to defend the status quo is more morally legitimate than force used to change it.

Manifestly, these questions cry out for more careful treatment, but I hope that I have established what I set out to, namely that there is a strong prima-facie case on individualist premises for drawing state boundaries so that they correspond with nationality, as I have defined it. I now want, in conclusion, to take up the aspect of nationalism that seems to me to pose some problems for

[50]Ibid., p. 219.

the individualist principle. This is cultural nationalism, the core of the romantic nationalism of the late eighteenth and early nineteenth centuries.

By no means all the claims that might be associated with cultural nationalism appear to me to create difficulties for individualism, and I shall begin by disposing of two that do not. First, there is nothing contrary to the individualist principle in saying that cultural similarity is a good basis for association. Anne Cohler, in her book *Rousseau and Nationalism,* treats similarity as a 'non-political' factor and draws all kinds of horrendous implications from such a factor's being the basis of political association.[51] Yet there are two quite straightforward advantages in cultural similarity. First, there is a strong causal link between cultural similarity and trust. Hans Kohn quotes Rudyard Kipling's poem 'The Stranger' as an illustration of a 'primitive feeling'.[52] But there is nothing primitive in the idea that the ability to interpret the behaviour of other people depends on a mass of shared understandings.

A second reason for having political units that are as culturally homogeneous as possible is that the provision of public goods is more feasible and their funding from tax revenues more equitable the more similar the tastes of the public. Again, this is simply the same analysis as Acton's with the opposite conclusion: Acton favoured heterogeneity to avoid any collective action beyond the bare minimum of 'law and order'; but if one takes the view that it is appropriate for states to provide collective benefits, especially where they are 'non-excludable' so that it would otherwise be difficult to raise the money for them, then it clearly follows that the more homogeneous the taxing unit the more scope there is for collective provision. It should, however, be said that this point bears on tax and service-provision units rather than on states, and could be met by making subordinate units correspond to areas with different cultures. Even where cultural differences do not cut along convenient geographical boundaries, it is possible to go some way towards public provision for each cultural group by having each person pay a tax (thus avoiding the 'free rider' problem) but permitting each to designate whether he wants it to

---

[51] Anne Cohler, *Rousseau and Nationalism* (New York, Basic Books, 1970).
[52] Kohn, *Idea of Nationalism*, p. 5.

go (say) to a Catholic or Protestant school system or television system, as in the Netherlands. Thus, the public goods argument for a culturally homogeneous state is not very strong in itself.

As far as linguistic homogeneity is concerned, we can again emphasize the relation between communication and trust, and press the view that, for democratic politics to work, the citizens must be able to communicate with one another, and must have access to the same forums of political debate. This was one of the bases of J. S. Mill's endorsement of linguistically-defined frontiers in *Considerations on Representative Government*; but Mill did not make it sufficiently clear that the rationale of linguistic homogeneity here has nothing to do with the usage of language (in the form of 'mother tongue') to establish ethnic group membership, that is to say, nationality in the 'objective' sense in which the sentiments of the people concerned don't count. The California Supreme Court has dealt a blow to this conception of the requirement of inter-communication by permitting the registration to vote of citizens lacking the ability to speak English, and it is quite likely that the requirement of competence in English for naturalization will come under attack in the courts in coming years. The basis for the California decision was that there were (in the Los Angeles area, where the case was brought) a sufficient number of Spanish news-papers, magazines, and television channels to enable monoglot Spanish speakers to collect enough information to be in a position to cast an informed vote. The model underlying this decision is clearly that of the voter having fixed interests which he looks around for a means of satisfying through the political system. The idea that there is an overriding collective interest in the mainten-ance of a single political community among those formally entitled to take part in political affairs is lacking in such reasoning. One can hardly avoid asking oneself what is the expected half-life of a political system in which the norm of politics as a means for the pursuit of individual interests, rather than as a process in which the conception of one's interests is constantly open to modification through societal communication, has penetrated so deeply that one of the most respected courts acts on it.

The aspect of cultural nationalism that seems to me to create some problems within the individualist paradigm is the claim that the state should be used to preserve the culture of the nation as it has come down and transmit it to the next generation. There are two variants on this which, whatever their merits, do not run into conflict with the individualist principle as I define it. The first is the one that Rousseau advanced in the *Considerations on the Government of Poland*. As Judith Shklar has emphasized, 'quite unlike the later nationalists Rousseau did not believe that the national self had any basis in nature'.[53] But he regarded it as essential for a country like Poland to have a national identity distinct from all others, and insisted that the educational system should stress national peculiarities, even if they were quite devoid of intrinsic value.

Rousseau's advice has begun to be taken in recent years by the governments of some Third World countries, which 'have discovered that independence must be taken a stage further [than that of formal political independence] into the cultural fold and pressure must be placed on the radio and television companies (which are normally state-owned) and on the newspapers (which are state-influenced and sometimes state-owned) to indigenize their output, to play down the imported entertainment material and emphasize local news, local and regional culture, indigenous entertainment.'[54]

This may be regarded as the obverse of the notion that cultural uniformity within the country makes for the kind of solidarity necessary for politics to work smoothly: the idea here is that difference from other countries also helps. It may be said, of course, that this other side is a good deal more sinister in that it seems inescapably bound up with the view that states are to be defined as being in (actual or potential) conflict with others. The situation of Poland in the eighteenth century was perhaps desperate enough to warrant extraordinary measures to play up national peculiarities. The conflict with neighbours was only too apparently present. But it seems hard to justify the fomenting of national peculiarities for purely political reasons as anything but a response to a dire threat of national extinction. The point for our present purpose is, however, that there is no difficulty in seeing how, if the appropriate factual assumptions are supplied, cultural nationalism can be derived from individualistic rather than holistic premises, since it can be argued to be conducive to individual interests.

[53] Judith N. Shklar, *Men and Citizens* (London, Cambridge University Press, 1969), p. 161.

[54] Anthony Smith, *The Geopolitics of Information: How Western Culture Dominates the World* (New York, Oxford University Press, 1980), p. 38.

The other notion of cultural nationalism that is consistent with the individualist principle is that of cultural imperialism. If you believe that German culture is better than Slav or that European culture is better than that of the 'natives' of India or Africa, in the sense that it is better *for people,* then you could deduce a 'civilizing mission' for the bearers of the superior culture from individualist premisses. This should perhaps count as another variant on the theory that it doesn't matter what the boundaries are so long as those within them are culturally heterogeneous: that it is a positively good thing for the culturally more 'advanced' to dominate the more 'backward' races. Acton, indeed, believed this too, and much of the essay on 'Nationality' is devoted to that theme.[55] It is a common idea among Victorian liberals: we can also find it in Mill and Sidgwick, for example. Clearly, in order to make this go, from an individualist standpoint, one must have a conception of interest that detaches it from preference, since 'natives' have usually had the poor taste to resist colonization. Most of us lack the certainties of the Victorians that we know what is best for alien peoples, though Americans seem to have continued to struggle with the White Man's Burden long after the European powers gave it up. Anyway, there is no need here to evaluate the theory of cultural imperialism. All we have to do is to note that, again with suitable adjuncts, it can be fitted into the individualist framework.

The version that does cause trouble is, ironically, one that is neither manipulative for ulterior political ends like Rousseau's nor arrogant like the cultural imperialists'. This is the idea that each culturally distinct group has a legitimate interest in maintaining the integrity of that culture and passing it on intact to the next generation. Notice that this is different in a basic respect from either of the views just canvassed because it posits that people attach an intrinsic value to their own culture. On Rousseau's theory, it would be perfectly all right to assimilate to a different

---

[55] As well as the cultural imperialist strand, one also has to take account of the Roman Catholic strand in Acton's thought. This comes out more clearly in another essay, where he wrote: 'Thus the theory of nationality, unknown to Catholic ages, is inconsistent both with political reason and with Christianity, which requires the dominion of race over race, and whose path was made straight by two universal empires. The missionary may outstrip, in his devoted zeal, the progress of trade or of arms; but the seed that he plants will not take root, unprotected by these ideas of right and duty which first came into the world with the tribes who destroyed the civilisation of antiquity, and whose descendants are in our day carrying those ideas to every quarter of the world.' Acton, *History of Freedom*, p. 247.

culture if this were politically necessary. Separate cultures are important only as the underpinnings of separate polities. And on the cultural imperialist theory it would be positively desirable if the culture to which one was assimilating had (on some sort of universalistic criterion) a language capable of handling more complex discriminations and a richer literature. The view in question is, however, distinct from both of these. According to it, my culture is best for me and yours is best for you. Each of us should preserve and transmit our own culture and respect the culture of others.

Now, it is quite clear that much resistance to assimilation can be related to (whether 'accounted for by' is another question) economic advantage. Cultural nationalism produces 'jobs for the boys', because the criteria for becoming a schoolteacher, a civil servant, and so on, change so that, instead of competing at a disadvantage in a second language, the members of the newly enfranchised language are at a comparative advantage. But it is impossible to explain the whole phenomenon in this way. Assimilation over a generation or so can be perfect so that the disadvantage would be transitional: in Belgium, for example, part of the tension in linguistic politics arose from Dutch-speaking parents in the Brussels area choosing to send their children to schools in which French was the language of instruction so that they could obtain better jobs in a French-speaking environment. The Fleming concerns taken up collectively through political action were not for the well-being of individual Flemings, many of whom were happy to have their children assimilate to French, but for the maintenance of the Fleming identity and culture. Similarly, in Quebec, one may explain in terms of self-interest the explosion of pressure on firms to create promotion opportunities for French speakers in the 1960s and 1970s. However, the same self-interest would dictate discouragement of assimilation to French among the rest of the population, yet the current education policies are designed to produce assimilation. Thus, there is (I almost apologize for having to say) a desire for a French-speaking province over and above the economic considerations.

The school of German nationalism stemming from Herder is the obvious place to look for the arguments. I have already cited Herder's notion of nations as natural growths, but his primary concern, as I understand it, was with the idea that 'the individual can attain his highest self-development only in the life of the group as a whole.'[56] Clearly, if it were true that Germans (say) were naturally (in the sense of biologically) suited to German language and German culture, it would be easy to see why it was important to stick to them. It may be that some people (perhaps including Herder) said things like this, though I suspect that we tend to read into them more differentiated ideas than they had, but anyway such an idea is too stupid to be worth attention. Even if we drop any such notion of the biological basis of particular cultures, we can of course agree that as a matter of biological necessity an individual, to flourish, must grow up and live in *some* culture.[57] But that still leaves us with the question why it is worth trying to protect one's own culture from being swamped by outside in-fluences—as many people believe it is—and worth trying to ensure that subsequent generations grow up sharing its ideas, reading its literature, and so on.

One possible answer would be that in practice cultural mixing is almost always for the worse. Rousseau's attacks on 'cosmopolitan' culture would obviously align him with this claim. In a contem-porary version, it might be argued that what will tend to be picked up are the quickly-gratifying, non-demanding, effort-saving, bland, and tasteless aspects of other cultures, at the expense of the more physically, intellectually, and morally strenuous features of the indigenous culture. This is the root of the widespread antipathy around the world to 'Americanization'. And the key to the invasive success of American culture is, perhaps, that it is itself the product of generations of assimilation and has thus selected out for exactly the features mentioned above: American food is notoriously lacking in sharp flavour or distinctive texture, for example, and even American language is oddly shapeless and diffuse, wholly lacking the sinewy precision of the best models of English[58].

[56] Ergang, *Herder*, p. 248.

[57] See Mary Midgley, *Beast and Man: The Roots of Human Nature* (Ithaca, N.Y., Cornell University Press, 1978), pp. 285–305. 'A culture is a way of awakening our faculties. Any culture does this to some extent. People proficient in one culture can usually make sense of another. There is no prison. We can always walk on if we want to enough. What we cannot do is something which is no loss—namely be nobody and nowhere. I do not mean that some people may not be very unlucky in their culture, either because it is generally bad, or because it suits them badly. But this is still nothing to the misfortune of having no culture at all.' (p. 291.)

[58] See Tibor Scitovsky, *The Joyless Economy* (New York, Oxford University Press, 1967).

I find this argument broadly persuasive, and thus sympathize strongly with the efforts of weaker countries to control the flow of communications across their borders—especially restricting the import of American television programmes.[59] The standard American criticisms of this seem to me to miss the point that, because tastes are changed by exposure, individual 'freedom to consume' cultural artefacts gives rise over time to a pervasive cultural drift within the society, which is a collective phenomenon and a legitimate subject of collective concern and regulation. Of course, to say that something is a legitimate matter for political intervention is not to underwrite any and every form of intervention, and most actual ones are open to criticism. But the point here is simply that, on a broad conception of interest, individual interests are certainly at stake here.

The argument up to this point is that whatever the existing culture is, it is probably better, not than alternative cultures, but than what would most likely result from the (inevitably partial) assimilation of this one to another. As Sir Arthur Evans said of the culture of the inhabitants of Knossos, the Palace of which he had excavated, 'A poor thing but Minoan.'

Surely, however, this cannot be the whole story. Many people care a lot about the preservation and transmission of their culture as an end in itself. They see themselves as standing in a position of trust between past and future generations. This notion of a culture as something continuous through time, with those currently alive as trustees, recalls to English-speaking readers Edmund Burke. But the idea is more fully developed by the German Romantic nationalists. We can find it in Herder, but it is much more fully expressed in Fichte's *Addresses to the German Nation,* especially the eighth. Does not the man of noble mind, he asks, 'wish to snatch from the jaws of death the spirit, the mind, and the moral sense' that he displayed in his own life? He invokes the German resistance to assimilation to Rome: 'All those blessings which the Romans offered them meant slavery to them,—they assumed as a matter of course that every man would rather die than become half a Roman, and that a true German could only live in order to be, and to remain, just a German and to bring up his children as

---

[59]'The free flow of one section of the globe merely swamps the culture of others.' Smith, *Geopolitics of Information*, p. 37.

Germans.'[60] If we steer clear of the references to laws of nature and laws of divine development with which Fichte's text is strewn, we may ask whether we can make any sense of what is left from within the individualist framework.

Here again, everything has to be referred back to the crucial concept of interest. If my interest is identified with my happiness or pleasure (or any other state of myself), it must be the case that I can have no interest in what happens on earth after my death —assuming that death is the termination of consciousness. By the same token, those who are no longer alive can have no interest in what happens now. However, it seems perfectly natural to say that our interests are for states of the world rather than only for states of ourselves. If I want something to happen, I don't merely want the satisfaction of believing that it happens; and if it happens, I have got what I want even if I never have the satisfaction of hearing about it. If it is reasonable to include in interests having certain things happen (whether one knows about them or not) while one is alive, it seems strange to draw the line at one's death.[61] If interests can include states of the world after one is dead, we have a possible way of justifying, on individualistic premises, a collective decision to try to pass on one's own culture intact, even if one believes that it could be transformed without being damaged. (It may be questioned whether such a judgement could be made, since the criteria for damage have to come from somewhere and the obvious candidate is the existing culture, in which case all change will be bad automatically. However, I assume that it is possible to gain some degree of detachment from one's culture and to conclude that some changes impoverish it and others enrich it.)

Obviously, the move to bring cultural nationalism within the individualist fold depends on the actual desire on the part of past and present people to pass on their culture. If that desire exists (or existed), we can talk about an interest and thus get to the answer that cultural transmission satisfies individual interests. What we cannot do, however, as far as I can see, is say that people ought to

[60] Johann Gottlieb Fichte, *Addresses to the German Nation*, trans. by R. F. Jones and G. H. Turnbull (Chicago, Open Court, 1922), pp. 132, 144.

[61] See Joel Feinberg, 'Harm and Self-Interest' in P. M. S. Hacker and J. Raz (eds.), *Law, Morality, and Society: Essays in Honour of H. L. A. Hart* (Oxford, Clarendon Press, 1977), pp. 285–308; reprinted in Joel Feinberg, *Rights, Justice and the Bounds of Liberty: Essays in Social Philosophy* (Princeton, Princeton University Press, 1980), pp. 45–68.

have an interest in passing on their culture, even if they do not in fact have one. We could try to persuade them that their lives would take on greater significance if they were to care about the texture of their descendants' lives. But if they still don't care, we have, I take it, reached the outer bounds of individualistic political philosophy. If we want to say that they are *wrong* not to care, then we have to be prepared to say that cultures have a value of their own and that human beings are, as it were, their biological instruments. At a pinch I could perhaps bring myself to believe this, but on the whole I am gratified to find how far one can get without having to resort to this kind of move.

Of course, what I have been saying in these last pages presupposes that it does make sense to talk about people having interests that survive them, and this is, in some people's view, an odd and paradoxical notion. Let me break it down, however, into two parts. The first is the assertion that people have interests in what happens after their deaths. For example, they may want their children to be well provided for rather then simply wanting the pleasure of believing now that their children will be well provided for. This seems to me fairly incontrovertible. If it were not true, large parts of human behaviour would be simply unintelligible. The second assertion, which is what some people gag on[62] is that when a person is dead he still has an interest in what happens. I think that Feinberg is right in supposing that, when one really thinks about it, it is actually quite hard to accept the first without accepting the second—or, to put it the other way round, the premisses required to reject the second will jeopardize the first as well.

Both are required if we wish to say that the interests of past as well as present generations are involved in cultural transmission. But only the first is required if we confine ourselves to saying that the members of the present generation have an interest in what happens to their culture in the future, including the time after they are dead. Moreover, it may be argued that we can still bring in the previous generations indirectly by saying that the present generation has more chance of having its own current interests with respect to what happens in the future served by future generations if it itself makes a point of playing up the fact that it is carrying out the

[62] See for example Ernest Partridge, 'Posthumous Interests and Posthumous Respect', *Ethics*, 91 (1981), pp. 243–64.

wishes that previous generations had for the future while they were alive.[63]

However, I am bound to say that for me this proposal brings out the difficulty of accepting the first assertion without the second. For if those now alive (the As) really care about what happens after they are dead and would like their descendants (the Ds) to regard the As' present concerns for the future as a basis for the Ds' actions then, why should the As not accept the past concerns for the present of earlier generations as a basis for the As' actions now?[64] Thus, I do not myself see that the halfway house is a satisfactory resting point. But I offer it in case it can be shown by some further argument to be internally consistent to accept the first assertion and deny the second.

I have in this paper traversed a large area, and I shall not attempt to summarize. Let me conclude, then, with the observation that the individualist moral theory, in its general form, is capable of generating a wide variety of alternative conclusions about the rights and wrongs of nationalism in various forms. Ultimately, the disagreements turn on the conception of interest that one plugs into the basic doctrine and on the ways of life that one believes conduce

[63] This is Partridge's own answer.

[64] An illustration of this point is provided by the case of Roger Lapham, a keen golfer who wanted to be cremated and have his ashes buried on his favourite golf course, Cypress Point on the Monterey Peninsula. 'He died in 1966, at the age of eighty-three, and Lewis, on receiving the news of his father's death, hurried out to the family home in San Francisco. Shortly after his arrival, he was informed by his brother that there had been a hitch in the plans: their mother had stated forcefully that she would not permit her husband's body to be cremated or to be buried at Cypress Point. ''Under California law at that time, a person did not control the disposition of his remains,'' Lewis Lapham has recalled. ''His executors could disregard his stipulations if they wished to. When I got together with my mother, I suggested that we have a shot of sherry—that seemed a good idea. Then we began discussing things, and I said to her, 'I don't think your position is reasonable. For example, I'm your heir and executor. What would you think if I were to disregard the instructions set down in your will?' 'You wouldn't dare,' she said. 'But consider this,' I went on. 'That is exactly what you are going to do with someone you lived with for fifty-nine years.' I suggested we have another sherry. The upshot was that my mother came round, and my father was cremated and buried on that little ridge overlooking Cypress Point, in sight of the tide rolling in on a small beach.''' Herbert Warren Wind, 'The Sporting Scene: From Linksland to Augusta', *The New Yorker*, 22 June 1981, 96–111, p. 104.

This *could* be interpreted in 'intergenerational social contract' terms, so that the widow complied with her late husband's wishes *in order to* get the son to comply with hers. But surely the way the story runs makes it clear that the crucial move is an argument from equity: that if you really care about what happens after your own death there is no valid reason for refusing to pay the same attention to the wishes that others had for what would happen after their deaths. And this is exactly the point advanced in the text.

to human interests so understood. Although my main intent here has been to explore the ways in which the argument can go, my not-so-hidden agenda has been to suggest that nationalism has been given a bum rap in recent political theory, and to try to show that the efforts of the Viennese liberals to conflate ethical individualism and anti-nationalism will not withstand scrutiny.

Political Equality and Majority Rule* †

Peter Jones
University of Newcastle

Disputes concerning democracy often seem fruitless exercises in assertion and counter-assertion. Given the favourable connotations that now attach to the adjective 'democratic', it is not surprising that politicians have manipulated its meaning as suits their purposes. Political theorists have neither the same need to exploit, nor therefore the same excuse for exploiting, the rhetorical potentialities of the term. Yet they seem no more agreed upon what democracy is, nor any less keen to defend their preferred definitions. Argument over the correct usage of 'democracy' and 'democratic' is not entirely pointless since there are criteria by which some uses can be judged more justified than others and by which still others can be dismissed as misuses. But these criteria still leave scope for disagreement and they do not tell us what, if anything, is so special about democracy.

Whatever democracy is, it is not self-justifying. If someone declared himself 'against justice', we would infer either that he intended some sort of irony or else that he had no understanding of what justice meant. There is nothing similarly puzzling, let alone incomprehensible, about someone's declaring himself 'against democracy'. Even those of us who are 'for' democracy may not be so unreservedly; we may believe it to be the right or best decision procedure for some sorts of decision but not for others. Democracy then is something that can be argued both for and against and, when it is argued for, quite different sorts of argument can be offered in its support. Granted this, instead of dealing with disputes over democracy as though they were mere battles of definition, it is more profitable to establish people's reasons for preferring the decision procedure that they deem 'democratic' so that the argument can become one about those reasons and what they

*© Peter Jones 1983.

† This paper has benefited from discussions I have had with many people. I am particularly grateful to Hugh Berrington, Tim Gray, Michael Lessnoff, David Miller, Robert Sugden, and Albert Weale for their helpful comments and criticism.

155

imply. Even where different reasons are offered in support of the same general conception of democracy, they may still imply differences of detail and emphasis.

It is with how different justifications bear upon one prominent 'detail' of democracy, its decision rule, that I shall be concerned in this paper. More particularly, my concern is with the status of the majority principle and with the issues raised by 'persistent minorities', that is, by groups of individuals who invariably find themselves on the losing side. Although I shall have to engage in a good deal of preliminary skirmishing, the issue I shall eventually confront is whether persistent minorities should regard their position as unfair or merely unfortunate.

When I use the term 'democracy' I shall have in mind a very simple and, I hope, uncontroversial model: an association of people who enjoy equal rights of participation in their decision procedure and who vote directly upon issues. By the 'majority principle' or 'majority rule' I shall mean simply the rule that a proposal should be adopted if it receives the support of at least 50 per cent + 1 of the votes cast. My excuse for using this simple model is that the general principle of what I have to say is unaffected by the complexities and modifications exhibited by actual 'democratic' political systems and there is no point in complicating the argument unnecessarily. Moreover, the argument I develop applies not only to the state but also to other associations for which democracy is thought the right or desirable form of decision procedure, and my simple model is less far removed from the reality of many such non-state associations.

JUSTIFYING DEMOCRACY

Why should democracy be regarded as the right or desirable decision procedure for some, if not all, associations? One sort of answer is consequentialist in character. It posits a condition as desirable and then commends democracy because it is the decision procedure which is guaranteed to produce that desirable condition or which is more likely to do so than any alternative decision procedure. Thus democracy has been defended because it results in wise policies, a just society, a free society, decisions which promote the public interest or the common good, which respect individual rights, which promote science and intellectual activity, and so on. The list is limited only by one's resourcefulness in enumerating the good things of life and the conviction with which one is able to argue that democracy will promote them.[1] Each of these justifications can also be urged in defence of the majority principle. Why should the vote of the majority be decisive? Because it will promote, or is most likely to promote, this or that desirable result.

Consequentialist justifications of the type I have instanced focus upon the intrinsic quality of democratic decisions. However, there is another type of consequentialist justification in which the appeal is not to the desirable content of democratic decisions but to the benefits that flow from the way in which those decisions are reached. Perhaps the most widely used justification of this sort is that particularly associated with J. S. Mill: the argument that, in participating in the decisions that are to govern his life, an individual is improved both intellectually and morally.[2] Claims that people are more ready to respect decisions reached democratically and that democracy has an integrative effect upon a community are also examples of this second type of consequentialist justification.

It is less easy to relate this second sort of consequentialist justification to any specific decision rule such as the majority principle. Clearly it implies widespread participation and participation implies the possibility of having an influence upon decisions. That, however, need not be of any specific type. Mill, for example, thought that his arguments for participation did not necessarily entail that participants should be granted equal voting rights.

Consequentialist justifications of democracy have an obvious rationale. It would be surprising if one's approval or disapproval of a form of government took no account of the quality of government that one could expect from it. Nevertheless there are a number of reasons why one might be less than wholly satisfied with justifying

---

[1] For examples of justifications of this kind, see Carl Cohen, *Democracy* (Athens, University of Georgia Press, 1971), ch. 14; Jack Lively, *Democracy* (Oxford, Basil Blackwell, 1975), ch. 4; Henry B. Mayo, *An Introduction to Democratic Theory* (New York, Oxford University Press, 1960), chs. 9 and 10; William N. Nelson, *On Justifying Democracy* (London, Routledge & Kegan Paul, 1980), ch. 6. Despite some equivocations, John Rawls's justifications of democracy and majority rule are essentially of this form; in his terms both are instances of 'imperfect procedural justice'. *A Theory of Justice* (London, Oxford University Press, 1972), sections 31, 36, 37, 53, 54.

[2] J. S. Mill, *Utilitarianism, Liberty and Representative Government* (London, Dent, 1910), pp. 202–18. See also Carole Pateman, *Participation and Democratic Theory* (Cambridge, Cambridge University Press, 1970); Peter Bachrach, *The Theory of Democratic Elitism: A Critique* (London, University of London Press, 1969) ch. 7; C. B. Macpherson, 'The Maximization of Democracy' in his *Democratic Theory: Essays in Retrieval* (Oxford, Oxford University Press, 1973).

democracy in this way. (These reasons apply with less force to one sort of consequentialist justification: the utilitarian justification of democracy in terms of the maximization of happiness or want-satisfaction. I shall deal with utilitarianism later.) Firstly, consequentialist justifications are contingent in character. They involve empirical assertions which may or may not hold true. For example, whether a society which respects certain sorts of individual right is a 'good' society is not an empirical question; whether a democratic system of government will ensure such a society most definitely is. The simple confidence with which some writers are prepared to make such empirical assertions in justifying democracy is, to say the least, quite remarkable. Moreover, given that consequentialist justifications have this contingent character, they do not constitute principled commitments to democracy as such. If it turned out that the desired result would be better achieved by a non-democratic system of government, then we should abandon democracy.

Secondly, and relatedly, consequentialist justifications fail to account for our sense that democracy constitutes a fair decision procedure. That is, they do not accommodate the idea that, irrespective of what decisions are made, a democratic system constitutes a fairer way of making decisions than one in which some are excluded from the process of decision-making and others are accorded a privileged status. More particularly, consequentialist justifications cannot provide a satisfactory account of the idea of an equal *right* of participation. The assertion of a right makes the focus of concern the well-being of the individual right-holder. Thus the assertion of a right to vote entails construing a vote as of benefit to the individual voter and the removal of that right as a disbenefit to him.[3] In consequentialist justifications of democracy, the establishment of equal voting rights is justified simply as a means to a

[3] The alleged beneficial effects of participation on the character of an individual could be represented as a benefit he receives from voting but, J. S. Mill notwithstanding, the picture of a body of disfranchised individuals protesting because they have been deprived thereby of the means of intellectual and moral self-improvement is somewhat fanciful. The argument that people should have equal voting rights because that is essential to their enjoying equal 'status' (understood as a social or psychological condition) also belongs to the second type of consequentialist justification that I have identified, but may provide a more plausible account of why people should have equal rights of participation. I consider this argument below, pp. 177–8.

desirable collective end.[4] If that collective end required unequal or selective voting rights there could be no ground for complaint. Even where the attainment of a collective end did require equal voting rights, the removal of those rights from an individual or group of individuals would be construed as a harm to society at large (because it endangered the attainment of the collective end) rather than as an injustice to the disfranchised individuals. Yet the arbitrary disfranchisement of a group of individuals is typically thought of as an infringement of *their* (pre-legal) rights, as an injustice to them in particular rather than merely a harm to society in general.

Thirdly, of less significance but still worth mentioning, democracy is a form of decision procedure thought appropriate to many associations other than the state. Several of the consequentialist justifications offered in support of democracy have little or no relevance to these non-state associations. For example, if a gardening club or a rambling association or a film society has a democratic constitution, it is unlikely to apologize for this by appeals to the promotion of justice or freedom. It may regard its democratic constitution as *embodying* ideas of justice and freedom but that is a different matter.

How else then might democracy be justified? The answer is clearly implied in the shortcomings of consequentialist justification. The alternative is to appeal to a principle which entails that democracy is the inherently right or fair way of making decisions. Here there is not a prospective appeal to a desirable consequence but a retrospective appeal to a principle which predicates the intrinsic rightness or fairness of the democratic process itself. When equality is appealed to not merely as a feature of democratic institutions but as a reason for having those institutions, democracy is being justified in this way. It is to the justification of democracy by way of equality that I shall give most of my attention. It is not the only form of non-consequentialist justification of democracy that there can be. If one believed that democracy was the divinely approved form of government (as some have believed in the past and, for all I know, as some may still believe now) that would clearly afford a non-consequentialist justification of democracy. Justifica-

---

[4]For purposes of this argument the goal of a society which institutes and respects individual rights counts as a 'collective' end, since it is an end general to the voters as a group.

tions which stress 'self-determination' will also usually be of this type. However, the appeal to equality is perhaps more frequently heard than any other.

EQUALITY AND THE MAJORITY PRINCIPLE

In a moment, I want to look at what sort of principle of equality can justify political equality. But since my interest is ultimately in the decision rule that a democracy should adopt, let me first of all indicate the very simple way in which the majority principle is often justified by way of equality. Political equality entails that each should have an equal right of participation and, in particular, that each should have a vote and that each vote should count equally. If there is a clash of preferences and if each vote is to count equally, then the proposal preferred by the majority must be adopted. To allow the will of the minority to prevail would be to give greater weight to the vote of each member of the minority than to the vote of each member of the majority, thus violating political equality. This argument can be used not only in defense of absolute majorities but also in defence of relative majorities if, for some reason, an absolute majority is unattainable.[5]

If we accept the spirit of this argument, does it require our unqualified acceptance of the majority principle? There are two widely canvassed limitations upon the majority principle which must be mentioned, though I mention them largely to emphasize their separateness from a third sort of limitation upon which I shall dwell.

1. *Majority rule and minority rights*

People often want to assert individual or minority rights as restrictions upon the scope of majority preference. Is this compatible with the argument from equality?

In answering this we need to distinguish between democratic and

---

[5] For examples of this form of argument for majority rule, see Robert A. Dahl and Charles E. Lindblom, *Politics, Economics and Welfare* (New York, Harper and Row, 1953), pp. 41–4; Robert A. Dahl, *A Preface to Democratic Theory* (Chicago, University of Chicago Press, 1956), pp. 37–8, 60–2; Austin Ranney and Willmoore Kendall, *Democracy and the American Party System* (New York, Harcourt, Brace & Co., 1956), pp. 29–37; Neal Riemer, 'The Case for Bare Majority Rule', *Ethics*, 62 (1951–2), 17–18; Nelson, *On Justifying Democracy,* pp. 18–20. (Nelson questions the relevance but not the logic of the argument.)

non-democratic rights.[6] By 'democratic rights' I understand those rights which are integral to the democratic process. Obviously these include the right to vote but also rights such as freedom of expression and freedom of association in so far as these are essential for an individual's participation in the democratic process. Anyone committed to democracy and to the rule of the majority of a pre-defined demos must require the maintenance of those rights. One reason is that those rights are sanctioned by the principle of equality which sanctions the majority principle itself. Another is that a majority which removes the democratic rights of part of a demos impairs the claim of future majorities to be majorities of that demos.

The case of non-democratic rights is perhaps more contentious. Rights such as the right of freedom of worship or the right to a fair trial rest upon some ground other than their being essential to the democratic process and are intended to limit the scope of that process. These rights are often called minority rights but that is misleading since they are usually rights ascribed to every individual in a community and not only to a specific minority. Presumably they are labelled minority rights because they are conceived as safeguards against possible ravages of the majority. As long as these rights are universal to each member of a demos, I cannot see how they can be impugned on grounds of equality. It is sometimes implied that the inhibition of majority preference by individual rights constitutes an inequality in favour of a minority. But the inequality involved in universal rights is not an inequality of persons, but an inequality in the status attributed to certain goods and is an inequality enjoyed by everyone.

This is not to say that democracy requires that such rights be recognized or respected. On the contrary, there would be nothing 'undemocratic' about their denial, removal, or infringement, although these might well be objectionable on other grounds. I am holding only that a society which restricts the scope of the democratic process, and therefore the will of the majority, by the institution of individual rights cannot be faulted on grounds of equality alone.

---

[6] This distinction corresponds to John Plamenatz's distinction between 'political' rights and 'private' rights (*Democracy and Illusion* (London, Longman, 1973), pp. 200–1).

2. *Apathetic majorities and intense minorities*

A second complication in moving from political equality to majority rule concerns intensity of preference. It is often considered a defect of the majority principle that it merely counts preferences and takes no account of the different intensities with which those preferences are held. It is not obviously right or desirable that the very mild preferences of a 52 per cent 'apathetic majority' should prevail over the strongly held preferences of a 48 per cent 'intense minority'.[7] Certainly any justification of democracy in terms of maximizing satisfactions implies that account should be taken of the intensity as well as the number of preferences. Nor would it be difficult to argue that equality allows, if it does not require, that account be taken of intensity of preference. If individuals are treated equally in respect of the criterion of intensity, the egalitarian *qua* egalitarian has no reason to complain.

There are large problems in devising procedures which take reliable account of intensity of preference and much disagreement about the sensitivity of Western representative democracies to differing intensities of preference. But, for the moment, my concern is only with whether it is right, in principle, to take account of intensity of preference. A feature of this criterion which may make one hesitate about it at this level is its subjectivity. Some people seem to feel more strongly than others about almost everything. Some become excited without good reason; others fail to become excited when they have good reason. Taking account of intensity of preference may therefore favour over-sensitive busybodies to the disadvantage of long-suffering stoics. The point here is not that recognized by Dahl: that overt behaviour may not always be a reliable indicator of individuals' states of mind. Rather it is that, even if X undoubtedly feels more strongly than Y, it is not clear that X should get his way if his strength of feeling seems 'unreasonable'. This element of subjectivity can be avoided by reformulating the principle in terms of interests, so that ideally a decision procedure would take account of the extent to which individuals' interests were affected beneficially or adversely even when this did not coincide with the sensitivities manifested by the individuals

[7] Dahl, *Preface to Democratic Theory*, pp. 48–50, 90–102.

themselves.[8] Certainly if the principle upon which political equality rests is that of an equal claim to the promotion of one's interests (as I shall argue), that implies that interests should be weighed as well as heads counted.

A further point of principle is that the case for taking account of intensity depends upon how the democratic process is conceived. If one thinks of it as computing wants or interests, there is a case for weighing as well as counting these. If, on the other hand, one takes a consequentialist view of democracy in which votes represent judgements rather than preferences, intensity may be irrelevant. As Rawls points out, those who have stronger feelings on an issue may do so because of their ignorance or prejudice, while those who have weaker feelings may do so because of their better appreciation of the complexities of the issue.[9] In other words, intensity of feeling is not a reliable indicator of quality of judgement.

However, having made these qualifications, there is clearly a strong case for allowing considerations of intensity to modify the majority principle (in so far as this is practicable), and a case which has more rather than less to be said for it in terms of equality of treatment.

WHAT PRINCIPLE OF EQUALITY?

Before taking up a third and more radical qualification of the majority principle, I want to return to the issue of equality itself and the principle which underlies a commitment to political equality.

Since democracy is a decision procedure, it may seem that the principle of equality relevant to democracy must be one concerning people's capacities as decision-makers. And, indeed, there are writers who assert or imply that adherence to democracy entails a presumption of the equality of competence of individuals on political matters. This presumption can be more or less strong. In its strongest form, the claim would be simply that people *are* equally competent to make political decisions. A slightly weaker claim would be that, although there are differences in competence

---

[8]For a reformulation of the notion of intensity of preference in terms of 'essential interests' and its application to the problem of 'tyranny', see James S. Fishkin, *Tyranny and Legitimacy* (Baltimore, The Johns Hopkins University Press, 1979), especially chs. 3–6. See also T. M. Scanlon, 'Preference and Urgency', *Journal of Philosophy* 72 (1975), 655–69.

[9]Rawls, *Theory of Justice*, pp. 230–1, 361.

between individuals, those differences are too slight to matter. A still weaker claim would be that, although some are more competent than others, those differences are insufficiently obvious for there to be agreement on who is more competent than whom and that therefore we have to treat people as if they were equally competent, even though they are not. Thus Singer suggests that the reason for rejecting Mill's proposal for plural votes for those with superior education and intelligence 'is not that it would be obviously unfair to give more votes to better qualified people, but rather that it would be impossible to get everyone to agree on who was to have the extra votes'. Thus, 'one person, one vote', represents a sort of practical compromise.[10]

One reason, possibly the main reason, why people have been induced to make these claims is that, historically, the most common objection to democracy has been the alleged incompetence of the many. This objection implies that the right to govern is dependent upon one's competence and, if the democrat accepts that implied premiss, he has to make his case in those terms. Nevertheless, this is an unpromising and unnecessary line of argument for a democrat to pursue. Firstly, the assertion of equality of political competence is an empirical one and one that it is difficult to find convincing. Secondly, it is not usually accepted that competence is a quality which, of itself, generates rights. Consider, for example, how we distinguish between being *in* authority and being *an* authority. To be in authority is to possess a right to determine the conduct of others. To be an authority is to be distinguished by one's competence on a matter but not therefore to be *in* a position of authority on that matter; that is, it does not give you an automatic right to decide on behalf of others. Others may be well advised to heed you, but you have no right to control their conduct and they have no duty to conform to your injunctions merely in virtue of your superior wisdom. Thirdly, if equality of competence were to figure at all in a justification of democracy, it would seem that it could figure only as an empirical presumption in a consequential justification and not as an autonomous justificatory principle.[11]

[10] Peter Singer, *Democracy and Disobedience* (Oxford, Oxford University Press, 1973), pp. 34–5.

[11] The argument for democracy in terms of competence is sometimes presented not as a claim about the individual abilities of citizens but as a claim about the wisdom they manifest as a collectivity, especially through the process of discussion. However, it is still difficult to see how this argument could be used to generate any strong theory of equal political rights.

*similar to
Beitz:
maker's &
matter*

The argument from equality is much more plausible if it focuses not upon people's qualities as *producers* of decisions but on their qualities as *consumers* of decisions.[12] The members of an association are each subject to the decisions of the association. They therefore each have an interest in the decisions that the association makes. Moreover, it is often, though not always, true that each member is equally interested in the decisions of the association. This can be true whether the members of the association are pursuing some collective purpose through the association or (as may be the case in a political association) simply making rules which provide a framework within which they can pursue their individual purposes. Even then, it may not be that each member is equally affected by each and every decision; a particular decision may affect some more than others and that is why it may be appropriate to weigh individuals' interests or to measure the intensities of their preferences. But we may still be able to say that, taking all decisions in the round, taking the 'set' of all decisions, any member is as interested in the outcomes of the decision procedure as any other. In particular it would seem reasonable to say this of individuals as members of states.

This account of the position of individuals as members of associations is partly analytic and partly empirical. It is not, or not obviously, moral. To derive a prescription for an egalitarian decision procedure we have to introduce an egalitarian principle. However, that principle need not be a particularly specific or strong principle of equality—simply one that entails that, *ceteris paribus*, the well-being of one person is to be valued as much as that of another. A principle such as the principle of equal human worth as elaborated by Gregory Vlastos would fit the bill.[13] For Vlastos an individual's worth is not the same as his merit. 'Merit' takes in all of those qualities by which we grade people. By contrast individuals' 'worth' is 'the value which persons have simply because they are persons'. It is because we attribute worth equally to persons *qua* persons that we hold that 'one man's well-being is as valuable as any other's'.[14] Following a principle such as this we may say that,

---

[12] The argument of the next few paragraphs is similar in many respects to the more detailed argument of Carl Cohen, *Democracy*, ch. 15.

[13] Gregory Vlastos, 'Justice and Equality' in Richard B. Brandt (ed.), *Social Justice* (Englewood Cliffs, N.J., Prentice-Hall, 1962), pp. 31–72.

[14] Ibid., pp. 48, 51.

where individuals' interests or wants are equally at stake (and that is the only relevant consideration),[15] each has an equal claim to have his interests promoted or his wants satisfied. This, in turn, implies that a decision procedure should be structured so that it respects the equal claim of each to have his interests promoted or his wants satisfied. ('His' here is, of course, meant to be sexless.) Thus a decision procedure is fair in so far as it respects equally this equal claim of each; unfair in so far as it does not.

The presumption that people's interests *are* equally at stake in the decision arena is as important to this conclusion as a principle of equal human worth. If some people's interests were more greatly at stake than others, then the principle of equal human worth would not merely allow but would require that account should be taken of those differences of interest. There are cases where the members of an association have different degrees of interest in the association, where the decision procedure reflects those differences, and where that arrangement seems perfectly acceptable. For example, in general terms, there is nothing unfair or otherwise objectionable about the shareholders of a company holding votes in proportion to the number of shares that they hold.[16]

Even now, the argument for democracy is not entirely complete. Given that each individual is equally interested in the decisions of an association, that interest may be interpreted as no more than that decisions should be, as far as possible, what he wants them to be. In that case we can move straight to the inference that the decision procedure should afford an equal opportunity for the expression of wants and take equal account of those wants. Alternatively, acknowledging the conceptual distinction between interests and wants (even if an individual's interests have, ultimately, to connect with his wants), one might argue entirely in terms of the interests of individuals. The democrat would then have to confront the well-

[15] By this qualification I mean to exclude the possibility that the issue is one in which certain sorts of want should not count at all or should not count equally with others, as would be the case, for example, if the rights of some individuals were at stake. Although my argument is largely structured in terms of want-satisfaction, I shall not take up the issue of whether and how some sorts of want should be 'censored' out of the democratic process since that issue arises whether one goes for majority, proportionate, equal, or random satisfaction or any other sort of decision rule.

[16] Cohen, *Democracy*, p. 246. However, this example presumes that one can circumscribe the interest of each member *qua* member. There is a sense in which a poor shareholder may have a greater interest in the fate of a company than a rich shareholder even though the poor shareholder holds fewer shares.

worn objection that a benevolent and informed despotism could promote the interests of a people as well, if not better than, a democracy. The usual reply to that objection is that we may presume that each individual is the best judge of his own interests. In fact the more relevant presumption is that each is the best promoter or, in Mill's words, the best 'guardian' of his interest since it benefits him nothing if his interest is better judged by another but then ignored. However, this is not the only strategy open to the democrat. He might argue that whatever an individual's competence as judge of his own interests, he and he alone has the right to be the final arbiter of that interest. I shall not assess the merits of either argument, partly because that would be a lengthy and probably inconclusive business, but mainly because that assessment is at some distance from my chief concern: the limits of majoritarianism. I shall simply presume that the care of each individual's interest is properly left in his own hands.

MAJORITY SATISFACTION AND PROPORTIONATE SATISFACTION

From the principles and presumptions that I have outlined we can derive the characteristic features of democracy, at least in its simple form: an equal right to vote, to participate in discussion, to place items on the agenda, and so on. Some might argue that this equalitarian position requires not only that these rights should be formally available to all, but also that socio-economic conditions should be adjusted to ensure that these rights constitute genuinely equal opportunities rather than merely formal entitlements. In addition it might be supposed that we can derive the majority principle in the way that I have already indicated. Individuals' interests or wants are to count equally, therefore votes are to count equally; if votes count equally and if there is a conflict of votes, then the votes of the majority must prevail. But is such an inference valid? Consider the following example.

There is a street whose residents control and pay for the amenities of the street and who decide democratically what those amenities shall be. Each resident has a vote and the vote of the majority is always decisive. They have three issues to decide upon, each of which they reckon equally important.

1. Whether to have asphalt or paved sidewalks. Asphalt is ugly but cheap. Paving stones are pleasant but more expensive.

2. Whether to keep the existing gas lighting which is picturesque and in keeping with the character of the street or to replace it with electric street-lighting which would be garish but provide the same amount of lighting more cheaply.

3. Whether to improve the appearance of the street by planting trees or to save money and plant no trees.

Two-thirds of the residents are economizers; one-third are aesthetes. Thus when each vote is taken the economizers win, the aesthetes lose. The street has asphalt instead of paved sidewalks, electric instead of gas lighting, and no trees. Is that result satisfactory?

If we took any decision in isolation the answer would be yes both for an orthodox utilitarian and for someone who adhered to the principle of equality that I have outlined. Utility has been maximized and each individual's wants or interests have been valued equally. But consider the decisions as a group. Again the utilitarian would find nothing to object to particularly if we assume, as seems reasonable in the example I have given, that successive wins do not have a declining marginal utility for the winning majority. Provided social utility has been maximized, it is of no concern to the utilitarian that, in each decision, it is the same individuals who have had their utilities promoted and the same individuals who have not.

However, this must be of concern to the democrat who is a democrat because he adheres to the principle of equality that I have outlined. He cannot be satisfied that the interests or wants of the members of a community are consistently opposed in a ratio of 2:1 but consistently satisfied in a ratio of 3:0. Those individuals who make up the persistent minority can properly complain that repeated applications of the majority principle are not consistent with their equal entitlement as individuals to want-satisfaction or interest-promotion. If that entitlement were respected the aesthetes would get their way on one of the three issues.

It might be objected that there is no justification for treating the three decisions as a group. Each is an independent decision, each individually meets the requirements of equality, and it should be accepted as merely fortuitous that the same people win or lose in each of the three decisions. That objection cannot be sustained. What links the three decisions is that each is part of a process of want-satisfaction or interest-promotion. Want-satisfaction or interest-promotion is a good and a good capable of different distributions which, in turn, can be examined in the light of distributive principles. The democratic process allocates that good and it is quite legitimate to assess the overall distribution of the good even though that distribution is made by way of a number of separate decisions. If, having made such an assessment, we discover that some individuals have received all of that good and others have received none, we have good reason to doubt that the equal claim of each individual to the promotion of his interests has been respected.[17]

This, of course, relates to an essential and oft-noted difference between principles such as equality or fairness on the one hand and utilitarianism on the other. Equality and fairness are distributive principles, whereas the maximization of social utility is an aggregative principle to which distributive considerations are entirely subordinate. It is true that utilitarians would generally follow Bentham's injunction that each should count for one and no more than one. But that is no more than a working assumption to be following in maximizing aggregate utility and, at most, yields a principle of impersonality or 'anonymity'. Maximizing social utility may entail taking equal account of each individual's interest, but that does not make it the same exercise as distributing satisfactions fairly.

It is for this reason that I have avoided a formula that is often presented in discussions of this sort: that each person is entitled to equal consideration or, more specifically, that each person's interest should be considered equally. The trouble with this formula is that it is not clear what it requires. Dahl, for example, gives the following as a principle which a procedure must satisfy to be 'democratic'.

Equal Consideration for all members: No distribution of socially allocated entities, whether actions, forbearances, or objects, is acceptable if it

---

[17] I say only 'good reason to doubt' to allow for the possibility that this result could be the outcome of the sort of lottery that I consider in the next section. Another objection to my argument here might be that what I have presented as three separate issues could be equally well regarded as a single issue: should the street have the cheapest or the most pleasant amenities? However, part of the thrust of the argument I develop here is that, wherever it is practicable to divide up issues so that a fairer satisfaction of preferences becomes possible, this should be done.

violates the principle that the good or interest of each member is entitled to equal consideration.[18]

But how demanding is this principle supposed to be? If 'equal consideration' requires merely 'taking equally into account', the utilitarian can claim to consider interests equally in maximizing social utility. If, on the other hand, 'equal consideration' means that equal claims of interest should be equally met, the principle sets a test which the utilitarian cannot pass—except in those few cases where, by a happy chance, maximizing utility coincides with meeting equal claims equally. Elsewhere in the same essay, Dahl enunciates another principle that is fundamental to procedural democracy: 'equally valid claims justify equal shares'.[19] He apparently thinks that 'this elementary principle of fairness' amounts to very little—'it falls just short of a tautology'. But it is just such an 'elementary' principle that a utilitarian cannot acknowledge. He can claim to consider interests equally in respect of the goal of maximum social utility; what he cannot do is to acknowledge the equal satisfaction of equal claims as a goal in its own right, for maximizing aggregate utility is not guaranteed to redeem each individual's equal claim to interest-promotion.

PROCEDURAL FAIRNESS AND EQUALITY OF OPPORTUNITY

A possible counter to my argument against majoritarianism is that a system in which people have equal chances or opportunities is compatible with the egalitarian principle I have outlined, and that decision by majority vote constitutes a system of equal chance or opportunity. I would accept the first proposition but not the second.

Suppose a group of individuals agreed to make the decisions which applied to them collectively by way of a lottery. For every issue there would be a lottery in which each individual held one and only one ticket. The individual who held the winning ticket for a

---

[18] Robert A. Dahl, 'Procedural Democracy' in Peter Laslett and James Fishkin (eds.), *Philosophy, Politics and Society*, 5th series (Oxford, Basil Blackwell, 1979), p. 125. See also Stanley I. Benn, 'Egalitarianism and the Equal Consideration of Interests' in J. Roland Pennock and John W. Chapman (eds.), *Nomos IX: Equality* (New York, Atherton Press, 1967).

[19] Dahl, 'Procedural Democracy', p. 99. Dahl himself refrains from deriving any specific decision rule from either principle of equality; ibid., pp. 101–2.

particular issue would have the right to decide on that issue on behalf of the whole group. Thus, for any issue, each individual *qua* individual would have an equal chance of being the decider. The odds in favour of any particular proposal being adopted would be proportionate to the number of individuals who favoured that alternative in the total group. However, the fairness of the lottery system would not depend upon its tendency, over time, to produce decisions roughly in proportion to the wishes of different sections of the population. Rather the procedure could be said to be inherently fair; it would be an example of what Rawls calls 'pure procedural justice'.[20] The mere fact that each individual's ticket counts for one and no more than one can be regarded as enough to satisfy the equal claim of each to want-satisfaction.

However, decision by majority vote cannot properly be represented as a lottery of this sort. When individuals enter the decision arena they may be ignorant of one another's preferences and therefore ignorant of whether they will be in the majority or the minority. In addition, they may be ignorant of one another's preferences on future issues. Indeed, they are likely to be ignorant of their own preferences on future issues since they will not know what all of those issues will be and therefore will not yet have formed preferences on them. But ignorance is not randomness; it is merely ignorance. That people are ignorant of the total configuration of preferences on all future issues, and therefore ignorant of how often they will find themselves in the majority or minority, does not mean that decision by majority vote amounts to a lottery in which people have equal chances of winning.

This may seem too short a way with majoritarianism. Have I not overlooked an important equality commonly claimed for majoritarian democracy: the equal opportunity of each to persuade the majority to his point of view? If the entitlement of each individual to that opportunity is respected, should that not remove our reservations about majoritarianism? There are at least three reasons why it should not. Firstly, a majority may simply be intransigent and not open to persuasion. Secondly, there are many issues—particularly those which arise from conflicting interests or wants—which are not really matters for persuasion. I do not know how the aesthetes in my street example could produce reasons which would 'persuade' the economizers to change their

---

[20] Rawls, *Theory of Justice*, p. 86.

preferences. (Issues which arise from conflicting judgements are a different matter which I shall consider separately in a moment.) Thirdly, this sort of equality presupposes what is at issue: the majority principle. Persuading the majority is simply set as the condition of a competition in which people have an equal opportunity to participate. That people have an equal right to participate in that competition does nothing to establish that the competition is itself satisfactory, that persuading the majority ought always to be the condition of promoting interests or satisfying wants.

What if people consent to majority rule, if not directly then indirectly by joining an association in which the majority principle is already an established part of the constitution? Does that not render majority rule fair? The problems involved in holding that people 'consent' to be members of states are well known. However, I have said that my reservations about majority rule apply equally to many non-state associations and we would normally have no qualms about describing membership of most of those associations as 'voluntary'. That people have consented to a form of government rather than having it imposed upon them must count for something. Nevertheless, it is still possible to assess the fairness of an argument independently of whether it has received the consent of those to whom it applies. Consider, for example, a lottery in which there are two sorts of ticket—one for Blacks, the other for Whites. All tickets are sold at the same price but those sold to Blacks carry half the chance of winning as those sold to Whites. All are aware of this and no one is obliged to buy a ticket, so that when a Black buys a ticket he does so freely and is therefore a 'consenting' participant in the lottery. Even so, it seems quite reasonable to say that, as far as Black participants are concerned, the lottery is unfair. Notice that if consent were a sufficient condition of fairness, we would have to describe as fair not just majority rule but *any* arrangement to which people consented no matter how morally grotesque it might be.[21] Thus, even where people have consented to be governed according to the majority principle, we may still say that that principle can work unfairly, though we may also feel that there is little reason to protest on behalf of a persistent minority that

[21] For a fuller examination of this issue, see Albert Weale, 'Procedural fairness and rationing the social services' in Noel Timms (ed.), *Social Welfare: Why and How?* (London Routledge and Kegan Paul, 1980), pp. 235–7.

has, more or less wittingly, consented to the position in which it finds itself.

CONCLUSION

The conclusion that I wish to draw from all that I have said will be obvious: where majority rule results in persistent minorities those minorities have reason to complain that they are being treated unfairly. This is a simple and perhaps unsurprising statement but it is one that democratic theorists have been remarkably reluctant to make. The common assumption seems to be that a democratic minority can legitimately complain only in two sorts of circumstance: (1) if its rights are infringed or if in some other way it is persecuted, oppressed, or exploited; (2) if its special interests are overridden by an 'apathetic majority'. If a minority is persistently on the losing side, but can make neither of these complaints, its position is usually regarded as merely unfortunate rather then unfair.[22]

Certainly persistent minorities are thought to be 'bad' or 'unhealthy' for a democracy. For one thing, persistent minorities are likely to become increasingly reluctant to bend to the majority's will. For another, persistent majorities, it is said,[23] are likely to abuse their position. Where there are fluctuating majorities, the individual who is in the majority today knows that he will be in the minority tomorrow. He therefore has an incentive not to abuse his majority position lest he, in turn, is abused when he is in the minority. The members of a persistent majority have no such incentive to play fair by the minority. However, neither of these points questions the fairness of majoritarianism itself. Both are simply empirical assertions about the way in which persistent majorities and minorities endanger the satisfactory working of democratic institutions, whereas I have tried to argue that a persistent minority has reason to complain in terms of the very principle of equality that underlies democracy.

---

[22]Some exceptions are J. Roland Pennock, *Democratic Political Theory* (Princeton, Princeton University Press, 1979), pp. 8–9, 374; Elias Berg, *Democracy and the Majority Principle* (Stockholm, Scandinavian University Books, 1965), pp. 153–59; Arthur Kuflik, 'Majority Rule Procedure' in J. Roland Pennock and John W. Chapman (eds.), *Nomos XVIII: Due Process* (New York, New York University Press, 1977), pp. 309–25.

[23]e.g. by Madison in *The Federalist*, No. 10 and by Cohen, *Democracy*, pp. 71–4.

SOME CONSEQUENT ISSUES

1. *Democracy and the Majority Principle*

Am I therefore saying that majoritarianism is 'undemocratic'? Any such assertion would contradict the main import of the remarks with which I began this paper. I have simply argued that one major justification for democracy, the argument from equality, is not always compatible with one typical feature of democratic systems—decision by majority vote. However, where majorities fluctuate so that want-satisfaction is fairly distributed, majority rule is unobjectionable in terms of that argument. Moreover, as I have indicated, there are other justifications of democracy, many of which are, at least in principle, quite compatible with straightforward majority rule.

2. *Proportionate Returns and Equal Returns*

Is the conclusion that I have drawn from my premises sufficiently radical? I have argued for proportionate levels of satisfaction but it might be thought that I should be arguing for equal levels of satisfaction. Suppose there were 100 individuals who were opposed 99 to 1 on every issue and the minority of 1 was always the same individual. If decisions were taken on 100 issues then, on my argument, the group of 99 would get their way 99 times and the lone dissenter would get his way once. Yet each member of the 99 is no less 'rewarded' by a winning vote merely because he shares it with 98 others. Should not the majority of 99 and the minority of 1 each get their way 50 per cent of the time? Assuming that each issue was equally significant, each member of the community would then enjoy equal levels of satisfaction or utility.

A committed egalitarian might well argue that this would be the right outcome.[24] Nevertheless, it is not the outcome required by my premises. I have argued that where individuals are equally interested in the outcomes of a decision procedure, that procedure

[24] Cf. the principle of equality elaborated by G. W. Mortimore, 'An Ideal of Equality', *Mind*, 77 (1968), 222–42, according to which the ideal state of society is one in which everyone enjoys an equal level of good. This would also be the outcome of the voting system proposed by Dennis C. Mueller, Robert D. Tollison, and Thomas D. Willett, 'On Equalizing the Distribution of Political Income', *Journal of Political Economy*, 82 (1974), 414–22. However, Mueller *et al.* do not so much 'equalize political incomes' (which is what I would require) as adjust political incomes by vote taxes and vote subsidies so that each individual receives equal levels of utility from the political system.

should value their interests equally. If we regard a vote as a political purchasing power, then each individual's vote should constitute the same sum of political money. No one should be required to spend that money for a nil return but neither should anyone be able to claim a larger sum of political money than anyone else. To allow the persistent minority of 1 to get his way as often as the persistent majority of 99 would be equivalent to giving him 99 times as much political purchasing power as any individual in the majority. The members of the 99 could then protest that their interests were not being given the same status as those of the lone dissenter.

This point is perhaps illustrated more graphically when it arises in relation to a single decision. Imagine a group of individuals are voting on a public good. Since the good will be equally available to each, it is agreed that each should be taxed equally in order to finance it. However, there can be more or less of the public good and the members of the group are divided over how much of their income they want to devote to it and therefore over how much of the public good there should be. The group is made up of four individuals whose preferences are as follows: A, B, and C each want 3 units, D wants 1 unit. Decision by majority vote would result in 3 units of the public good. My principle of taking equal account of the preferences of each individual would entail adopting the average preference: 2.5 units. The equivalent of giving equal weight to the preferences of the lone dissenter as to the collective preferences of the 99 in my earlier example, would be to observe that A, B, and C each have the same preference and to hold that that preference should therefore enter the calculation only once. Thus the decision would be that there should be only 2 units of the public good. It is true that, if this were the decision, D would suffer no greater disutility than A or B or C. However, A, B, and C could quite properly protest that they were then being treated unfairly since each of them is a distinct individual with distinct, if identical, wants, yet the decision to have only 2 units of the public good gives only a third of the value to each of their wants as to those of D.

3. *Preferences and Judgements*

My argument has been developed entirely in terms of decisions on whose interests are to be promoted or whose wants satisfied, and that is a crucial feature of the argument. Sometimes votes are interpreted not as expressions of interests or wants (i.e. preferences) but as judgements—judgements about what is right, true, efficacious, etc. Unfortunately writers on democracy are inclined to describe the democratic process either entirely in terms of preferences or entirely in terms of judgements, whereas in most associations some decisions are of one kind and some of the other. Is majoritarianism subject to the criticisms I have made where votes express judgements rather than preferences?

The example of a jury shows clearly that it is not. A jury is a body in which a decision has to receive the support of a majority, although in this case the majority has to be at least 10 to 2. Imagine I am one of twelve members of a jury which judges 12 cases. In each case there is disagreement amongst the jurors and in each case I find myself in the minority of 2. Even so it would be quite misplaced for me to complain that my fellow-jurors were treating me unfairly and that my judgement should prevail on at least one of the 12 cases. The reason is simple. The purpose of a jury is to judge guilt or innocence and not to distribute goods amongst the jurors themselves. I may complain that my fellow-jurors are making the wrong judgements and that the innocent are being convicted and the guilty going free; but I cannot complain that they are being unjust *to me* in not deferring to my judgement on at least one occasion.

A jury is a special sort of body but this point is not at all special to juries. If votes express judgements and nothing but judgements—judgements about what is true or false, right or wrong, expedient or inexpedient—then they are necessarily disinterested. I can therefore have no interest in my judgement's prevailing over those of others merely because it is *my* judgement. This is so not only where my judgements bear only upon others (as in a jury) but also where my judgements bear upon myself. Consider a decision which is not about whose interest is to be promoted but simply about how a desired result is best achieved. We all agree that X is desirable and the vote is simply upon the most effective way of securing X. If every individual's vote, including my own, expresses a judgement and only a judgement on that issue then, as I have said, I have no interest in my judgement prevailing simply because it is my judgement. I have an interest in the right or best judgement prevailing, but that is a different matter. Of course, if I had reason to suppose that my judgement were superior to that of others then I would have an interest in its being given greater weight, simply because it was more likely to be right. But then everyone else would have the same interest in my judgement's being given greater weight. By the same token, if there was reason to suppose that my judgement was inferior to those of others then I, as well as everyone else, would have an interest in its being given less weight.

Thus the argument from an equal claim to want-satisfaction or interest-promotion against simple majoritarianism does not apply where votes express pure judgements. One might still have reservations about majoritarianism where votes are of this kind, but those would be reservations of a different sort.

It would be convenient if the issue of preferences and judgements could be dismissed so easily. Unfortunately there are a number of considerations which muddy the simple clarity of the distinction I have drawn. For one thing, the distinction between preferences and judgements may not always be easy to apply in practice. Considerations of personal interest will often intrude into votes that are ostensibly pure judgements. In addition there are some issues which are not clearly either issues of preferences or issues of judgement. Votes on abortion, blood sports, pornography, the interests of future generations, are likely to straddle this distinction. The distinction is likely to be most difficult to maintain where decisions are of a moral rather than a purely technical nature. Nevertheless, it remains true that the argument that I have developed up till now applies only if, and in so far as, individuals can be shown to have an interest in their votes being decisive.

Suppose that an issue is clearly one of pure judgement. I have argued that an individual then has no interest in account being taken of his judgement simply because it is *his* judgement. This simple view may be insufficiently sensitive to the realities of human relationships. David Miller has argued that 'in modern societies political equality has come to symbolise the basic human equality between the members of a given community in such a way that everyone who is excluded from, or treated unequally in, the political realm will suffer a loss of self-respect'. The claim for equal voting rights is 'essentially a claim for status'.[25] If this is true then

---

[25] David Miller, 'Democracy and Social Justice' in Pierre Birnbaum, Jack Lively, and Geraint Parry (eds.), *Democracy, Consensus and Social Contract* (London, Sage, 1978), pp. 92, 95–6.

an individual can have an interest in his being granted an equal voice in matters of judgement, for his self-esteem may be no less damaged by having his judgements discounted than by having his preferences ignored. In Rawls's theory every significant political decision is conceived as a judgement, yet he too insists that equal rights of political participation are required by the primary good of self-respect. If some individuals held less than equal political rights that would 'have the effect of publicly establishing their inferiority' which would be 'humiliating and destructive of self-esteem'.[26] However there is not a simple logical link between these arguments for political equality and the reservations I have expressed about the majority principle. The constraints that equality of status places upon the decision rule that a society may adopt would seem to be entirely dependent upon what the members of that society feel is compatible with their being accorded equal respect. In particular, since the relevant interest here is not an interest in the outcomes of the decision procedure but simply an interest in being a participant in that procedure, there may be no serious tension between equality of status and majority rule.

A somewhat different matter is the 'psychic' interest that an individual may have in his judgement's prevailing. People often have a considerable emotional investment in their opinions and are consequently gratified when their views prevail and displeased when they do not. Our estimation of these feelings may vary— 'worthy' if they derive from a concern to see right done, 'unworthy' if they are merely the self-gratification of victory or the pique of defeat. Either way, there are obvious reasons why this sort of utility should be ignored by decision procedures. To mention but one, if they were not ignored, we could be faced with an embarrassing choice between the decision rule which distributed psychic satisfactions fairly (or maximised such satisfactions, if that was our concern) and the rule which seemed most likely to yield the right substantive decision. (The same dilemma may confront those who emphasize the importance of political equality to equality of social status. The decision rule which is most desirable in terms of equal status may not be the rule that is most likely to yield the correct result.)

Finally, consider the following case. The members of an associ-

---

[26] Rawls, *Theory of Justice*, pp. 234, 544–5. See also Pennock, *Democratic Political Theory*, pp. 153–4.

ation have to make a number of decisions, each of which is concerned not with what they want but with what they believe to be right. On each decision there is disagreement and each member is equally convinced that his judgement is correct: that is, each is equally unconvinced that the judgement of any other member or members is superior to his own. There is no independent source of wisdom to which the members can resort, nor is there any shared conviction that a particular decision rule, such as majority vote, is likely to issue in the right answers. How should the members resolve their disagreements?

The answer suggested by Peter Singer is by a decision procedure in which each member has an equal voice.[27] This is not because an equal franchise is required by an equal right of self-government or by other principles of equality, appeal to which Singer abjures.[28] Rather it is because, in these circumstances, 'one person, one vote' constitutes a 'fair compromise'. Each member is convinced that he is right, but each has to recognize that that is equally true of every other member. A democratic decision procedure 'makes it possible for everyone to refrain from acting on his own judgement about particular issues without giving up more than the theoretical minimum which it is essential for everyone to give up in order to achieve the benefits of a peaceful solution to disputes'.[29] Singer also apparently accepts that 'one person, one vote' entails decision by majority vote. The majority principle should be embraced therefore, not because it is likely to issue in correct judgements, but because it is part of the fair compromise.

This is not a case in which disputes can be represented as conflicts of interest. Each member is impelled solely by his wish to see right done together with his sincere conviction that he knows what is right. Indeed, what a member judges to be right could run counter to his personal interests. Nevertheless, since, for Singer, the merit of democracy consists in its fairness, albeit its 'compromise' fairness, rather than in its propensity to produce right answers, the logic of proportionality would seem to apply just as strongly in this kind of case as in cases of conflicting interests. This is especially so where conflicting judgements are consistently those of fixed majorities and minorities. Singer recognizes that his argument may run into

[27] Singer, *Democracy and Disobedience*, pp. 30–41.
[28] Ibid., pp. 26–30.
[29] Ibid., p. 32.

trouble where there are permanent majorities and minorities. However, he believes that the fairness of the compromise holds provided that a permanent majority does not use its votes to the constant disadvantage of the minority.[30] What he fails to recognize is that the logic of his argument requires not merely that the minority be treated fairly in whatever decisions the majority makes but that a fair proportion of decisions should be made *by* that minority.[31]

4. *From Principle to Practice*

My chief concern has been to consider what constitutes fair treatment of minorities by a decision procedure and, in particular, to explain why we should (and often do) feel unhappy about the position of persistent minorities under majority rule. However, what I have said raises some important practical issues. One of these, which I shall have to leave undiscussed, is how the plight of persistent minorities under majority rule affects their obligation to conform to the decisions of the many. More particularly, how would the answer to this question be affected by whether, and to what extent, membership of an association was voluntary? Another practical issue is how the principle of proportionality can be implemented. Again this is a subject which requires more attention than I can give to it here, but I can hardly escape without saying something about the problem of implementation.

If life were always as simple as in my street example, implementing the principle of proportionality would present no great difficulty. For example, the residents could first reveal their preferences on the three issues of sidewalks, street-lighting, and trees. Noticing that there was a consistent division of 2:1 on each issue, they could then agree that the aesthetes should get their way on one of the issues. That would still leave the question of which of

[30] Ibid., pp. 42–5.

[31] Nelson, *On Justifying Democracy*, pp. 22–4, criticizes Singer's general approach to democracy on the ground that, where a decision is about what is right, what matters is not the intrinsic fairness of a decision procedure, but its probability of producing the correct outcome. 'If there are independent standards for evaluating legislation, and if the procedure most likely to produce legislation acceptable by those standards is not a fair compromise, then, in fact, we ought to adopt this unfair procedure.' (p. 24.) But his criticism is of no force in the circumstances that Singer contemplates: if there is no generally agreed standard for assessing outcomes and therefore no agreed standard for assessing decision procedures in terms of outcomes, how are we to proceed?

the three issues should go the minority's way. This could be determined randomly. Alternatively, if the minority held slightly more intense preferences or the majority slightly less intense preferences on one of the issues, that would provide a rationale for selecting that issue as the one on which the minority should get its way.

Unfortunately, life is not usually so simple either in the state or in associations which confront fewer and less complex issues than the state. There are four obvious difficulties that are likely to arise in any attempt to implement the principle of proportionality.

1. Issues are not always as easily separable as in the street example. If the residents decide upon asphalt rather than paved sidewalks that is unlikely to pre-empt their choice between gas or electric lighting and trees or no trees. But issues are often more interrelated than these so that one cannot extend a measure of satisfaction to everyone and still have a coherent set of decisions. (However, this may also be a problem under the majority rule where there are fluctuating majorities.)

2. The membership of majorities and minorities is unlikely to be absolutely stable on all issues. This does not make the principle of proportionality either irrelevant or inapplicable but it does make its application more complicated.

3. It is not enough merely to count wins and losses. Account also has to be taken of the different importances of issues and therefore of the different importances of wins and losses. This can be done, but again it complicates matters considerably.

4. A decision process is often 'open-ended' in that there is no point at which it is obviously appropriate to call a halt while one takes account of and adjusts for the total distribution of wins and losses to date.

The principle of proportionality is widely, though not universally, accepted as the correct principle for one aspect of modern democratic systems: representation. The problems of implementation that I have listed may go some way to explaining people's reluctance to apply the same principle to decisions upon issues. There are fairly simple ways in which the principle can be implemented, albeit in a rough and ready fashion. In associations which prefer (and can afford) to reach decisions by agreement and accommodation rather than by simple votes, deference can be, and often is, paid to the principle of proportionality. What I have said also indicates that 'power-sharing', such as has been tried (unsuccessfully) in Northern Ireland, can be looked upon as more thaﬁ a shabby compromise which departs from the 'truly democratic' principle of majority rule. However, a precise implementation of the principle would require a voting system which continually adjusted individuals' voting powers to take account of how often they have been on the winning and losing sides, the proportions involved, and the different importances of the issues voted upon.

No doubt such a voting system could be devised but it is difficult to see how it could be other than cumbersome, complex, and time-consuming in its application.[32] Thus those who recognize the claims of proportionality might still conclude that these have to be sacrificed in the interest of efficient and coherent decision-making. Nevertheless, it is still worth establishing that a sacrifice is involved and that the majority principle is not always consistent with the principle that inspires our commitment to political equality.

---

[32] Something akin to the required voting system can be found in Mueller, Tollison, and Willett, 'On Equalizing the Distribution of Political Income', although, as I explained earlier (n. 24), their voting system is geared to equal rather than proportionate satisfaction.

The Roles of Rules*

Geoffrey Marshall
The Queen's College, Oxford

Sometimes ideas or terms in political, social, or legal theory go up and down in public estimation. Something like this seems to have happened with rules. Much use has been made of the term 'rule' in both moral and legal contexts. But more recently it has been argued both that law is not a system of rules[1] and that moral judgment is not a matter of rule application.[2] One of the difficulties is that the idea of a rule is itself a general and an unclear one. Professor Max Black once noted that it was like a playing-card used in many games but that he could not find any satisfactory examination of its meaning.[3]

RULES AND INSTANCES

The idea of a rule certainly cuts across distinctions between imperative, hortative, commendatory, and predictive locutions: 'The younger children are never to leave the garden alone'; 'Always respect your parents'; 'Let workers of the world unite'; and 'Guinness is good for you' are all rules of a sort. Being a rule therefore cannot properly be contrasted with being an order. Some rules are orders and some orders are rules—along with some mottoes, some moralizing and some manifestos. On the other hand some prescriptions are not framed in terms of rules: 'You ought to do that now' or 'Get dressed immediately' are not rules. Orders and prescriptions can be either particular or general. Rules clearly cannot be particular and must in some sense be general; but what the requirement of generality amounts to, is not easy to say. It has been traditionally supposed that both rules and laws must in their nature be general and that this is what distinguishes rule by law

---

*© Geoffrey Marshall 1983.

[1] Ronald Dworkin, 'The Model of Rules' in *Taking Rights Seriously,* 2nd Impression (London, Duckworth, 1978), chs. 2 and 3.

[2] G. J. Warnock, *The Object of Morality* (London, Methuen, 1971), chs. 4 and 5.

[3] *Models and Metaphors* (New York, Cornell University Press, 1962), p. 106. Professor Black suggested that there were four main senses of the term which fit the ideas of 'regulation', 'instruction', 'precept', and 'principle'.

from regulation by fiat or Act of Attainder. Order and predictability flow, it is hoped, from generality and the assumption that like cases are treated alike. But it is not clear what restrictions this imposes on the formulation of something that can be called a rule. When Rousseau in the *Contrat Social* tried to specify what the characteristics of a general rule were (since the legislative pronouncements of the General Will were confined to such manifestations) he suggested that a general rule must ignore particular cases; must know only the totality of persons subject to legislation; and treat all alike, in the sense of placing no burden on one that is not placed on another. Some of this might perhaps be counted as going to the question whether a rule is a fair or just rule rather than to the issue of its existence as a rule. How particular, inequitable, or neglectful of the equal merits of like cases can a rule be whilst still being a rule? Between a single individual identified by name or description and the totality of all persons in the system subject to rule there are infinite gradations. Clearly there is no more need for all self-respecting rules to deal with all persons than to apply to all objects or to govern all times and places. Rousseau's requirements picture the element of generality solely in terms of persons, and even so his criteria of particularity are vague. Would a rule or law that applied only to persons convicted of crime be particular in referring to a special group, or general because referring to a class of persons? What about a rule dealing only with convicts whose surnames begin with Q? Could we have a rule for a single person? 'Whenever Convict 99 complains, his complaint should be referred to the prison Governor' might well be described as 'the rule for dealing with Convict 99's complaints'. What is necessary is that a rule deals with a class of *cases* (whether persons, objects, or occasions) and that the necessary degree of generality, whatever it is, can be acquired in any of these dimensions.

RULES, HABITS, AND PRACTICES

Rule-following may not be easy to distinguish from forms of convergent behaviour commonly described as habits or general practices. The distinction itself is difficult to make since there is no single term that can be easily contrasted with what happens when rules are consciously followed. Words like 'practice' and 'custom' are themselves often used to refer to rules having prescriptive force (as in the law, practice, usage, and customs of Parliament).

'Conforming' is also applied both to rules and patterns, though individual acts or instances might more appropriately be said to fit rather than conform to a pattern. If the term 'practice' can be wiped clean of its normative implications so as to describe a repeated pattern of behaviour, it is not obviously synonymous with 'habit'. A practice may be followed without being habitually followed. Habits are acquired or contracted rather than conformed to or followed. ('I make it a habit to clean my teeth three times a day.') But here it is the practice we are following as if it were, or until it becomes, an acquired reaction or habitual act.

In *The Concept of Law*[4] Professor Hart suggested some criteria for distinguishing the kind of behaviour that is in question when a social rule is being followed from that which is being manifested in the occurrence of a general or group habit (though perhaps 'practice' would be the better general term). What, he asked, distinguishes a pattern of behaviour such as regularly attending a cinema performance every Saturday, from general obedience to a social rule, such as regularly baring the head when entering a church? In both cases there is a pattern or convergence of behaviour, but one is rule-governed and the other is not. What makes the difference, he argued, is first that in the rule-governed case deviation from the standard behaviour meets with criticism. Secondly such deviation is regarded as a legitimate ground for criticism. Thirdly each individual has a 'critical reflective attitude' towards the practice or standard, so that he regards it as a common standard and, in discussing it, typically makes use of such words as 'right', 'wrong', 'must', 'should', and 'ought'. It need not be the case that each and every member of the group always adopts the relevant critical stances. A minority may not only deviate from the practice but also fail or refuse to look upon it as a standard either for themselves or others.[5] How many of the group must treat the regular mode of behaviour as a standard of criticism and how often and for how long are indefinite matters. It would presumably, however, not simply be a matter of majority acceptance. There is a difference between something's being generally accepted in a society and its being accepted even by a large majority. A practice

---

[4] H. L. A. Hart, *The Concept of Law* (Oxford, Clarendon Press, 1961), pp. 9–11 and 54–9. Cf. P. Winch, *The Idea of a Social Science* (London, Routledge, 1958), chs. 2 and 3.

[5] Perhaps it is worth noting that in such cases rule-breaking in general, or the breaking of all rules of a particular kind, may be the subject of *praise* as well as of criticism.

might be said to be generally accepted even if quite large numbers of different people from time to time on different occasions ignored or neglected it. But if, say, a group within a society consistently and reflectively rejected the practice in question it would be more difficult, even if the dissenting minority were a small one, to say that the society had an accepted rule in the matter.

What is under consideration here is informal or unmade social rules rather than made or formal rules. A formal rule exists when it has emerged from the carrying-out of a recognized procedure of creation or promulgation and its existence simply is its having such a source. There is more difficulty about the existence of informal rules. Moreover the question 'How do we distinguish rule-following from other forms of convergent behaviour?' may be a confusing one. Three possibly different inquiries may be involved. One is 'Is there a rule to be followed in a particular case?' Another is 'How do we know when people are following (i.e. as distinct from deviating from or breaking) rules?' A third is 'How do we detect whether people think that they are in the presence of rules as distinct from something quite different, namely habits, orders, or customs?' What significance is to be placed on the fact that deviation from a standard form of behaviour may meet with criticism? Might it not be objected that the actual occurrence of criticism for deviations seems to relate mainly to the third question? Though it would be very odd for there to be a universal misconception about the existence of an informal rule, it is not at all impossible for there to be quite widespread misconceptions and for many people to be mistaken about their obligations or the obligations of others. Consider for example many problems that arise within the informal rules of etiquette or social behaviour. Doubts may often arise about the existence of a rule of behaviour to be followed in particular circumstances because it may be unclear how an accepted general standard is to be applied to the circumstances in question. Should old men, for example, give up their seats to younger women? There being no court of social appeal, there may be no way of deciding definitely what the rule is in such a case but the question is not always or obviously to be settled by observing whether critical pressure is brought to bear on deviant Old Age Pensioners; and if there are two views about such a social rule— one group contending that the particular rule exists and another contending that it does not—what they are arguing about is not whether it is true they are criticizing and pressurizing each other.

If it is supposed that the essence of the matter is that the social disputants will be arguing about the *propriety* or legitimacy of criticism that might be directed at a given pattern of behaviour then it would seem that they would be in effect simply arguing about the propriety or rightness of the behaviour itself and the notion of 'criticism' seems redundant. Criticism is also an unclear notion. Carping, denunciation, or condemnation or any adverse articulated reaction are forms of criticism. What sort of criticism is in question? The only appropriate sort seems to be *moral* criticism and the identification of that as involving the characteristic use of words such as 'right', 'wrong', 'should', and 'ought', seems to presuppose an understanding of rules as much as elucidate it independently. The contrast between rules and habits seems to need no more than the assertion that they are the kinds of things that put upon those who are subject to them an obligation to conform; there being as many forms of obligation as there are types of rule. If we understand our legal, moral, religious, charitable, and sporting obligations we know how to recognize the corresponding rules.

RULE USES AND FUNCTIONS

A plausible answer to the question 'What do rules do?' sounds as if it might be that rules regulate, or prescribe. But these terms do not seem to set off rules from other phenomena. Moreover, they misdescribe some of the many things that rules do. Much the same may be true of the remark that rules have a normative force. Unhappily we are not much clearer about what it is exactly that norms do. We may conclude rightly, but with insufficient particularity, that they form or guide conduct. 'It is common to all norms, legal or otherwise, that they guide human behaviour.'[6] But there are a great many sorts and sources of guidance (cf. advice-bureaux, sheep-dogs, travel agencies, Samaritans, and cake recipes). In any case the question 'What do rules do?' is itself not very clear. This can easily be seen in the case of legal rules. We can ask what functions such rules have and decide for

---

[6] J. Raz, 'On the Functions of Law' in A. W. B. Simpson (ed.), *Oxford Essays in Jurisprudence*, 2nd Series (Oxford, Clarendon Press, 1973), p. 281.

example that amongst other things they discourage deviant behaviour; that they make possible various private arrangements between individuals; that they allow the settlement of disputes; and that they provide for the distribution of resources.[7] There can also be distinguished various 'techniques'[8] through which these aims or purposes are achieved. Though there is frequently a typical connection between a particular type of legal rule and a social purpose—for example between prohibitory rules and the penal purpose of discouraging deviant behaviour—this need not be so. Conferring benefits or redistributing resources, for instance, could be achieved by many different types of rule, including prohibitory rules (penalizing drunkenness could have a benefit-conferral function). The upshot is that if we try to list the number of different activities displayed by legal rules or to say what it is that such rules do, we need a very long list. Among other things, legal rules penalize, prohibit, require, obligate, prescribe, inform, guide, empower, permit, license, enable, facilitate, entitle, command, define, designate, constitute, distribute, describe, exempt and identify. There is no common grammatical form or shape of sentence that is common to all these. So there is perhaps neither any single thing that rules typically, usually, or always do, nor any single linguistic form in which they do it.

RULES, MERITS, AND DISCRETION

Following rules and acting in accordance with rules is sometimes contrasted with considering the merits of particular cases. What a rule does, it is said, is 'to exclude from practical consideration the particular merits of particular cases by specifying in advance what *is to* be done whatever the circumstances of particular cases may be'.[9] Thus a cricket umpire terminates an over after six balls have been bowled because there is a rule to that effect and not because on each occasion there is a good reason to do so. To say that he

---

[7] Raz instances these as 'social' functions of law.

[8] Robert S. Summers in 'The Technique Element in Law', 59 *California Law Review* 733 (1971) suggests five such basic techniques—the penal, the grievance-remedial, the administrative-regulatory, the benefit-conferral, and the private arrangement techniques. See also Hans Kelsen's essay 'The Law as a Specific Social Technique', 9 *University of Chicago Law Review* 75 (1941).

[9] Warnock, *The Object of Morality*, p. 65.

applies or follows the rule is to say that he does not consider whether there might be good grounds for prolonging the over in a particular case.[10]

There is, however, a special feature about this example of rule-following which helps to conceal what is often involved in applying rules to particular cases. The 'six balls to an over' rule mentioned by Warnock is a reasonably clear and unambiguous rule. At least it is unambiguous if the point that we are considering is the propriety of a seventh ball. There is one sense of merits in which we might say that the reason for not considering the seventh ball on its merits is simply that the merits are clear and it has none. There might be some grounds to do with charity or kindness to children for sometimes permitting somebody to bowl more than six balls but in terms of cricketing propriety there are no grounds at all and no merits.

Most rules, however, do not display this specificity. They may say, for example, that 'A player guilty of ungentlemanly conduct shall be cautioned'; or (leaving the sports-field) 'The number of accesses permitted on to a trunk road is to be severely limited'; or 'Congress shall make no law abridging the freedom of speech'. It is still true that following these rules involves excluding from consideration the merits of the deliberate breaking of opponents' legs or of an unlimited number of trunk road accesses or of wholesale censorship. Following a rule necessarily rules out without discussion of its merits whatever the rule properly interpreted excludes. In the case of rules whose terms are non-specific the problems of rule application are indeed to do with deciding what it is that a rule when properly interpreted both excludes and includes, and whether a particular thing or situation is covered and governed or excluded by the rule. There is a different problem about rules and particular cases when what is in issue is whether a rule should be extended or changed or modified to include a fresh situation or instance. This is most obvious where the rules in question are flexible and when their application is deliberately intended to invoke an element of discretion. An

---

[10] This is one of a number of reasons given by Warnock in support of the view that morality, in the sense of holding moral views and making moral judgments, is not a matter of accepting and applying moral rules (since in moral judgment there should be 'the constantly repeated attempt to achieve the best judgment on the full concrete merits of each individual case'). *The Object of Morality*, p. 67.

area in which this often occurs is the issue of licences or permits. Here a contrast may sometimes be drawn between considering a case 'on its merits' and having or following a rule or policy. But it may be possible for a body both to exercise a discretion and to have a rule or policy. This has sometimes been thought permissible provided that the persons deciding the issue hold themselves open to consider exceptions to the policy in particular cases.[11] This is to say that they have to keep their minds open[12] to the need to formulate a wider or modified or different rule that accommodates the new instance. Here, the merits of the situation cannot be simply contrasted with the results of following the rule. The particular situation is not considered on its merits as they might be if the rule did not exist. The rule exerts some sort of pressure on the situation which would be missing if there were no rule. The question whether a particular liquor licence should be granted might well be decided differently, in the absence of any rule or policy, from the way in which it might be decided in the light of a rule or policy to the effect that additional licences ought to be discouraged. However, the particular case also brings pressure to bear on the rule, since it prevents the rule from being a fetter on or nullifying the exercise of discretion and it may succeed in changing or modifying the rule. In principle it should be possible to distinguish between (1) considering at large whether something ought to be the case in the absence of any pre-existing rule; (2) considering whether something already falls within a rule as it stands, and (3) considering whether in the light of a rule a fresh but in some way related instance ought to give rise to a modified rule.

RULES AND PRINCIPLES

A great deal is sometimes thought to turn upon the varieties of uncertainty or indeterminacy that occur in the rules of a legal system. Indeed the model of law as a body of rules has been said to stand in danger of demolition if it can be shown that there is no such set of *determinate*[13] rules in developed societies; that there is no commonly recognized single test for *determining* which standards

---

[11] *Ex parte Kynoch Ltd.* [1919] 1 K.B. 176 *R.* v. *Flintshire County Council Licensing Committee ex parte Barrett* [1957] 1 Q.B. 350.

[12] Or, it has been said, at least ajar.

[13] A rather indeterminate term.

are to count as law; and that the law does not even consist exclusively of rules, since in its application it is necessary to invoke the use of 'principles' which are not themselves legal *rules* (though they are legal in character and part of the law).[14] If it can be added that the delineation of and arbitration between such principles requires an appeal to arguments that make reference to moral and political policies, then it may be urged that legal positivism must be false and that 'in countries like the United States and Britain . . no ultimate distinction can be made between legal and moral standards'.[15] If so it may also be argued that in such countries it cannot ever be finally determined what the law is or whether anybody who breaks what others (including the courts) believe to be the law is behaving lawlessly.

Precisely this attack has been mounted on the positivist 'rules model'. The argument has been that the application of determinate rules cannot decide all cases that arise in a legal system. When the consideration of established rules does not yield a clear result, judges invoke 'principles' which, not being legal rules, cannot be derived from any master test for legal rules. They cannot, moreover, be weighed one against another except by the invocation of arguments about moral and political policies or principles[16] which take lawyers outside the field of what positivists would be prepared to call law. Part of what is at issue here if a 'rules model' of law is to be defended, is whether a clear distinction between rules and principles can be discerned. Professor Dworkin's proposal—and it seems reminiscent of Warnock's (six balls to an over) image of rules—is that rules are determinate in their application. Principles on the other hand do not determine a result. They may point towards a result; they may conflict and they have to be weighed against each other. They represent or resemble policies (or perhaps values or objectives) and are embodied in such statements as that 'litigants should not be permitted to profit by their own wrongdoing' or that 'automobile accidents should be decreased'.

---

[14] R. M. Dworkin, 'Social Rules and Legal Theory', 81 *Yale Law Journal* 855 (1972).

[15] Ibid., p. 855.

[16] Subsequently Professor Dworkin (in 'Hard Cases', 88 *Harvard Law Review* 1057 (1975)) has drawn a firm distinction between 'principles' and 'policies', arguing that all adjudication must be in terms of the former, not the latter. See also *Taking Rights Seriously*, pp. 14–80 and pp. 241–368; and 'No Right Answer' in P. M. S. Hacker and J. Raz (eds.), *Law, Morality, and Society* (Oxford, Clarendon Press, 1977), p. 58.

But there may be a question whether such principles clearly differ from 'rules' of law. It may be that they differ only in ways that rules differ amongst themselves—in terms of specificity, complexity, completeness, and comprehensiveness. A rule may be comprehensive but not specific—for example the American rule that 'No state shall deny to any person within its jurisdiction the equal protection of the laws'. A rule may also be fairly specific but incomplete or not comprehensive—for example a rule about the inadmissibility of hearsay evidence.

Whether we speak of rules or principles it seems clear that indeterminacy may arise in their application. For example a proposed statement of a legal rule may be incomplete. There may be either rival formulations of the rule or suggested conflicts with other alleged rules. A complete formulation will require distinctions to be made, inconsistencies resolved, and exceptions stated and accommodated.

Again, where the formulation of the rule is not in doubt (say because it is set out in a statute or constitution or other instrument), the sense to be given to particular words or phrases may be unclear because the terms in question are ambiguous or general or in various ways unclear. Some words and phrases (e.g. 'the interest of the State' in the Official Secrets Act, 1911 or 'discrimination' in the Race Relations Acts) are fairly general. But no word in any rule or principle is proof against doubt or uncertainty. (Consider, for example, the forensic nightmare brought on by the word 'driving' in the Road Traffic Acts.)

FORMS OF RULE UNCERTAINTY

Since rules and principles are formulated in words they may suffer from all the sources of uncertainty that infect words themselves. Some of these are as follows:

(a) *Ambiguity.* There may be alternative possible senses for words of identical form or ambiguities relating to syntax.

(b) *Generality.* A rule may contain abstract concepts or words indicating quality or degree or terms of which different forms or varieties occur.

(c) *Rival criteria.* There may be competing criteria for the application of a term.

(*d*) *Breadth.* A fairly clear choice may exist between a wider and a narrower application of a term.

(*e*) *Technicality.* Doubt may exist as to whether a term has been given or is to be understood in a special, technical, or scientific sense as against an ordinary or popular sense.

(*f*) *Obscurity.* Use may be made of an obscure or unusual expression or term with no commonly accepted application.

(*g*) *Complexity.* There may be complexities of grammar or phraseology or inconsistencies or complicated relationships between different sections or sentences making up the formulation of the rule.

(*h*) *Historicality.* Doubt may exist as between a historical and a contemporary sense of a word or as to what a particular historical sense was.

(*i*) *Marginal vagueness.* Questions of degree may cause uncertainty. Or it may arise from doubts as to the propriety of including something in a list or group of related things.

(*j*) *Translation difficulties.* Possible differences may exist between versions of the same rule in different languages.

The ways in which uncertainty is resolved can also be classified. Sometimes, in the case of a very general concept, subsidiary tests or interpretive rules may be introduced to guide the application of the general term. Thus in the United States the Supreme Court may interpret the free speech guarantee in the First Amendment with the aid of a subsidiary 'clear and present danger test' (which may itself then have to be modified, refined, or extended), or the common law will elucidate the general concept of 'negligent behaviour' by way of interpretive tests about, say, 'remoteness of damage'.

Another technique, continuously present, is that in which definitions or explanations are given of the meaning and application of general terms. Yet another recourse is the making of explorations (of a limited and tentative kind under English rules of interpretation) into the intentions or purposes of the legislators and draftsmen who originated the rules. In this area a subsidiary legal technique may be to invoke common knowledge and suggest that the meaning of some words is a question of fact[17] not

---

[17]*Brutus* v. *Cozens* [1972] 2 All E.R. 1297: *R.* v. *Feeley* [1973] 1 All E.R. 341. The distinction between 'ordinary words in the English language' whose meaning is a question of

requiring judicial elaboration and determinable by the instincts of jurymen and magistrates.

The conclusion might well be that all of these types of indeterminacy or lack of specificity may be present in rules, principles, tests, policies, and maxims and that in particular they are present within rules. So little is to be gained by separating rules from principles; and little is to be lost by saying that law consists in the main of different kinds of rules.

THE RULE PEDIGREE

It may well be, however, that this conclusion will not mollify the anti-rule critic. Even if he is persuaded that nothing hangs upon resisting the application of the term 'rule' to what he wants to call 'principles', he will still want to say that when legal rights are determined judges have to make determinate the general, vague, ambiguous, partial, or competing rules; and that the law so produced is not then characterized or identified by reference to any *single* test. If not, then, he will say, there is no single test, rule, or standard for determining what is or is not law within the legal system and the model of a rule system derived from a single master or pedigree rule can be rejected.

The force of this assault on the rules model (of which Hart's *Concept of Law* is held to be a major, though not sole, representative) perhaps depends upon the senses in which a single pedigree rule or (in Hart's terminology) a secondary Rule of Recognition might be said to provide a 'test for law'; or legal results or decisions be said to be *determined* by ultimate constitutional or pedigree rules.

It seems unlikely that theorists who have treated legal systems as hierarchies of rules have intended to say that the most general rule in an ascending series could be used as a 'test for law' in the system, in the sense that any particular legal issue arising anywhere in the system could be simply determined, or resolved, or an alleged resolution of the issue be identified as law or non-law, by the mere use or invocation of the pedigree rule or rule of recognition and of nothing else. The connection between a simple

---

fact and extraordinary words whose meaning raises a question of law has become rather unclear. We now know that 'insult' and 'dishonest' are plain and ordinary words; but not (presumably) 'theft' or 'attempt' or 'incest'.

pedigree rule such as 'What Parliament enacts is law in the United Kingdom' and some particular thing done under Parliamentary authority is not a deductive one. A recognition rule works more like a signpost than a measuring-rod. Moreover pedigree rules of recognition may need to be formulated in a fairly complex way. They may prescribe multiple sources of legal obligation (for example legislation, custom, or precedent). They may also specify the modes of delegated legislative activity. In turn legislators may specify judicial techniques for resolving indeterminacies that emerge from the competition of competing sources of obligation, or from the generality of legal terms, or from the incompleteness of the rules and principles generated by the legal process. Adjudicators may receive from interpretation statutes instructions to follow particular interpretive principles, of which a wide range is available (e.g. 'Think of what the legislators would have done knowing what you know of their general purpose.'; 'Promote substantial justice in cases of uncertainty.'; 'Use literal or grammatical construction.'; 'Search the legislative records.'; 'Ignore the legislative record.' etc.). The end results of this process only derive from the more general authorizing rules in the sense that these latter state the general conditions under which they may be generated. The law that emerges could not be predicted or deduced by someone simply in possession of a statement of the authorizing conditions (any more than a recital of the rule that the MCC has the authority to lay down the laws of cricket would in itself answer the question whether a particular batsman was in or out).

A CONCLUSION

Belief in law as rules does not imply a belief in law as a *fixed* or *clear* or *determinate* body of rules or in either a discovery theory or a legislative theory of adjudication. This being so, nothing that we have discovered about the complexities of rule application or adjudication is inconsistent with the 'model of rules.' The rules model does not therefore suggest misleading answers to any fundamental questions of legal theory.

Hobbes, Toleration, and the Inner Life*

Alan Ryan
New College, Oxford

It always surprised me that John Plamenatz wrote so perceptively, so incisively, and so well about Thomas Hobbes.[1] On the face of it he ought to have found Hobbes as little to his liking as he found Bentham and James Mill.[2] Hobbes's famous injunction to consider men in the state of nature as if they were sprung out of the ground like mushrooms, without engagements to one another, seems to be what Plamenatz deplored as the root of bad practice in social thought. The *idée maîtresse* of *Man and Society* is just that: social and political arrangements are not matters of artifice, not constructed for the pre-social and pre-political purposes of self-contained individuals. The Hegelian emphasis on the organic unity of society may reflect an unintelligible metaphysics, but it rests on a sound methodological instinct. Individuals are *essentially* social, and their aspirations are such as only members of a social and political community could conceive. What we count as individual achievements, individual hopes, even individual miseries, could not come into existence except in a social setting. It is not only Hegel who is praised for seeing this, of course; Rousseau is sometimes chided for incoherence but he is always praised for his understanding of the degree to which our relations with our society are internal relations. Even Pascal, of whom it is certainly true that the anarchy he fears is a spiritual anarchy whose cure lies in submission to God, must be credited with a subtler sense than Hobbes of the genesis of our restlessness and our vanity, and a subtler sense of how society may do something to control them.[3]

John Plamenatz certainly enjoyed the vigour and the crispness

---

*© Alan Ryan 1983.

[1] See particularly, John Plamenatz, *Man and Society* (London, Longman, 1963), vol. I, ch. 4; his Introduction to *Leviathan* (London, Collins, 1962), pp. 3–55; and 'Mr Warrender's Hobbes', *Political Studies*, 5 (1957), 295–308.

[2] John Plamenatz, *The English Utilitarians* (Oxford, Blackwell, 1958), chs. 4 and 6.

[3] Plamenatz, *Man and Society*, vol. I, p. 207.

of Hobbes's thinking and writing. Whether reading Plamenatz or arguing with him in tutorial, there was no mistaking the pleasure that Hobbes's 'brisk witt' gave him. Hobbes's own aggressiveness and self-confidence evidently encouraged a like response; no one need have qualms about arguing against Hobbes with every weapon he possessed. Hobbes's description of the man armed with science as an utterly invulnerable fencer almost reads like an invitation to the duel, and everything we know of Hobbes's own behaviour as a controversialist suggests that the cut and thrust of argument did much to give him pleasure; better, perhaps, a strenuously and confidently wrong-headed thinker like Hobbes than a muddled and slackly right-minded one like J. S. Mill.[4]

What follows is intended to explore what I imagine Plamenatz himself would have thought a non-existent subject. Is it not verging on the frivolous to suggest that Hobbes has anything to say about the inner life? No doubt, he has a good deal to say about the infinitesimal interior motions, or endeavours, which are the beginnings of voluntary action. He has a good deal to say about how perception as well as emotion is to be explained by internal pressures; but these are not part of our inner lives in anything except a flatly physiological sense. Can it be said that such matters as our religious convictions, our moral aspirations, our views on the meaning of life and so on, get anything but the roughest and most peremptory treatment? Whether the materialism which leads Hobbes to explain our thoughts and beliefs in terms of 'phantasms' with physiological causes is intrinsically inimical to a serious concern for the private moral and intellectual aspirations we generally reckon as our 'inner life' is arguable; what seems less so is that Hobbes was a materialist who gave the inner life short shrift.

Even those who would allow that there is more to be said about it than that would still generally deny that what Hobbes speaks to is the inner life. When Professor Wolin explains Hobbes as something like an illiberal proto-liberal, it is because Hobbes thinks that a man's rational concerns are essentially with his private interests, and that politics matters only in so far as it impinges upon those interests. The end result on Wolin's account

[4] Plamenatz, Introduction to *Leviathan*, p. 55.

'was to destroy the distinctive identity of the "political" by merging it with interest'[5] but for our purposes two points alone are worth noticing. Hobbes certainly attacks classical and republican conceptions of politics; in the process, he invents a new meaning for the term 'Liberty', which he uses to deny that republics possess liberty while monarchies do not, and, indeed, uses positively to insist that a man may live with more security against intervention in a monarchy than under a popular government. Liberty as unimpededness is the only sort of liberty there is, and what men rationally desire is to be as little impeded as possible in the pursuit of their own interests. The first point is that among the sorts of liberty to which Hobbes displays any tenderness, liberty of conscience is not one, the second that this 'privatization' of our aspirations is tender to private economic aims not to an interest in our inner lives. For it to have been anything of the latter sort, Hobbes should surely have shown a sympathy towards religious sects and small communities of believers which he was very far from showing.

It is commonplace and true that throughout *Leviathan* Hobbes is hostile to religious dissent and claims for freedom of speech; he is eager to keep universities firmly under control, and shows no scruples about what is and what is not under government control. Nor is Hobbes casual in his illiberalism; he does not suggest that sometimes and in dire emergency we can resort to censorship, nor does he say that because men's opinions on religion and morality are of little importance, it is all one whether governments choose to control them or not. He argues exactly the opposite: states that take no care to secure doctrinal and liturgical uniformity are storing up trouble for themselves; precisely because opinion does matter, the sovereign must ensure a good deal of uniformity in opinion. Hobbes insisted that 'It belongeth therefore to him that hath the Soveraign Power, to be Judge, or constitute all Judges of Opinions and Doctrines, as a thing necessary to Peace; thereby to prevent Discord and Civill Warre.'[6] This requires that he must decide 'on what occasions, how farre, and what, men are to be trusted withall, in speaking to Multitudes of people; and who shall examine the Doctrines of all bookes before they be published'.[7] And this is

[5] S. Wolin, *Politics and Vision* (London, Allen and Unwin, 1961), p. 280.
[6] T. Hobbes, *Leviathan* (London, Dent, 1914), ch. 18, p. 93.
[7] Ibid.

because 'the Actions of men proceed from their Opinions, and in the wel governing of Opinions, consisteth the well governing of mens Actions, in order to their Peace, and Concord'.[8]

The question this raises is how far that control of opinion can go, and how far Hobbes thought it should go. That Hobbes did not think complete uniformity of opinion or desire would ever be achieved is evident enough from the way he contrasts the sociability of those non-human creatures which simply coincide in their aims and behaviour with the contrived sociability of human beings.[9] Even so, it might be said that once an artificial society had been constructed and a sovereign instituted, there was room for the remaking of human nature by educating men into a new uniformity of opinion and desire. That *something* of the sort is proposed by Hobbes is a reasonable inference from the famous footnote to *de Cive* in which he insists that 'all men, because they are born in infancy, are born unapt for society . . . man is made fit for society not by nature, but by education'.[10] This, however, leaves us with three possible interpretations of Hobbes's position. The first would suggest that somehow or other the sovereign could and should exercise complete control over our opinions, and render dissidence literally unthinkable. This imputes a very totalitarian ambition to Hobbes, and I shall later suggest that something of the same ambition can be found even in paradigmatically liberal writers like Mill and Russell. The second view is the most usual one, and essentially amounts to saying that he was extremely anxious to secure uniformity of *profession* in matters of religion and jurisprudence (the latter category embracing the former, in his view)[11] but minded about little else. Public profession could be divorced from private conviction, and the control of opinion therefore amounted to no more than the control of opinion's public expression.[12] The third view is that Hobbes had more positive concern for freedom of speech and for the exercise of individual conscientiousness than is generally thought. I shall end by coming

[8] Ibid.

[9] Ibid., ch. 17, pp. 88–9.

[10] Sir Wm. Molesworth (ed.), *The English Works of Thomas Hobbes (EW)*, (London, John Bohn, 1841), vol. 2, p. 2.

[11] *E.W.* 2. pp. 292–7.

[12] M. M. Goldsmith, *Hobbes's Science of Politics* (New York, Columbia University Press, 1966), pp. 214–20.

back to the usual view, but I hope to show that there is a good deal in Hobbes to which it does not do justice.

It is a commonplace that Hobbes saw two great causes of civil strife in England. The first was a lack of agreement on the legal supremacy of the Crown; the other was the eagerness of private persons to set up their religious intuitions as a guide to themselves and everyone else—one consequence of which was the extreme quarrelsomeness that men must feel if they think their eternal salvation depends on their political disputes.[13] These disagreements opened the way for interested parties to claim an overriding authority—judges, Members of Parliament, Presbyterians, and Papists among them. It is worth noting that Hobbes's intellectualism is not so extreme as to suggest that the Civil War sprang solely from intellectual errors about the nature of authority. Men will believe whatever fosters their power, so that although it is true that some men's power springs from the acceptance of error, it is also true that the disposition to accept these errors rests on the search for power. Hobbes was very attached to the view that peace might be preserved indefinitely if sound doctrines were widely diffused—if *Leviathan* was prescribed as a textbook in the universities; but he was quick to say that interested error could not be eliminated by argument alone.

The importance of securing doctrinal agreement is obvious from the way in which half of *Leviathan* and *de Cive* are devoted to the subject. The twentieth-century reader of *Leviathan* pays little attention to Books III and IV, and even for those who do pay attention to them, it is rather puzzling that Hobbes should have been so alarmed by the Papacy's contribution to the Kingdome of Darknesse as late as 1651, unless this reflects his experiences in Paris.[14] None the less, the last two books crucially complement the first two. Once Hobbes has explained the matter and generation of the commonwealth in secular, naturalistic, and this-worldly terms as a contrivance of men's hands for their this-worldly welfare, he needs to show that a Christian commonwealth is not *qua* commonwealth affected by being a *Christian* commonwealth. It is worth noting that Hobbes has to approach this topic from a particular

---

[13] 'Behemoth', *E. W.* 6, pp. 167–9.

[14] L. Stephen, *Hobbes* (Ann Arbor, University of Michigan Press, 1961), pp. 31, 34; his hostility is unabated in 'Behemoth', *E. W.* 6, pp. 169–75.

direction; he has to ask whether and in what way the obligations of a subject are affected by the subject's being a Christian, and, again, whether and in what way the rights of sovereigns are affected by their being Christian sovereigns. The target, always, is the suggestion that ecclesiastical authority can be different from, or even superior to, lay authority, with its implication that some religious authority can release the subject from his obedience to the sovereign. Hobbes's main concern, in both *de Cive* and *Leviathan*, is to argue that the City and the Church are one—that there is one and only one test of the lawfulness of doctrines and practices, and that is whether it has pleased the magistrate to permit or forbid them. What we ordinarily call the authority of the church in spiritual matters is the power vested in 'pastors lawfully ordained, and who have to that end authority given them by the city'.[15]

The implied premiss here comes from Hobbes's views about the motive for obedience. Since we cannot be obliged to do anything that threatens our lives, and since the earthly sovereign can only threaten our earthly lives, while God can threaten our lives in eternity, any suggestion of a clash between the commands of God and the commands of earthly rulers has to be avoided. To this end, Hobbes argues over and over again that the only thing we are commanded by Christ is to believe in Him; since we cannot believe in Him unless we believe in God the Father, we must profess our belief in Him too. It follows that no minimally Christian sovereign ever gives us ground for disobedience; the criterion for his being a minimally Christian sovereign is that he cannot command his subjects 'to deny Christ, or to offer him any contumely'.[16] since to do that would just be to profess himself not a Christian. Everything else is a matter of doctrinal speculation; crucially, everything else, on Hobbes's account of it, is a matter on which God has not *commanded* us to say or think something in particular. Evidently, this leaves open the question of how the Christian must treat the commands of a non-Christian sovereign. In matters temporal, insists Hobbes, obedience must be absolute, and if, in matters spiritual, we cannot obey, Hobbes's only advice is 'Go to Christ by martyrdom'.[17] What is not clear is when this moment might arrive; given that Hobbes seems to be convinced

[15] *E. W.* 2, p. 315.
[16] Ibid.
[17] Ibid., p. 316; but cf. *Leviathan*, p. 328.

that we could safely worship graven images or even deny Christ if commanded and escape the consequences by mental reservation, we might wonder whether anyone of Hobbes's views would ever go to Christ by martyrdom.

The purpose of Hobbes's arguments seems to be to drive scriptural considerations out of politics, in order to deprive the church of any independent political power. At a time when those who thought about political morality at all generally did so by reference to the Bible, this was a bold move, but essential if Hobbes was to demolish the aspirations of those who thought that the goal of politics was to establish God's kingdom here in England. Hobbes says, in *Leviathan* and many other places, that there is no useful sense in which any earthly kingdom can be identified with God's kingdom. The divines speak of God's kingdom metaphorically, as meaning the life hereafter, but he wishes to confine the name of God's kingdom to the one case in which God did indeed rule over His chosen people by covenant. God's government of the Jews was 'constituted by the Votes of the People of Israel in peculiar manner; wherein they chose God for their King by Covenant made with him, upon Gods promising them the possession of the land of Canaan'.[18] The kingdom of God by nature, on the other hand, is not and cannot be instituted; God rules all those who have the wit to recognize His existence and follow His laws, that is to say, all those who can work out that there must be a God and that the laws of nature must be His laws. He also, in a manner of speaking, rules those who acknowledge no such thing, since his irresistible power can rightly be unleashed against anything and anyone. But, viewed from the side of God's subjects, it is only those who believe and who acknowledge his laws who can properly be termed *subjects*. The rest are, in Hobbes's technical sense of the term, *enemies*. There is one obvious implication of this, which is that atheism is no injustice and no sin, though loss of faith might well be held to be such. It is the fool, not the sinner, who says in his heart, 'there is no God'. The important conclusion, though, is that since God no longer licenses prophets, there is no question of re-creating the special relationship He enjoyed with the Jews; no band of religious enthusiasts can be taken seriously in their desires for re-creating God's kingdom on earth, since their aims are either unrealizable or realized already.

[18] *Leviathan*, p. 219.

Part of the object here is, evidently, to defuse the thought that the Bible might itself be an independent source of authority. Over and over, Hobbes insisted that the only way an interpretation of Scripture could become uniquely lawful or be made unlawful is by command of the sovereign. All the same, Hobbes did not wholly oppose the translation of the Bible into the vernacular, and was not fearful of the results of independent judgement, so long as proper distinctions were drawn between what we might call speculative questions about the origin and nature of the universe and its government on the one hand, and practical questions about liturgical conventions on the other. Hobbes's arguments in favour of uniformity in the latter area—always drawn from the consideration that what one man thinks a way of honouring God another might think ridiculous—are entirely consistent with the defence of a large measure of speculative freedom, though they suggest a circumspect view about *publication*. The energy with which *Leviathan* berates scholastic philosophy might suggest that Hobbes was simply hostile to philosophical speculation; but that is belied by his defence of true philosophy and Hobbes is more usually at odds with the power-hungry clerics who seek political influence by heresy hunting. Hobbes's undistinguished little history of heresy shows a decided hankering after the original sense of the word—'which signified no more than a private opinion, without reference to truth or falsehood'—or, failing that, a return to the legislative restraint of Constantine, when heresy had 'by virtue of a law of the Emperor, made only for the peace of the church, become a crime in a pastor'.[19] The implication is obvious: doctrinal uniformity may be a necessity in the officers of a church, since otherwise the organization will suffer, but that does not suggest that laymen need be chased after by zealots for orthodoxy.

It is for all that certainly true that Hobbes laid it down as an important task for the sovereign to tell teachers and subjects how to interpret the Scriptures. He does so as part of a general doctrine about the sovereign's role in intellectual matters, a doctrine which he himself applied to *Leviathan*. In his 'review and conclusion' Hobbes reports that on looking through his work he thinks that it is true and demonstrable, and he hopes that it may occur to someone to have it printed and taught in the universities. (In fact, his

[19] *E.W.* 4, p. 388; cf. *E.W.* 6, p. 174.

own university had it burned in the Bodleian quadrangle.) The reason is that 'the Universities are the Fountains of Civill and Morall Doctrine, from whence the Preachers and the Gentry, drawing such water as they find, use to sprinkle the same (both from the Pulpit and in their Conversation) upon the people.'[20]

Hobbes was also anxious to insist that he had looked to see if anything he had said was unlawful, and that he thought nothing was. Moreover, in such unsettled times a novel doctrine could not be accused of upsetting the (non-existent) peace, and precisely because times were unsettled there was all the more reason to explore this avenue to peace. Hobbes seems to be asserting both that what he writes is true and that it would be usefully imposed as an orthodoxy—that is, given a unique place as the only doctrine publishable. Hobbes also distinguishes the question of the truth of his doctrine from his right to *publish* it, for he readily admits that if the sovereign had forbidden its publication, he would have had no right to publish. This raises the obvious questions of how truth, utility, and publishability are connected, of how far the sovereign can go in imposing doctrines, of what frame of mind the search for uniformity is supposed to achieve in subjects, and of what limits, if any, government activity in this area is subject to.

An extreme view might be culled from what Hobbes says in *de Cive* about the way in which an agreement on terms creates truth. The proposition that $2 + 3 = 5$ is said to depend on our will, for we have decided that 'the number //is called two, /// is called three, and ///// is called five', and by the will of those who have thus called them, 'it comes to pass that this proposition is true, *two and three taken together make five*'.[21] Since agreement on meanings depends on the existence of a linguistic community, and the existence of a community depends on the existence of a sovereign, we might infer either that *all* truth depends on the sovereign, or, more minimally, that some truths will depend on the meanings he imposes. This would imply that there was no room for disbelief in what the sovereign lays down as truth, and that subjects would simply have to believe it. There could be no room for objection, so long as the meanings thus imposed did indeed lead to peace. The picture is not wholly intelligible, once it is scrutinized in detail, however;

[20] *Leviathan*, p. 391.
[21] *E.W.* 2, p. 203.

even in the example Hobbes offers, it is only the linguistic expression of the mathematical truth that is conventional. The only sense in which $2 + 8 = 5$ could be made true is if '8' was to be employed as '3' is now; nothing else is amenable to linguistic fiat.

This does not entail that there is no useful role to be played by laying down a vocabulary; if coherence is not the whole of the truth, ambiguity is certainly inimical to the pursuit of truth. It is not too fanciful to see Hobbes groping after the analogy of the draughtsman's blueprint; here, in a manner of speaking, it is the will of the draughtsman which determines whether an actual object 'truly' conforms to what he has laid down. Statecraft for Hobbes is very obviously a matter of laying down blueprints, and, of course, just as there is no pre-existing object for the blueprint of a new model of car, say, to copy, so there is no such natural thing as a 'natural' state for Hobbes's blueprint to copy. But whether a motor car made according to the blueprint will actually work is not a question of anyone's will, but one of fact. Evidently, it is a pre-condition of it working that there are no incoherent instructions in the blueprint, but another condition is that it should not demand impossibilities of the material out of which the vehicle is to be built. Moreover, it is a matter of what people want from the vehicle that determines how good a car it is at last. Analogously, we may lay down a geometry or a number system; whether it is coherent, accurate, and useful is something we do not lay down but discover. If this is so, we may credit Hobbes with a milder doctrine, that truth and utility cannot for long diverge, and that where there is no question of truth (or truth is impossible to ascertain) the sovereign must simply lay down conventions. The subject who understands Hobbes's philosophy will not demur at this, even if his private opinion is different from the sovereign's; and the sovereign who understands Hobbes's philosophy will remember the injunction of *de Corpore Politico* to leave his subjects as much natural liberty as he can. He will not stretch their willingness to obey him in things necessary to peace by enquiring minutely into their private opinions.[22] This suggests that the view we offered as commonplace—that Hobbes is the illiberal forebear of liberalism—is not quite right; Hobbes's reticence about securing intellectual uniformity is liberal enough in its own right.

[22] *E. W.* 4, p. 215; cf. *E. W.* 2, pp. 178–80; Stephen, *Hobbes*, p. 31.

What allows Hobbes to occupy this position is partly the inclination towards nominalism that we have seen above, and partly a kind of non-naturalism in his ethics. By non-naturalism here, I do not mean that Hobbes lays the foundations of his ethics anywhere other than in human nature;[23] but that Hobbes insists that evaluations are not descriptions. The goodness or badness, as much as the justice or injustice, of actions and states of affairs implies a human agent (and in the case of notions like sin, a divine agent) by reference to whose desires these attributions make sense. For 'whatsoever is the object of any mans Appetite or Desire; that it is, which for his part calleth *Good*: And the object of his Hate, and Aversion, *Evill*: And of his Contempt, *Vile* and *Inconsiderable*. For these words of Good, Evill, and Contemptible, are ever used with relation to the person that useth them: There being nothing simply and absolutely so; nor any common Rule of Good and Evill to be taken from the nature of the objects themselves. . . .'[24] There is therefore no question of the truth or falsity of such judgements, though what *is* true is that peace depends upon our being got to utter harmonious appraisals on the same occasions. That is, only if I can be got to regard it as 'good' that, say, you walk quietly down the road as you desire and already think good, will I easily live in peace with you.

Even more important than Hobbes's appreciation of the role of convention here is the effect of his scepticism about the amount of information to be derived from natural theology about the nature and wishes of God, for it is this scepticism which allows him to detach the essentially political question of who ought to interpret the Scriptures authoritatively from the metaphysical question of who made the world and decided how it worked. The effect is to make uniform public worship a political good and not a religious issue in the usual sense, while strongly suggesting that private opinion can be left unfettered—a view we have already come to by one route, and will come to again. How valuable the liberty is is another question; so often we find Hobbes seeming to suggest that freedom of thought is necessarily secure, because one man cannot pry into another's mind, that it is easy to think him uninterested in it. It can, however, at least be said that one objection to minute enquiry into our private thoughts is not just that we

---

[23] D. D. Raphael, *Hobbes* (London, Allen and Unwin, 1977), p. 33.

[24] *Leviathan*, p. 24.

can dissimulate them, but that we have little control over them and cannot justly be held to account for them. Thoughts and desires break in upon the mind, and we cannot be compelled to keep them out when this is impossible; what we may be compelled to is some discretion in divulging them—'The secret thoughts of a man run over all things, holy, prophane, clean, obscene, grave, and light, without shame or blame; which verball discourse cannot do, farther than the Judgement shall approve of the Time, Place, and Persons.'[25] Security would be threatened by much prying, so much prying is condemned. Of course, this is light years away from Mill's insistence in *Liberty* that freedom of thought means nothing without freedom of speech; Hobbes's point is precisely that we can conjoin private liberty and public regulation.[26]

Hobbes's briskly sceptical account of religion is familiar enough: anxiety about relations of cause and effect makes us work backwards from effects to causes until we 'come to this thought at last, that there is some cause, whereof there is no former cause, but is eternall; which is it men call God'.[27] All the same, we hardly understand the conclusion we draw, since we 'cannot have any Idea of him in the mind, answerable to his nature'.[28] We are like blind men warming themselves at the fire; we know that something warms us, but we know not what. Many commentators have said that Hobbes was an atheist, even the father of atheism, but we need not draw any such conclusion. He is always eager to insist that we know that God is omnipotent; and he seems sincere enough in holding that the Gospels provide men with a clear and adequate moral code, their allegiance to which ought not to be shaken by sectarian wrangling.

Still, it is true that Hobbesian natural theology is extremely agnostic. Since we can form no clear idea of God we can infer nothing about Him. Most of what we say about God is grammatically misleading, for it is really affirmed of our *in*capacities rather than His capacities. To call God omnipotent is not to say how much power God has, but to admit our incapacity to say how

[25] Ibid., p. 34.

[26] J. S. Mill, *Three Essays* (London, Oxford University Press, 1975), pp. 22–3; *Leviathan*, pp. 283–4.

[27] *Leviathan*, p. 53.

[28] Ibid.

powerful He is. 'Hee that will attribute to God, nothing but what is warranted by naturall Reason, must either use such Negative Attributes, as *Infinite, Eternall, Incomprehensible;* or Superlatives, as *Most High, most Great,* and the like; or Indefinite, as *Good, Just, Holy, Creator*; and in such sense, as if he meant not to declare what he is, (for that were to circumscribe him within the limits of our Fancy,) but how much wee admire him, and how ready we would be to obey him. . . .'[29] Although Hobbes mocks those who call God a 'spirit incorporeal', which is a mere contradiction, he agrees that the description may not be absurd *in use.* The expression may be used not *'Dogmatically,* with intention to make the Divine Nature understood; but *Piously,* to honour him with attributes, of significations, as remote as they can be from the grossenesse of Bodies Visible.'[30] The view is obviously attractive; when we shout 'may the King live for ever' at his coronation, we know that he can do no such thing, but the wish is neither insincere nor absurd.

This suggests that one thing which is likely to be lost from our private concerns is an anxious attention to exactly what God requires from us for our salvation. By reason we know that He requires us to keep His laws, but those we can work out by rational reflection—they are 'theorems' first and divine commands second.[31] Faith in Christ in the sense of secure conviction is a gift of God, but we are obliged—by revelation rather than reason—to try to have that faith. Given the extent to which absolutely everything else may lawfully be determined by the sovereign, it is hard to see why anyone should worry very much about meeting God's requirements. Hobbes's insistence that He only demands a minimal amount of faith, plus obedience to the civil laws, seems to render the anxious inner life of Puritanism more than somewhat pointless.

This does presuppose that once we have cleared the decks for an extreme conventionalism in regard to religious practice, there will be no difficulty in carrying out the programme. On the face of it, the distinction between private views about the nature of the world and public conventions about *what counts as* worship in this state rather than some other is an easy one to maintain. Yet this seems to understate the extent to which beliefs about the Deity

[29] Ibid., p. 194.
[30] Ibid., p. 56.
[31] Ibid., p. 83.

infect attitudes to conventions. If God delights not in burnt offerings, will He not delight even less in five-part masses? A man who has read the first in Scripture will find it hard to confine himself to saying that he does not know whether God likes music, and that he is prepared to leave the question for God and the sovereign to settle in due course. Most of the doctrines Hobbes is eager to control are ones which claim secular power for ecclesiastical bodies, but if conviction and convention are implicated more than he suggests, the sovereign must either go farther towards securing uniform belief than Hobbes seems to want or less far towards securing any sort of uniformity.

Perhaps the difficulty we face here is the result of taking Hobbes less radically than we should. That is, Hobbes's claim throughout is that religion is a matter of law not of truth; and his aim always is to show that there is no way in which our duty to obey God can conflict with our duty to obey (at any rate Christian) sovereigns. If we keep this point steadily in mind, we end up accepting that Hobbes thought that his own sceptical account of the bearing of Scripture on politics was simply the truth, and that it ought to be taught as an orthodoxy in order to calm the passions which led to civil strife. Whether or not it was true, it would certainly be a useful doctrine to have believed, since it would prevent strife; but, given an audience which genuinely minded about its prospects for eternal life, it would make no sense to say *that*. Hobbes had to claim that his view was true and useful.

This, however, throws the issue of private judgement and its lawful expression back from religion in particular to law in general. That is, we still have the question of how far the sovereign may or must go to secure convinced or committed allegiance to his laws. The thought that we may think what we like, and want what we like, so long as we obey the law is an obvious first thought, here; the question, of course, is once again whether we can so completely detach private judgement from outward allegiance. Now, it is clear that Hobbes's central claim is always that any society needs a single sovereign of legally unlimited authority, but this does not at all imply that the wielders of authority only impose laws. They can, and are morally obliged to, ask perfectly straightforward questions about what laws would best achieve the ends of civil society. The question, what would be the best way to legislate on a given issue, is a perfectly straightforward question, and it can be answered on a commonsensical basis, by the sovereign or anyone else with the appropriate knowledge. Hobbes thinks the sovereign ought to get the best advice he can about the answer—this being part of what Professor Hood calls the 'moral constitutionalism' of the theory.[12] Hobbes himself suggests in his *Dialogue of the Common Law* that excessive litigation is the result of the lack of a proper system for registering land titles.[33] So there is no doubt that questions about the desirability of law are issues for individual judgement. The main burden of the *Dialogue,* however, is the familiar one: what the law *is* is a different question from that of what it *ought* to be. There is no direct connection between the reason of anyone and the validity of the law—not even where it is the reason of the very rational Sir Edward Coke. Origin not content determines the validity of law; bad laws laid down by 'him that by right hath command' are still laws. The subject may say to himself that the law is a bad law; none the less, he must obey it and must do nothing to discourage others from obeying it.

Need the sovereign go farther than this demand for outward obedience? Or, to put it differently, does the Hobbesian state require a deeper consensus than this? One suggestion that it does might be thought to be implicit in Hobbes's account of the natural dissensus of desire. After arguing, as quoted earlier, that terms like good and evil apply to objects, not in virtue of properties of the objects but in virtue of the desires of agents in respect of those objects, he goes on to say that the goodness and badness of anything is in a commonwealth to be taken from 'the Person that representeth it; or from an Arbitrator or Judge, whom men disagreeing shall by consent set up, and make his sentence the Rule thereof'.[34] Now, given Hobbes's redefining of 'justice' and 'injustice' to mean legal and illegal, it is not difficult to see how we have to admit that what the sovereign *declares* for justice and injustice *are* justice and injustice. What is less obvious is how we are to take the claim that we are to take for good and evil what the sovereign declares for such.

It seems that we might take two different views, one of which would not really involve any new evaluations, the other of which

[32] F. C. Hood, *The Divine Politics of Thomas Hobbes* (Oxford, Clarendon Press, 1964), pp. 180–1.

[33] *E.W.* 6, p. 45.

[34] *Leviathan,* p. 24.

would; it would then be a separate but related question whether either of these tied the goodness and badness of things directly to the sovereign's say-so. The first view is that the sovereign's ability to punish us for transgressing his rules makes situations good and bad in ways they were not before, but not in any sense in which they were not before. Thus, in the state of nature, I regard your having the apple you now have as bad and the state of affairs which would obtain if I had it instead as good. (That is, I want it, and I therefore dislike your having it.) In the commonwealth, your possession is ownership, and I should be punished for interfering with it; anticipating the punishment, I now think that your having the apple is (relatively) good. But this does not seem to have introduced rules for judging goodness and badness; it only seems to have introduced new consequences. I do not think your having the apple is in itself good, or my having an apple which is not mine as bad; it is only my-having-the-apple-and-being-punished which I regard as bad. There are common rules all right, but they seem not to be rules for evaluation, and one might claim that unless they were rules for evaluation they would not lend legal observance the moral support it actually needs.

The other view is that we do have a shift in evaluation. Anticipating the kind of account of the growth of conscience which is a commonplace of Mill's utilitarianism, Hobbes may be suggesting that what we come to think is that my-having-an-apple-owned-by-you is bad in itself, and that coming to think that is just what it is to develop a conscience.[35] Punishment may be necessary to instil such a conscience in us; but once instilled, its judgements are not consequentialist. Now it is certainly true that Hobbes shares with later utilitarians a tendency to vacillate between a view of society which sees fully formed adults setting it up *de novo* and a view which rightly recognizes this as a methodological fiction and which then tends to take society for granted and enquire about how to socialize children into apt members of it.[36] It is an odd aspect of the English liberal tradition—or its utilitarian wing—that it places a great deal of the burden of preserving social order on the educational system in this way, but one can see how

[35] J. S. Mill, 'Utilitarianism', *Collected Works*, vol. 10 (Toronto, Toronto University Press, 1969), pp. 229–32.

[36] *E. W.* 2, pp. 1–3.

there would be two rather different images of what difference the sovereign makes. Self-interested adults contracting in to a new political society would presumably apply their old evaluative habits to new situations—would value stolen fruit as highly as ever, but not want it for consequential reasons; their children would simply not want stolen fruit because they had been taught to disvalue it. In this second case, it does seem plausible to say that the sovereign has laid down rules for judging as opposed to simply attaching consequences of a novel kind.

As to the directness of the connection between the sovereign's say-so and new evaluations, we may distinguish three possibilities. The first picks up the first line of thought suggested above: we see the point of the sovereign's rules, and we see them creating instrumental goods. Without those rules there would be no property, and without property no secure enjoyment; therefore we think enforceable rules about property are good. We and the sovereign share evaluations, but this rests simply on the facts of the situation. The second possibility is rather different; it is that once there is security, things appeal to us intrinsically that did not do so before, and which perhaps hardly could do so before. There is a pleasure to be had from keeping promises, showing ourselves faithful to our friends, and so on; but this is a pleasure which can only emerge once we are safe enough to engage in morally satisfactory dealings with one another, and which is in a sense a second-order or emergent good. It therefore marks a rather larger break with the condition of mere nature. All the same, this is the sort of good which, as it were, grows naturally in fertile soil, and our thinking these things good seems to owe nothing to the sovereign's calling them good. Thirdly, then, there is the possibility that the sovereign simply conditions us into calling good those things which he calls good, presumably by conditioning us into desiring what it is that he desires that we should desire.

It is the possibility of his doing this that forms what one might call the soft underbelly of liberalism. Liberalism insists against the gloomier forms of Christianity that human nature is not irretrievably wicked, and that the right environment can mould beliefs and desires in the right direction. Critics of J. S. Mill have often argued that Mill's liberalism is essentially a *faute de mieux* solution to the problem of achieving a society in which happiness is scientifically pursued and secured.[37] Huxley's *Brave New World* may be to some extent a parody of the aspiration towards the scientific manipulation of human nature for the sake of happiness, but it struck the normally liberal Russell as one recipe for peace and perhaps a recipe that we ought to swallow.[38] What is characteristic of the Brave New World is that its inhabitants are so conditioned that they cannot think their way round the possibilities it offers; gammas are glad to be gammas and think green is the nicest of colours, while betas are equally pleased with their lot and much admire blue. They do not want the same things in the sense that they can agree whether blue or green is the prettier; but they want what it is good for harmony in society that they should want.

One difference between this sort of conditioning and anything apparently envisaged by Hobbes is that Hobbes seems to want to circumscribe our choices by way of imposition of names and agreement on definitions. It is a seemingly more intellectualist and less associationist theory altogether, although readers of Orwell's *1984* will wonder whether Hobbes hasn't pre-invented 'newspeak'. As much as Wittgenstein, Hobbes seems to think that the limits of language are the limits of our world, so that if the sovereign can secure the necessary grip on our language he can secure that our whole world, inner and outer, is under his control. Why should Hobbes be so eager to insist on his account of terms like 'injustice' if not because he hopes that once we think it is a definitional truth that the sovereign can commit no injustice, we shan't rebel against 'iniquity' but will think ourselves unable to rebel with a good conscience at all?

I hope that what has been said already is sufficient to cast doubt on the idea that Hobbes was hoping to define us into through-and-through conformity, and that the fact that Hobbes places so much weight on definitions and not on the association of ideas casts sufficient doubt on the idea that he was eager to condition us into parroting the sovereign's judgements of good and evil. In spite of the marvellous frontispiece to *Leviathan,* in which subjects are depicted as literally making up the body of the state, and in

[37] Maurice Cowling, *Mill and Liberalism* (Cambridge, Cambridge University Press, 1963); cf. S. Letwin, *The Pursuit of Certainty* (Cambridge, Cambridge University Press, 1965), ch. 21.

[38] This is not wholly surprising: he thought *Brave New World* had been lifted from his own book, *The Scientific Outlook.* R. W. Clark, *The Life of Bertrand Russell* (Harmondsworth, Penguin, 1978), p. 566.

spite of Hobbes's assurances that when a state is founded, 'it is a reall Unitie of them all, in one and the same Person',[39] there is no submergence of individual substances in some superior whole. Hobbes is neither Rousseau nor Hegel, and we ought not to try to turn him into either. There is still one obvious question which we ought to answer, however: if Hobbes is not bent on abolishing the individual, and yet certainly shows no great enthusiasm for moral and spiritual individualism; if he is not particularly delicate about the inner life but is tolerably clear that the interest of states is the interest of their members, then what interests do we have, and do any of them amount to an interest in our own inner lives?

The temptation is to make Hobbes into the spokesman of the bourgeois—or even of the suburban middle classes of today.[40] When Hobbes lists the horrors of the state of nature, the worst is the fear of violent death; but the state exists for more than mere survival. It exists for commodious living. This can readily attract a commercial gloss: luxury goods cannot be imported in the absence of maps and navigators, ships and sailors, merchants and bankers; we cannot live in decent stone houses with glass windows and non-smoking fires unless we have roads, and quarries and literate architects. It would be silly to underestimate Hobbes's attachment to *useful* knowledge; he may be less millenarian than Bacon, but he is as ready to assume that reason lights the way to peace and prosperity. But we ought not to go too far down the path of making him a spokesman for the nascent capitalist and the rising bourgeoisie.[41] His utilitarianism makes him accept as much freedom of trade as is for the general good and no more; nor does he think that property rights are sacred. We own what the sovereign says we own, and on the terms the sovereign lays down.[42] If the sovereign takes your property and gives it to a favourite, you have no grounds for complaint—though the sovereign ought not to do it in the first place, your rights are good only against fellow subjects. Again, Hobbes's views on the virtues have been described as bourgeois.[43] He was extremely hostile to the excesses of the

[39] *Leviathan*, p. 89.

[40] Wolin, *Politics and Vision*, p. 281.

[41] K. Thomas, 'The Social Origins of Hobbes's Political Thought', in Keith C. Brown (ed.), *Hobbes Studies* (Oxford, Blackwell, 1965), pp. 185–236.

[42] *Leviathan*, p. 131; cf. *E.W.* 2, pp. 157 and 178 where sumptuary laws are recommended.

[43] Leo Strauss, *The Political Philosophy of Hobbes* (Oxford, Clarendon Press, 1936), p. 121.

aristocratic concern for honour; men who seize on the slightest excuse to pick a quarrel are menaces to the peace. Yet Hobbes was not exactly a bourgeois apologist; his patron the Earl of Devonshire may have been interested in iron smelting, but he was no bourgeois, and the virtues of fidelity and a willingness to forget old grudges are, if not classless, the virtues of a gentleman.

To put it somewhat differently, there is certainly something about Hobbes's account of human psychology which irresistibly suggests the behaviour of an indefinitely expanding enterprise, in a *'race* we must suppose to have no other *goal,* nor other *garland,* but being foremost . . .';[44] but this picture of men without any natural standards of success and failure other than the envy or contempt of others is not a picture of commercially minded man. The pleasures of civilized men are not themselves commercial or mercenary enjoyments; the affection of our friends, the disinterested search for knowledge, and the pursuit of literary excellence are all private goods in their own right. It may be true that when we enjoy an intellectual discovery we experience the enhanced vital motions resulting from a sense of our talent for discovery, but we must be careful not to deflate Hobbes too far. Self-congratulation is an inescapable property of the physical organism, not the discovery of a cynical Hobbes. Hobbes has no quarrel with the claim that we enjoy one another's company quite disinterestedly, nor with the usual distinction between self-interested and disinterested intellectual activity.

I incline, therefore, to think that most of what we ordinarily think is valuable in the inner life was thought valuable by Hobbes. The worth of peace and security is that they enable us to enjoy civilized pleasures. These include the pleasures of having a quiet conscience and an easy mind; knowing that we have been generous, kindly, and charitable to the needy is the sort of pleasure Hobbes approved of.[45] It is one of the rewards of decent behaviour which is unavailable in the state of nature; it is, for all that, not imposed upon us by the sovereign, even though it intrinsically inclines us to peace, and will further incline us to obedience when we think of its dependence on the existence of good order. This being so, we can see again that the sovereign need not do anything very extra-

---

[44] *E. W.* 4, p. 53.

[45] Stephen, *Hobbes*, pp. 23–4; Thomas, 'Social Origins,' pp. 220–1.

ordinary to induce us to behave peacefully; he does not need to engage in thought-control or in the invention of 'newspeak' because our private occupations will in any case engross us. These occupations are, as we agreed earlier, the occupations of a-political men, of subjects rather than citizens. For all that, Hobbes commends those which yield pleasure to the mind, not the satisfaction of sensual appetite.

It ought to be stressed, however, that the farthest this can take us in finding a case for intellectual liberty and mutual toleration is no farther than a utilitarian argument can go. The degree to which it is worth the sovereign's while to intervene for the sake of peace seems to be an issue of technique not principle—that it is only for the sake of peace that he ought to intervene is the only principle in the case. Hobbes's sovereign cannot condition children as the Director in *Brave New World* can, and therefore should not try. There is no evident reason of principle to stop him applying the techniques when they are discovered. Just as Hobbes shares with avowed liberals like Mill and Russell a tendency to vacillate between adapting society to adults and conditioning children into society, so he shares with them the difficulty of providing a principled stopping-place for government control of the mind. That the sovereign *need* not control most intellectual activities is one thing; that he *may* not even if he wishes to and knows how to is another. Mill and Russell evade the issue somewhat by appealing to a principle of 'growth', which requires a liberal environment.[46] Hobbes is tougher and more consistent in simply employing the rule that the search for conformity is self-defeating if it only maddens the unorthodox.

Taking this together with what we saw earlier about the limits to the power of 'imposing names', we can now end by suggesting that the sense in which Hobbes has principled reasons for toleration must always and only be that he has epistemologically principled reasons, never morally principled reasons. There are things we cannot get people to think, and where we cannot we ought not to try. All else is a matter of expediency in that large sense in which the laws of nature bind sovereigns to act expediently rather than selfishly or arbitrarily. That Hobbes is inclined to let men alone but not to offer a principled defence of toleration is un-

[46] B. Russell, *Principles of Social Reconstruction* (London, Allen and Unwin, 1916), ch. 1; Mill, *Three Essays*, p. 73.

surprising. He paints a vivid picture of some parts of our inner lives—of anxiety, fear of ghosts, practical and impractical curiosity. But a man whose enthusiasm for music seems to have been limited to an appreciation of the good effects of singing upon his lungs is unlikely to get much further than that. He would no doubt have understood the fears of Soviet poets and writers in the face of Stalin's arbitrary cultural diktats; but it seems unlikely that he would have appreciated how far they minded about their art rather than their skins.

Rousseau and Marx[*]

Robert Wokler
University of Manchester

I

The political theories of Rousseau and Marx arouse stronger feelings than do most doctrines, and they have exercised a greater influence on the course of social revolutions than have the ideas of any other modern writers. But while each continues to attract widespread interest, they are seldom compared with one another, and only in Italy has there been any extensive discussion of the nature of the conceptual relations between them. Bobbio, Cotta, Mondolfo, and Marramao have all written on the subject over the past forty years or so,[1] and Galvano della Volpe and Lucio Colletti have each devoted books to it which proved sufficiently popular to warrant several editions.[2] English readers, accordingly, should be thankful to New Left Books and Lawrence and Wishart for recently publishing translations of the two main works about Rousseau and Marx in that tradition—della Volpe's *Rousseau e Marx* and Colletti's *Ideologia e società*[3]—though some may wonder at the bearing of these texts upon their subject, once they have been shorn from the world of Italian Marxism to which they belong. Della Volpe's book, whose English edition appeared in 1978, is a collection of essays written for the most part over twenty years earlier, in which the author's principal aim is to assess what he takes to be the limited egalitarianism of Rousseau and Marx and to rescue this doctrine from some of its Stalinist mis-

[*]© Robert Wokler 1983.

[1] See Norberto Bobbio, *Politica e cultura* (Turin, Einaudi, 1955), ch. xi; Sergio Cotta, 'La position du problème de la politique chez Rousseau' in *Études sur le 'Contrat social' de Rousseau* (Paris, Société Les Belles Lettres, 1964), pp. 177–90; Rodolfo Mondolfo, *Umanismo di Marx* (Turin, Einaudi, 1968); and Giacomo Marramao, *Marxismo e revisionismo in Italia* (Bari, De Donato, 1971).

[2] Galvano della Volpe's *Rousseau e Marx*, first published in Rome in 1964, passed through four editions over the next ten years; Lucio Colletti's *Ideologia e società*, first published in Bari in 1969, appeared in two further editions by 1972.

[3] See Galvano della Volpe, *Rousseau and Marx*, translated by John Fraser (London, Lawrence and Wishart, 1978), and Lucio Colletti, *From Rousseau to Lenin*, translated by John Merrington and Judith White (London, New Left Books, 1972).

interpreters. Colletti's more engaging and better argued work confronts the views of della Volpe in the manner of a courteous critic, invoking the authority of scholarly essays drawn from the most respectable, and bourgeois, French and English academic journals. To my mind each of these books offers a provocative but not always illuminating treatment of the subject, largely because in translation they have been plucked from their time and context. Together with Touchstone in *As You Like It,* I think it can be said about them that 'When they were at home, they were in a better place'. Far more satisfactory, in my view, though regrettably less familiar even to English readers, is the commentary by John Plamenatz in his account of *Karl Marx's Philosophy of Man,*[4] to which my remarks here owe an intellectual debt I am happy to acknowledge.

Such links as would connect the philosophies of Rousseau and Marx ought, of course, to form a subject of interest in themselves, not least to historians of ideas engaged in tracing Rousseau's influence or locating Marx's sources. From time to time scholars have in fact attempted to establish the intellectual influence exercised by Rousseau over Marx, particularly as it may have been mediated by Marx's father, who, according to Eleanor Marx, knew his Rousseau and Voltaire 'by heart'.[5] A few commentators have been intrigued, too, by the fact that in 1843 Marx turned to a meticulous reading of the *Social Contract* and in his Kreuznach notebooks transcribed no less than 103 passages from that work, all of which, incidentally, are still readily identifiable today.[6] And if we know from Marx himself that he read Rousseau's most important study of politics with such diligent care, it might appear from Engels's testimony that he was at least equally if not more impressed by Rousseau's second major contribution to political thought, that is, the *Discourse on Inequality,* since, in *Anti-Dühring*, Engels observed that this work includes a sequence of ideas which, in its dialectical detail, corresponds exactly ('gleich auf ein Haar') with Marx's own masterpiece, *Capital.*[7]

[4] John Plamenatz, *Karl Marx's Philosophy of Man* (Oxford, Clarendon Press, 1975).

[5] See *Mohr und General. Erinnerungen an Marx und Engels* (Berlin, Dietz, 1970), p. 158.

[6] See the Marx and Engels *Historisch-kritische-Gesamtausgabe* (*MEGA*), ed. D. Rjazanov (Berlin and Moscow, Marx-Engels Institute, 1927–36), I. 1. ii. 120–1.

[7] See Engels, *Anti-Dühring*, in *Marx-Engels Werke* (hereafter *MEW*), 39 vols. in 41 (Berlin, Dietz, 1957–68), XX. 130–1.

Yet if such evidence seems fertile ground for plotting the course of a historical influence, or mapping the extent of a historical debt, it is fertile ground stretched thinly over unnegotiable channels. As both della Volpe and Colletti have ruefully observed, Marx, despite his considerable debt to Rousseau, 'never gave any indication of being remotely aware of it'.[8] There are no more than some twenty-two references to Rousseau anywhere in the corpus of Marx's published writings, including his letters, and most of these are just passing citations.[9] His father may have known his Rousseau and Voltaire by heart, but Karl seemed scarcely able to distinguish them, and on at least one of the occasions that he mentions Rousseau he speaks of the philosophy of 'Rousseau-Voltaire',[10] as if this pair of mortal enemies of the Enlightenment formed a GilbertonSullivan compound, each standing for much the same as the other. Marx must have left his painstaking notes from the *Social Contract* behind when, in his introduction to the *Grundrisse*, he likened the citizens of Rousseau's ideal state to naturally independent Robinson Crusoes, coming together through covenants to engage in freely competitive social relations on the model later elaborated by Smith and Ricardo.[11] For though *Robinson Crusoe* is, indeed, a book Rousseau admired, it is in *Émile*

---

[8]Colletti, *From Rousseau to Lenin*, p. 187. See also della Volpe, *Rousseau and Marx*, p. 149.

[9]See *MEW* I. 80 (*Das philosophische Manifest der historischen Rechtsschule*); *MEW* I. 103, 104 ('Die leitende Artikel in Nr. 179 der *Kölnischen Zeitung*'); *MEW* I. 370 (*Zur Judenfrage*); *MEW* III, 75, 317, 386, 387, 512–13 (*Deutsche Ideologie*), and the passage from this text, first published in 1962, in *The German Ideology* (Moscow, Progress Publishers, 1964), p. 213; *MEW* IV. 353 ('Die moralisierende Kritik und die kritisierende Moral'); *MEW* XIII. 280 ('Die Kriegsaussichten in Preußen'); *MEW* XIII. 615 (*Einleitung* [*zur Kritik der politischen Ökonomie*], i.e. *Grundrisse*); *MEW* XIV. 588 (*Herr Vogt*); *MEW* XV. 69 ('Interessantes aus Preußen'), *New York Daily Tribune*, 30 June 1860; *MEW* XVI. 31, 32 ('Über Proudhon'); *MEW* XIX. 16 (*Kritik des Gothaer Programms*); *MEW* XXIII. 774 (*Kapital* I); *MEW* XXVII. 297 (Marx to Engels, 8 Aug. 1851); *MEW* XXVII. 314 (Marx to Engels, 14 Aug. 1851). Apart from *MEW* III. 512–13, where Rousseau is mentioned thirteen times (always in passing, and that mainly by way of quotations or paraphrases from Cabet and Grünn), reference to him, or to a 'Rousseauschen Sinne', appears only once on each of these pages, while *MEW* III. 75 does not mention his name at all but cites a passage from the *Contrat social*. The only reference I have found anywhere in Marx to Rousseau's most famous political concept, the 'volonté générale', appears in *MEW* XV. 69.

[10]See *MEW* XVI. 32. Cf. *MEW* XIII. 280.

[11]See Marx, *Grundrisse* (Harmondsworth, Penguin, 1973), Introduction, p. 83; *MEW* XIII. 615; and Karl Marx, *Texts on Method,* ed. Terrell Carver (Oxford, Blackwell, 1975), pp. 48 and 91–2.

that he commends it[12] and nowhere in the *Social Contract*, and neither a desert state nor one of freely competitive social relations has any place at all in the political argument of that work. Marx's misreading of the *Social Contract*, moreover, is no small matter of his memory having failed him during the fourteen-year interval between 1843 and 1857, when his mind would have been absorbed by other ideas. For the sense of the passage in the *Grundrisse* to which I have just referred closely follows a similar misreading of the *Social Contract* that figures in the *Jewish Question* which Marx drafted in the same year he culled Rousseau so assiduously and ought, presumably, to have been most under his sway. There Marx quotes at length from some lines in Rousseau's chapter on the legislator, which he had actually transcribed himself, dealing with the metamorphosis of human nature and the moral transformation of man through the pact of association.[13] Commentators have often been struck by the similarity between Rousseau's account of the abrupt change in human nature brought about by the social compact, and Marx's description of the proletarian redemption of our human essence through the revolutionary movement of communism, in his *Critique of Hegel's Philosophy of Right* and *Economic and Philosophical Manuscripts*,[14] also dating from this period. We might have expected that Marx himself, if he did not acknowledge Rousseau as his source, would at least have been impressed by these parallels, but in the *Jewish Question* he addressed himself to Rousseau's argument precisely in order to oppose it. Rousseau's conception of an uplifted form of popular morality was, he claimed, artificial and abstract, because it set the citizen apart from the individual in his everyday life and thus failed to recognize that human emancipation must have a social as well as a political objective. What a blundering misconstruction of the text that is. Marx need only have turned to Book I, chapter 9 or

---

[12] See *Émile*, III, in Rousseau's *Œuvres complètes* (hereafter *OC*). ed. Bernard Gagnebin and Marcel Raymond *et al.* (Paris, Bibliothèque de la Pléiade, 1959–64), IV. 454–5. In *Émile* Rousseau cites *Robinson Crusoe* as a most useful book of natural education. See also *OC* I. 644, 812, 826, and 1605.

[13] See Marx, *On the Jewish Question*, in *Early Texts*, translated and edited by David McLellan (Oxford, Blackwell, 1972), pp. 107–8; *MEW* I. 370; and Rousseau, *Contrat social*, II. 7, *OC* III. 381–2.

[14] See Marx, *Early Texts*, pp. 127–8 and 148; *MEW* I. 390 and sup. vol. I. 536. See also Rousseau, *Contrat social*, I. 8, *OC* III. 364–5.

Book II, chapter 11 of the *Social Contract* to see just how deeply committed Rousseau was to the social framework, and, indeed, institutions of economic equality, without which he believed the true liberty of morally transformed individuals could never be secured. Rousseau's doctrine of human nature, radically transformed in accordance with the terms of a social compact, may be nonsense, but if so, then Marx's central arguments of the *Jewish Question* and the *Economic and Philosophical Manuscripts* which so closely resemble that doctrine in both substance and style ought to be regarded as implausible for practically the same reasons.

What, then, are we to make of Engels's remark that the *Discourse on Inequality* corresponds to *Capital* in exact dialectical detail? Even if we make allowances for Engels's hyperbole—for the fact that he sometimes uncovered extraordinary similarities between Marx and other thinkers while at the same time praising him for his profoundly original genius—there ought to be no doubt that in the *Discourse on Inequality* Marx found precisely that focus upon the social relations of men whose absence from the *Social Contract* he deplored. There *should* be no doubt about this, but doubt there must be, since Marx gives no sign of having found anything of the sort in the *Discourse on Inequality*. We know that he corresponded with Engels about *Anti-Dühring* and even drafted a manuscript on the same subject, of which Engels incorporated an edited version in his published text.[15] In the preface to the second edition of *Anti-Dühring* Engels actually asserts that he had read the whole manuscript of the book to Marx before it was printed[16]—an unsubstantiated statement, though it suggests Marx had at least two opportunities, once in person, and once in print, to remark upon the fact that his closest collaborator was informing the world that his greatest work, the product of a lifetime's reflection, had already been anticipated by Rousseau in the *Discourse on Inequality*. This was not a trivial claim, and it is difficult to imagine that Marx was unaware that Engels had made it. Yet we have no reason for supposing that Marx ever attempted to refute, or disavow, or even take stock of it. He seems to have said nothing at all about the subject, and there the matter rests.

[15] See Terrell Carver, 'Marx, Engels and Dialectics', *Political Studies*, 28 (1980), 354–8, and *MEW* XX. 9 and 624.
[16] See Carver, 'Marx, Engels and Dialectics', p. 357, and *MEW* XX. 9.

Worse still for scholars convinced of Rousseau's influence on Marx is the fact that—so far as I am aware, at least—we have no evidence to suggest that Marx even read the *Discourse on Inequality*. Apart from his references to the *Social Contract* there are occasional citations in his writings of Rousseau's *Encyclopédie* article on political economy, but no mention at all of the *Discourse on Inequality*, not so much as an allusion to this most Marxist of all Rousseau's works. Nor, to my knowledge, did Marx ever refer to any of the other compositions which bear testimony to the radical philosophy of Rousseau and to the social and economic dimensions of his doctrine—to the *Discourse on the Arts and Sciences*, for instance, the *Letter on the Theatre,* the *Essay on Languages,* and all the rest. We can only speculate on what Marx might have said about Rousseau if he had taken the trouble to read these texts; one hopes that he might at least have found in them a doctrine more congenial to his own views, as well as some incentive to look at the *Social Contract* in a fresh light. It seems difficult to appreciate that Marx, who was so widely read in such a broad range of subjects, and whose major writings were so often set out as commentaries on the ideas of others, should have taken so little notice and—when he did notice—held such a poor opinion, of the social theory of a figure already regarded in his day as one of his main precursors. Yet there is no denying the fact that, as Plamenatz has observed, 'Marx's references to Rousseau are few, and on the whole unflattering and unperceptive'.[17]

Why Marx took such scant notice of Rousseau is a problem whose solution we are unlikely ever to discover. Conceivably, Marx may actually have known Rousseau's writings too well instead of too little, and he may have been better disposed to them than he ever admitted. We should not forget that Hegel's immense influence on the *Grundrisse* received scant acknowledgement from Marx, and sometimes he manifestly not only neglected to commend his sources but even poured his greatest scorn upon those figures—among them Proudhon and Bakunin—whose doctrines his own views resembled most.

Another, rather more plausible, answer leads in almost the opposite direction, and it is suggested to me by the fact that Marx's lengthiest discussion on Rousseau—that is, his

---

[17] Plamenatz, *Karl Marx's Philosophy of Man*, p. 60.

commentary in the *Jewish Question*—incorporates a critique of Rousseau's abstract citizen in a more general censure of the juridical rights of man, including property, equality, and security, won by the French Revolutionaries and proclaimed by them in the Declarations of the Rights of Man and their Constitutions of 1793 and 1795.[18] Now we know from *Anti-Dühring*[19] that Engels supposed the Revolution had marked the bourgeois and republican fulfilment of the abstract principles expressed in the *Social Contract*, and some such view seems also to be what Marx had in mind in his introduction to the *Grundrisse*. If so, it would appear to follow that Rousseau's ideals, as Marx conceived them, must have come to practical fruition in a revolution which, on his own testimony elsewhere,[20] had failed to achieve man's true social emancipation. According to Engels, moreover, Rousseau's social contract principles had been put into practice not only by the Revolutionary constitutions; they had also been realized in the Jacobin Terror.[21] This was a thesis advanced earlier in the nineteenth century by Maistre and especially Hegel, among others, and it had been implied even before that in the writings of Burke. As several commentators have remarked—not least della Volpe and Colletti[22]—Marx probably drew much of what he did know about Rousseau from his reading of Hegel, whose own misrenderings of the *Social Contract* stemmed from what he took to be their practical application in the course of the French Revolution. Marx, I believe, was, like Hegel, less concerned with the sense of Rousseau's doctrine than with its significance as an

[18] See Marx, *Early Texts*, pp. 101–5; *MEW* I. 362–7.

[19] See *MEW* XX. 17, or the same passage in *MEW* XIX. 190. See also della Volpe, *Rousseau and Marx*, pp. 85–6. It should be noted that Engels's own references to Rousseau are scarcely more numerous than those of Marx, with the great majority concentrated in *Anti-Dühring* alone: *MEGA* I. 2. 129 ('Rationalismus und Pietismus'), *Morgenblatt für gebildete Leser,* 17 Oct. 1840; *MEW* I. 469 and 475 ('Briefe aus London'), *Schweizerischer Republikaner,* 16 May and 9 June 1843; *MEW* IV. 295 (*Der ökonomische Kongreß*); *MEW* IV. 428 ('Louis Blancs Rede auf dem Bankett zu Dijon'); *MEW* XVI. 161 ('Was hat die Arbeiterklasse mit Polen zu tun?'); *MEW* XIX. 190, 192, 202 (*Die Entwicklung des Sozialismus von der Utopie zur Wissenschaft*); *MEW* XX. 17, 19, 91, 95, 129–31, 134, 142, 239, 292 (*Anti-Dühring*); *MEW* XX. 580, 584 ('Materielen zum *Anti-Dühring*'); *MEW* XXI. 282 (*Ludwig Feuerbach und der Ausgang der klassischen deutschen Philosophie*); *MEW* XXVII. 318 (Engels to Marx, 21 Aug. 1851); *MEW* XXXVII. 364 (Engels to Lafargue, 7 Mar. 1890); *MEW* XXXIX. 97 (Engels to Mehring, 14 July 1893).

[20] See, for instance, *On the Jewish Question*, in *Early Texts*, p. 108 (*MEW* I. 370).

[21] See *MEW* XX. 239 or *MEW* XIX. 192.

[22] See della Volpe, *Rousseau and Marx*, pp. 75–6 and 144, and Colletti, *From Rousseau to Lenin*, p. 188.

ideological expression of the aims and achievements of the French
Revolutionaries, but whereas Hegel saw that significance largely
in the Terror, I suspect Marx may have seen it more in the
establishment of a bourgeois Republic. In one case, that is, the
Social Contract was held to be a blueprint for a revolution that had
gone too far; in the other, in what was perhaps good dialectical
fashion, it may have been understood as the manifesto of a
revolution that had not gone far enough. In both cases, however,
if my guess is correct, the attempt to link the *Social Contract* directly
to the Revolution led to striking misinterpretations of its author's
meaning. It may be one of the ironies of his poor scholarship that,
by appraising Rousseau's works in the artificial glare of a revolutionary doctrine he regarded as defunct, Marx not only failed to
see, or neglected to state, how closely they in fact approximate the
substance of his own writings. He also failed to notice how much
revolutionary light, and even heat, they could shed upon the
darker and colder corners of his philosophy. All of this, however,
opens up a new field, full of unturned stones. I have not
undertaken that research, and my remarks in this paragraph are
less provisional than speculative.

Of course nothing I have said so far should be taken to imply
that I regard Rousseau and Marx as proponents of unrelated
social theories. On the contrary, the lack of a direct historical
influence joining the two thinkers is a matter of interest only
because we had good reason to expect that some such link might
elucidate the striking conceptual similarities between them. At
least a few of the works of Rousseau evidently did figure as part of
Marx's education, and it is in the light of their theoretical
affinities that I find it surprising that Marx drew so little
inspiration from the ideas of a writer I believe he ought to have
admired more. Theirs is not a resemblance, such as that between
Leibniz and Newton with regard to the differential calculus, or
between Darwin and Wallace with regard to natural selection, of
two men at about the same time coming more or less independently to similar conclusions. The fact, moreover, that the social
theories of Rousseau and Marx *do* correspond closely, one with
the other, seems to me manifestly clear. We have only to compare
Rousseau's conception of property in the *Discourse on Inequality*
with that of Marx in the *Economic and Philosophical Manuscripts* to
see this relation. We have only to juxtapose their respective

philosophies of history in which class conflict is the vehicle of revolutionary change, and the substitution of egalitarian for inegalitarian property relations the condition of society to which men should aspire. I shall in a few moments try to identify important differences pertaining to just these matters, but I have no doubt that, at least initially, the resemblances are more striking still. Something akin to Rousseau's conception of the general will was perceived by Marx to have been realized in practice by the Paris Commune. In his account of communist society, moreover, no less than in Rousseau's social contract state, Marx anticipated that men would be brought together by fraternal bonds through which not only equality but also moral liberty could finally be won. However little each thinker had to say about the institutions of future society, both saw mankind under contemporary social systems as alienated from its human essence by forces of which individuals were at once the authors and victims, and by forms of economic exploitation made binding through the exercise of legal and political authority. No one has investigated these links more perceptively than Plamenatz, whose academic career was in part devoted to the rescue of both Rousseau and Marx, together with Hegel, from the ill-informed disdain shown towards their supposedly obscure ideas by political philosophers of an earlier generation. More tenuous, no doubt, but still striking are those links of practical significance and application with which commentators have drawn together at least some of the principles of Rousseau and Marx. A good many of Rousseau's political detractors have held the doctrines of Marx to be loathsome for much the same reasons that they regard the views of Rousseau as insufferable, while his admirers, on the other hand, have often, as with Fidel Castro, seen the *Social Contract* and the *Communist Manifesto* as landmarks in the same magnificent revolutionary tradition. Can anyone deny that in Rousseau's republic of virtue, just as in Marx's classless state, each citizen will contribute only as much as he is able and, in turn, will receive as much as he needs?[23]

---

[23] Of course, as John Hope Mason reminds me, any putative likeness drawn between the satisfaction of needs in Rousseau's social theory and in that of Marx should not conflate their different perspectives on human needs and the manner of their satisfaction. For Rousseau our needs were fulfilled mainly through acts of self-reliance and political co-operation, rather than economic production. For Marx communist society would

Such resemblances and parallels, and many more like them, may turn out to be profound and significant when fully elaborated, and I set them aside here only because I fear that even if they could be drawn in convincing fashion they would shed too little light on the peculiar genius of either man. For both Rousseau and Marx, as with most major thinkers, we shall generally come closer to an understanding of their meaning if we study their ideas against the background of the sources they tried to refute rather than those they managed to reflect. Too often our attempts to trace historical lineages from conceptual parallels do injustice to putative creditors and borrowers alike. If, on the one hand, Marx voiced only what Rousseau asserted first, then why should we listen to the stubborn mule, who may not have been attentive to the message anyway, when we can still put our ear to the horse's mouth?[24] If, on the other hand, Marx maintained what Rousseau said, but better, then why should we look for the fluff on the lamb when we can already fleece the wool from the sheep? In the absence of a demonstrably certain and direct philosophical debt, for which so many scholars have hunted or fished in vain, I should like to offer, as an alternative, a few points of criticism which betoken some contrasts between the doctrines of Rousseau and Marx rather than any lines of historical influence.

II

It is one of the many curious features of Rousseau's intellectual biography that this continually uprooted, solitary vagabond held fast to a single guiding principle which, on his own testimony, informed all his major writings—to wit, that Nature made man happy and good, while society made him miserable and depraved.[25] Marx, on the other hand, was for many years firmly rooted to his seat at the British Museum and long betrothed to the Revolution beyond it, but he sometimes appears to have stood his ground on little else, and his shifts of focus and interest, which led

---

promote a progressively expanding rather than deliberately contracted set of needs, satisfied in accordance with some principle of proportional distribution based on relative requirements.

[24] As Plamenatz has observed in another context (*German Marxism and Russian Communism*, London, Longman, 1954, p. 191), 'Passing from German to Russian Marxism, we leave the horses and come to the mules.'

[25] See, for instance, *Émile*, I, *OC* IV. 245, and *Rousseau juge de Jean Jacques*, III, *OC* I. 934.

him to abandon many of his works before publication, have been the bane of his interpreters ever since. Persistent efforts by scholars to understand Marx's exact meaning have, accordingly, suffered much the same fate as attempts by others to establish what became of Rousseau's forsaken children. In the seemingly endless disputes about the compatibility of his humanist and scientific doctrines several issues have been raised time and again, and I trust I may be forgiven—at least for the reason that I mean to be brief—for resuscitating two of these issues here: first, Marx's account of the correspondence of relations to forces of production in his theory of history; and, second, his views about the moral status or implications of that historical theory.

In a profoundly original account and defence of historical materialism, Jerry Cohen has recently argued that the correspondence between forces and relations of production described by Marx[26] invariably attests to the primacy of the former over the latter.[27] Some commentators have instead alleged that our relations of production, as Marx conceived them, must be so linked with any underlying forces that they cannot in fact be abstracted from or initially determined by them,[28] but this claim is said to betray a fundamental misunderstanding of Marx's view. For while neither of these features of society can exist independently of the other, they are, according to Cohen, functionally related in such a way that one may account for the other's character,[29] with no circularity of *explicans* and *explicandum*.[30] On this interpretation the forces are primary since, though they are themselves conditioned by changing relations, it is they which promote, or select, such relations as are conducive to their own further development.[31] Productive forces so envisaged, moreover, are actually seen to incorporate an element of human agency

---

[26] Especially in his *Preface to a Contribution to the Critique of Political Economy* (see *MEW* XIII. 8–9).

[27] See G. A. Cohen, *Karl Marx's Theory of History: A Defence* (Princeton, Princeton University Press, 1978), pp. 28–9, 137–8, and 143–4.

[28] On this point Cohen (see *Karl Marx's Theory of History,* pp. 167–9) takes H. B. Acton and Plamenatz specially to task.

[29] See Cohen, *Karl Marx's Theory of History,* pp. 134–74.

[30] Among revisionist contributions to Marxism, Perry Anderson's account of the relation between a society's economic base and its superstructure in different historical epochs is challenged by Cohen (see *Karl Marx's Theory of History*, pp. 247–8) particularly with respect to this point.

[31] See Cohen, *Karl Marx's Theory of History*, pp. 160–3.

rather than exclude it, so that, as Cohen puts this thesis, 'once we notice that the development of the forces is centrally an enrichment of human labour power the emphasis on technology loses its dehumanizing appearance'.[32]

Now for a number of reasons which cannot be pursued here I am persuaded that Cohen's argument provides a more sophisticated interpretation of historical materialism than any we have had before.[33] And while I share some of the doubts of his reviewers as to the accuracy of his account of Marx's meaning,[34] I believe his occasional infidelity to the texts he explains tends to improve upon the original theory rather than detract from it. A defence which reformulates a thesis and manages to escape from some of its awkward corollaries seems to me all the more creditable for that, and as I mean here to invoke the philosophy of Rousseau in order to criticize not Cohen but Marx, I am content to accept Cohen's revisions as if they had been made on Marx's authority and with his assent. If I find Cohen unconvincing that is mainly because in defending Marx he has offered a defence of

[32] Ibid., p. 147.

[33] Until the recent spate of commentaries on Marx's philosophy of history by, among others, D. Ross Gandy, Melvin Rader, and William Shaw as well as Cohen, full-length book treatments of the subject have been scarce. For generations the most authoritative text was M. M. Bober's *Karl Marx's Interpretation of History*, first published in 1927.

[34] See, for instance, the comments of Walter Adamson in *History and Theory*, 19 (1980), 196–201; Jon Elster in *Political Studies*, 28 (1980), 123–7; Richard Miller in the *Philosophical Review*, 90 (1981), 91–117; and Peter Singer in the *New York Review of Books*, 26 (Dec. 1980), 46–7. Cohen's attempt to rebut other interpretations of historical materialism has been found by several reviewers to be more ingenious than convincing, largely because he seems to have paid too high a price for his gains. For one thing, his functional explanations appear out of keeping with the form and character of the arguments they purport to make clear, especially when applied to Marx's other claims about the correspondence between certain primary and secondary factors in social life, such as his views about the link between existence and consciousness, or between economic base and political superstructure. A functional explanation of Marx's theory of history, moreover, leaves us without a clear grasp of what he took to be the causal mechanisms of change and how they operate, whereas previously, following the perspective now regarded as insufficiently illuminating by Cohen, the prime examples of such mechanisms were thought to be social revolutions ('the locomotives of history'), initiated by classes at a certain stage in the development of the material forces of production of an economic system (see Cohen, *Karl Marx's Theory of History*, pp. 148–9 and 292). What I find particularly curious, too, and inadequately substantiated by any passages drawn from Marx himself, is Cohen's attachment of the idea of human agency and the rational exercise of labour power to his account of the technological forces of production, since Marx regarded productive forces in pre-communist societies as 'alien' powers, passing through stages 'independent of', and even governing, human will—see Marx and Engels, *The German Ideology* pp. 46 and 82 (*MEW* III. 34 and 67).

historical materialism too, and in that aim I think he has failed, for a host of reasons, among which at least a few can be drawn from the social theory of Rousseau. Let me turn, then, to some of Rousseau's ideas which may be taken to intersect with those of Marx, and which I believe Marx might have sought to confront, rebut, or accommodate, if only he had been aware of them.

It seems to me, firstly, that Rousseau would have regarded the Marxist—or Marx–Cohen—doctrine of historical materialism as too much encumbered by stratified forces and relations which operate 'independently of our will', as Marx often put it,[35] and which, according to Cohen, can be seen to correspond with one another in terms of non-purposive functional explanations.[36] Why, I believe Rousseau might have asked, should so much weight be placed upon the absence of will, and upon explanations of a non-purposive kind? His account of property relations in the *Discourse on Inequality* and elsewhere[37] suggests that he would have had little difficulty in agreeing with Marx that the ties which this institution engenders are essentially legal bonds arising from the division of labour characteristic of particular economic systems,[38] but, unlike Marx, he emphasized the specifically wilful character of that bondage—the fact that it depends upon consent, persuasion, deception, and language.

We have only to cast a glance over their respective ideas of property to see this most striking difference between each author's account of the economic foundations of society. For Marx our property rights were established by formal rules which constituted part of our intellectual or ideological superstructures whose features were ultimately determined by our underlying material forces of production. Since such rights could only be defined within a superstructure, they could not directly figure as part of the economic base of any class society.[39] For Rousseau, on the other hand, private property did form the basic element of every

[35] See *The German Ideology*, p. 46, and the *Preface to a Contribution to the Critique of Political Economy*, in Marx and Engels, *Selected Works* (hereafter *SW*), 3 vols. (Moscow, Progress Publishers, 1968–70), I. 503 (*MEW* III. 34 and XIII. 8).

[36] See Cohen, *Karl Marx's Theory of History*, p. 290.

[37] See especially the *Discours sur l'inégalité*, *OC* III. 173–4 and 177–8; the 'Dernière réponse' [to Charles Borde], *OC* III. 80; and the preface to *Narcisse*, *OC* II. 969–70n

[38] A thesis developed by Marx above all in *The German Ideology*—see pp. 32–6, 77–84, and 379–91 (*MEW* III. 22–5, 61–8, and 331–42).

[39] For an elucidating treatment of this subject see Cohen, *Karl Marx's Theory of History*, pp. 216–34.

existing social system, and that it did so was precisely due to its ideological character. The importance of his conjunction of the origin of civil society with the first claim to private property in the *Discourse on Inequality* lies in the fact that he conceived it as an entitlement enjoyed by some individuals to which others are required to give their assent. The private ownership of land, he believed, could only be established deliberately on the part of those who possess it and must be authorized even by those who do not. It was instituted by principles which require approval and legitimation, and he would not have accepted that the class divisions which rights of property express were really rooted in material forces independent of human will. Yet that claim must surely be the corner-stone of Marx's theory of history, however Cohen or others interpret it. Society, wrote Marx, is not founded upon the law, but the law upon society, whose needs arise from the prevailing material mode of production.[40] Engels also perceived this fact clearly enough when he asserted that we must eat and drink before we pursue politics and that, therefore, the economic production of the immediate means of subsistence forms the foundation on which our state institutions have evolved, and in the light of which our legal concepts must be explained.[41] This was, he remarked, the great law of human history Marx had discovered, and it was informed by Marx's own charge against his idealist precursors—made, for instance, in *The German Ideology* and repeated in his *Preface to the Critique of Political Economy*—that consciousness is determined by life rather than life by consciousness.[42] Cohen, who rightly subjects each of those works to a most rigorous interpretation, never refers to this statement in his defence of Marx's theory of history.[43] But if, as Engels supposed,

---

[40] In the *Neue Rheinische Zeitung*, no. 231, 25 Feb. 1849, *MEW* VI. 245.

[41] For instance in his celebrated speech at Marx's graveside, *SW* III. 162.

[42] See *The German Ideology*, p. 38, and the *Preface to a Contribution to the Critique of Political Economy, SW* I. 503 (*MEW* III. 27 and XIII. 9). The verb Marx employed in each of these passages is 'bestimmen'. See also *The German Ideology*, p. 42 (*MEW* III. 30–1), where Marx speaks of consciousness as a social product. In *Capital* I. 19 (17) he portrays certain ideas of political economists as 'imaginary expressions' which only represent relations of production. See Marx, *Capital*, 3 vols. (Moscow, Foreign Languages Publishing House, 1954–62), I. 535–42 (*MEW* XXIII. 557–64).

[43] Cohen's neglect of the passage might appear understandable in view of the stress he places upon human agency and rational purpose as features of the technological forces of production Marx describes (see Cohen, *Karl Marx's Theory of History*, p. 147). That would be an utterly misleading impression, however, since Cohen has elsewhere devoted

it forms a crucial part of his mentor's greatest discovery, I think Rousseau would have viewed it as his most profound mistake. For, by contrast with Marx, he surmised that consciousness— indeed belief of a kind which Marxists later termed 'false consciousness'—was so inextricably bound up with life that no primacy of any sort could be ascribed to material existence over modes of thought.

The significance he attached to the concept of authority, and to wilful behaviour and rule-governed conduct linked with that concept, led Rousseau into fields of social thought, especially linguistics, which were largely unexplored by Marx. Since economic domination depends upon the legitimacy of rules, and since these can only be established by consent, then the devices employed to elicit that consent, Rousseau supposed, must also occupy an essential place in any satisfactory theory of our history. He believed that our main instrument of subjugation has been much the same as the medium through which we conjugate too, that is, language. For his part Marx was so preoccupied with the unintended consequences of our actions that he had relatively little to say about the role of language in human affairs. Just as consciousness was determined by life, so too, he claimed in *The German Ideology*, was language: 'The problem of descending from the world of thoughts to the actual world', he insisted, '[turns] into the problem of descending from language to life. . . . Neither thoughts nor language in themselves form a realm of their own . . . they are only *manifestations* of actual life.'[44] Rousseau, on the other hand, regarded language as of central importance as a determinant of man's behaviour. The founder of civil society needed to find people foolish enough to believe him. In order to secure his entitlement to the land he had to induce others to renounce any claims of their own in his favour, and the institution

---

a whole article to the subject of 'Being, Consciousness and Roles: On the Foundations of Historical Materialism', in *Essays in honour of E. H. Carr*, ed. Chimen Abramsky and Beryl Williams (London, Macmillan, 1974), pp. 82–97. There he discusses the remark from the *Preface* and takes issue with Plamenatz over its interpretation (in Plamenatz's *Ideology* (London, Pall Mall, 1971), chs. 2 and 3), claiming (p. 95) that 'a person's "being", in the sense of Marx's thesis, is the economic role he occupies'. I am extremely grateful to Jerry Cohen for drawing my attention to that essay and thus sparing me a most embarrassing oversight, but I still cannot see how he reconciles the meaning of this passage with the theory of history he attributes to Marx, in so far as that theory is said to allow a determinant place to what rational men do.

[44] Marx, *The German Ideology*, pp. 491–2 (*MEW* III. 432–3).

of property itself depended upon the continual renunciation of a right by individuals who had not subscribed to the initial agreement but were persuaded of its justice. All that persuasion, of course, required the most artful eloquence and deception, the terms of which Rousseau recounts in several passages of the *Discourse on Inequality* and elsewhere, and which rather resemble, in a different context, the sublime rhetoric of the legislator of the *Social Contract*, who, we will recall, must also persuade without convincing.[45] So inextricably was language bound up with the foundation of society, in Rousseau's judgement, that he was actually unable to decide whether language was fundamentally a social institution or society itself a linguistic artefact.[46] Not only the institution of property but all our interpersonal ties were characteristically conceived by him in a linguistic framework, embracing artificially fixed meanings and symbolic representations which we employ to identify and distinguish one another and mark out what later came to be termed our station and its duties. It was from the ways in which we ascribe sense and especially attribute moral significance to our behaviour and the behaviour of others that society was constructed, and from the linguistic base of our specification of terms stemmed the moral emblems of our specialization of roles, and ultimately the fixation of social man in an abstract world of his own making. The ideological principles enunciated in language were thus not divorced from the real substance of social life; they were its very foundation.[47]

I have here addressed myself very briefly to Rousseau's views

---

[45] See the *Discours sur l'inégalité*, *OC* III. 164 and 177–8, and the *Contrat social*, II. 7, *OC* III. 383.

[46] See the *Discours sur l'inégalité*, *OC* III. 151, and my 'Perfectible Apes in Decadent Cultures: Rousseau's Anthropology Revisited', *Daedalus* (Summer 1978), 118–20.'

[47] Against the general drift of my argument here David McLellan reminds me that Marx likewise believed that men make their own history, while Terrell Carver and Michael Evans perceive a more prominent place for language in Marx's thought—in the 'fetishism of commodities', the 'riddle of money', and indeed his whole theory of ideology—than I have allowed. But it is economic producers, according to Marx, rather than moral agents, who characteristically shape our history, and its main patterns are not determined by individual, collective, or even conflicting, choice. Equally it is the illusory or 'fantastic', rather than linguistic, character of ideology and fetishism on which Marx lavishes most of his attention, at the same time pointing to an underlying reality which these abstractions are said to betoken or conceal: 'The verbal masquerade only has meaning when it is the unconscious or deliberate expression of an actual masquerade' (*The German Ideology*, p. 449, *MEW* III. 394).

on language mainly to show how, unlike Marx, he believed the conception and expression of our ideas to be of prime consideration in determining the nature of our economic modes of life. It was Rousseau's focus upon thought as it was bound up with life which led him to regard property as shaped as much by our authority relations as by the material forces of production to which those relations correspond. It was the same focus which prompted him, so much more than Marx, to consider the symbolic and cultural features of human behaviour responsible for both the character and origin of man's exploitation by man. If property, as he conceived it, displayed the deliberate, wilful purpose of our economic ties—if this institution was in some measure explicable as the consequence of a performative linguistic act such as the issue of a command or a promise to obey—it was equally through language, he argued, that the subterfuge, the deceit, hypocrisy, and false values which underlay our allegiances were articulated and expressed. More perceptively, perhaps, than any other thinker before him, and certainly more perceptively than Marx, Rousseau recognized the importance of imagery and illusion as constitutive elements of our social bonds. We act upon reflection, but our reflection is misled, even depraved, he observed,[48] and through language what we believe we see plainly turns out to be *trompe-l'œil*. In our undertakings to respect the private property of others we envisage ourselves in a position to enjoy the same entitlements, even though all the land we could acquire is already in private hands. In political society we think ourselves free but run headlong into our chains,[49] lured by the semblance of liberty. Everywhere we meekly accept the yoke of despotism because it is wrapped around us like a mantle of justice.

The whole of Rousseau's theory of culture, in fact, reinforces this conception of illusory bonds which form the nexus of society. What are our arts, letters, and sciences but, as he put it, those 'garlands of flowers woven round the iron chains by which men are weighed down'?[50] What is contemporary theatre, he asked, but the adornment of vice behind the mask of eloquence which moves audiences to approve the most terrible crimes? What has our music become, now that it has been displaced from its springs

[48] See the *Discours sur l'inégalité*, *OC* III. 138.
[49] See the *Discours sur l'inégalité*, *OC* III. 177.
[50] Rousseau, *Discours sur les sciences et les arts*, *OC* III. 7.

of poetry and melody, but a collection of artificial scales and listless harmonies echoed, in speech, by the prosaic rhetoric of mountebank kings, counterfeit scholars, and charlatan priests? Everywhere we are confronted by incantations and diatribes, by recitations from the pulpit and proclamations from the throne, distracted by the demons of art, stupefied by preaching and shouting devoid of sense. In music, he wrote, 'the calculation of intervals [has been] substituted for the finesse of inflexions',[51] but this calculation of intervals was only a variant form of the divisive moral relations by which individuals have become equally enthralled in civilized society. Just as we have ceased to assemble together to determine our civic ideals, so, similarly, through art, science, and religion we have been numbed and made passive, displaced from the centre of cultural life and herded into its pit and pews. Transformed from agents of what we do into witnesses of what happens to us, we are, in the modern world, turned into a hushed audience and taught deference and timidity. In the arts, no less than in our political relations, Rousseau observed in his *Essay on the Origin of Languages*, 'it is necessary to keep subjects apart; that is the first maxim of contemporary politics'.[52] Such, I believe, was the essence of his view of culture, and it is an aspect of his social theory as a whole from which Marx, if he had been familiar with it, might have drawn some inspiration but also, perhaps, a number of correctives to his own approach as well.

These elements of Rousseau's philosophy of culture, together with his conception of property, thus embrace a wider—more political, linguistic, aesthetic, and scientific—spectrum of human activities than Marx allowed to be of central significance, and, of course, my aim here has been to stress the greater scope of Rousseau's vision of our civilization's decline as compared with Marx's account of the factors which shape our historical epochs. But equally, this is just to say that Rousseau relied *less* than Marx upon the thesis that mankind is essentially *Homo faber*, that we are distinguished from animals, as Marx sometimes observed, by virtue of the fact that we produce our own means of subsistence,

[51] Rousseau, *Essai sur l'origine des langues*, ed. Charles Porset (Bordeaux, Ducros, 1970), ch. 19, p. 187. For an assessment of some political aspects of Rousseau's theory of music see my 'Rousseau on Rameau and Revolution', *Studies in the Eighteenth Century*, 4, ed. R. F. Brissenden and J. C. Eade (Canberra, Australian National University Press, 1979), pp. 251–83.

[52] Rousseau, *Essai sur l'origine des langues*, ch. 20, p. 199.

so that what individuals truly are, 'depends on the material conditions determining their production'.[53] For Rousseau, what individuals are depends as much upon the patterns of their fixation in abstract worlds of their own making as upon either their material relations, or their technological forces, of production. A conception of *Homo faber* lies at the heart of his own theory no less than at the base of Marxism, but what he adds to Marx is a richer anthropological theory[54] of the exploitative nature of social relations in class-divided societies. He believed our chains were as much of cultural as of economic origin, and that it was through culture that *Homo faber* had become *Homo fabulator* and our species as a whole, not *Homo sapiens* but *Homo deceptus*. Marx taught us that we have nothing to lose apart from our chains, but if he had read Rousseau attentively he would have found explanations of more links in those chains than he ever perceived himself.

III

The second contrast between Rousseau and Marx I wish to consider has to do with the place of moral values in their doctrines. As I have already suggested, there are many similarities between their accounts of the defects characteristic of class society—their conceptions of man's self-estrangement, their views of the dehumanizing effects of the division of labour, their perspectives on the suffering caused by social inequality generally. As Marx himself implies in the *Jewish Question*, the main difference between them seems to be that Rousseau's principles were articulated in a political frame of reference, emphasizing such terms as sovereignty, equality, and liberty, whereas in his focus upon our 'species-being' he instead stressed the social, rather than political, essence of man. On this reading of their disagreement it appears that Marx was just as much concerned with liberty as Rousseau

---

[53] Marx, *The German Ideology*, p. 32 (*MEW* III. 21). This famous line actually concludes a paragraph in which Marx speaks of the mode of production as a 'definite form of activity' of individuals which gives expression to their life. It is worth noting, therefore, as McLellan points out to me, that the final sentence seems a *non sequitur*, though I cannot agree that the preceding sentences 'entirely accord with Rousseau'.

[54] Especially towards the end of his life Marx did read widely and meticulously through much of the current literature in cultural anthropology (see *The Ethnological Notebooks of Karl Marx*, ed. L. Krader, Assen, Van Gorcum, 1974). But he did not show as much interest in the subject or its literature as Rousseau had done in the 1750s, and he never shared Rousseau's (nor even Engels's) fascination for physical anthropology.

was, though he conceived the context of human emancipation in another way. As we know from a familiar passage of *Capital*, he believed that the true realm of freedom only begins when labour is no longer determined by external purposes. 'Freedom', he wrote, 'can only consist in socialized man, the associated producers, rationally regulating their interchange with Nature . . . instead of being ruled by it as by [some blind power].'[55] The agents whose freedom must be truly realized are not abstract citizens but real producers, and Marx was prompted by this approach to the question of freedom to voice some of his most eloquent pleas on behalf of human liberty in terms of free time. A man who is so occupied in working for the capitalists that he has no free time is 'less than a beast of burden', he commented in *Wages, Price and Profit*,[56] so that in place of the pompous catalogue of the inalienable rights of man he put forward what he termed 'the modest Magna Charta of a legally limited working-day, which shall make clear when the time which the worker sells is ended and when his own begins'.[57] The freedom to which Marx was committed thus appears to be as important a moral concept in his philosophy as freedom conceived in terms of sovereignty and the exercise of the general will was for Rousseau. On this interpretation we might even say that Marx's theory is a corrective to that of Rousseau, based, as it was, upon a sharper awareness than Rousseau had, or could have had, of the economic forces and constraints which render us unfree even when we enjoy civil liberty and political independence.

Yet to render the contrast between their views of liberty in that way is also misleading, in so far as Marx was less concerned to ground abstract moral principles in our economic relations than to deny their direct relevance to his account of human history as a whole. 'Communists do not preach morality at all,' he remarked in *The German Ideology*. Only discontented schoolmasters base their arguments for revolution on their moral dissatisfaction.[58] Because Marx regarded most conservative moral doctrines as ideological, and most radical moral doctrines as utopian—above all because he saw morality itself as part of the intellectual superstructure of

[55] Marx, *Capital* III. 48, p. 800 (*MEW* XXV. 828).
[56] Marx, *Wages, Price and Profit*, ch. xiii, *SW* II. 68 (*MEW* XVI. 144).
[57] Marx, *Capital* I. 10, p. 302 (*MEW* XXIII. 320).
[58] See *The German Ideology*, pp. 267 and 413 (*MEW* III. 229 and 362).

any economic system—he went to great lengths to expunge moral ideals from his social theory. Morality and all such 'phantoms [of] the human brain', he wrote, have no independence, no history, no development of their own. They are products of thought which derive their real existence from the material production of man.[59] Now in adopting this stance Marx undermined much of the force of his own condemnation of capitalism. Since our moral ideas were shaped by the modes of production to which they correspond, he believed that they could only be assessed in terms of that correspondence and not with respect to their inherent merit or attractiveness. As he put it in *Capital* and reiterated in the *Critique of the Gotha Programme*, the justice of transactions which take place between agents of production depends upon the extent to which they adequately express those relations; justice cannot be invoked as a standard by which to judge them: '[Their] content is just whenever it corresponds, is appropriate, to the mode of production. It is unjust whenever it contradicts that mode.'[60] It therefore followed that whereas slavery or fraud was unjust with regard to the capitalist mode of production, there could be no injustice within the market itself—no such thing as an unjust wage, no unjust extraction of surplus value from a worker's labour power. Because it was not an abuse of capitalist production but a manifestation of it, exploitation, in short, was not unjust.[61] Indeed, any reform of capitalism which was designed to re-distribute profits in such a way as to abolish the exploitation of workers must violate fundamental property rights sustained by the capitalist mode of production and hence would itself be an unjust imposition of a principle incompatible with it.[62] The correspondence of moral ideals with their underlying modes of production precludes our calling upon any supposed universal

[59] See *The German Ideology*, pp. 37–8 (*MEW* III. 26–7).

[60] *Capital* III. 21, pp. 333–4 (*MEW* XXV. 351–2). In the *Critique of the Gotha Programme* (*SW* III. 16, *MEW* XIX. 18) the point is made as follows: 'Is not [the present-day distribution] the only "fair" distribution on the basis of the present-day mode of production? Are economic relations regulated by legal conceptions or do not, on the contrary, legal relations arise from economic ones?'

[61] These propositions are elaborated in an engaging essay by Allen Wood ('The Marxian Critique of Justice', *Philosophy and Public Affairs*, 1 (1972), 244–82), to which my remarks in this paragraph are much indebted (see especially pp. 260–75). For replies to Wood by Ziyad Husami and George Brenkert, and for Wood's rejoinder, see also *Philosophy and Public Affairs*, 8 (1978–9), 27–64, 122–47, and 267–95.

[62] See Wood, 'The Marxian Critique of Justice', pp. 265 and 268–9.

standards in judgement of the merits of a particular economic system. From this point of view, justice, and indeed the rightness of all moral principles,[63] is determined in something like the manner Hobbes thought necessary—that is, our values are established by a predominant *de facto* power whose control over human affairs they express and legitimate—with this crucial difference, of course, that the sovereign power described by Hobbes shapes our moral principles through an act of will, whereas that of Marx operates at a deeper level independently of our will. Marx's mistrust of the language of morals, it seems, has its roots in just those misgivings which inform his doubts regarding the place of will and consciousness as determinants of human affairs in his theory of history.

On this point, at any rate, Marx is quite explicit. 'Right', he remarked in his *Critique of the Gotha Programme*,[64] 'can never be higher than the economic structure of [the] society' to which it applies. Not only was he unwilling to accommodate any so-called rights of man in his philosophy, but he could find no room either, he said, for what this or that proletarian, or indeed even the whole proletarian movement, might imagine to be its aim, since the only question worth considering was what the proletariat *is*, and what, historically, it is compelled to do.[65] Communism, therefore, was unconcerned with the pursuit of lofty moral principles. It is not an idea, he insisted, to which reality must somehow adjust itself. It is the actual movement transcending the present state of affairs, resulting from premises already in existence.[66] However much other socialists might aspire to bend the laws of history, Marx himself suffered from none of their illusions and advocated no utopia of his own. The visionary authors of the Gotha Programme could hardly have suffered a sharper insult from him than his acid

[63] In 'Freedom and Private Property in Marx', *Philosophy and Public Affairs*, 8 (1979), 122–47, Brenkert argues that Marx's conception of freedom is a moral ideal, even if his view of justice is not, while McLellan informs me that Marx probably judged communism to be better than capitalism in terms of his picture of human nature and needs. Both of these claims, however, seem to me to draw their strength more from what Marx must have meant than from what he actually said.

[64] Marx, *Critique of the Gotha Programme*, *SW* III. 19 (*MEW* XIX. 21). I find it difficult to agree with Cohen that this passage implies that Marx thought moralities might be assessed one against another, some being found 'higher'.

[65] See Marx and Engels, *The Holy Family* (Moscow, Foreign Languages Publishing House, 1956), p. 53 (*MEW* II. 38).

[66] See *The German Ideology*, p. 47 (*MEW* III. 35).

remark that they 'could just as well have copied the whole of Rousseau'.[67]

Let me conclude, then, with the reply which I believe Rousseau would have made to these claims. The proposition that morality must always be explained in terms of our material modes of production is a thesis I have already dealt with in my remarks about his account of property and his theory of culture. The point Rousseau invites us to consider, we should recall, is that our ideas, including our moral ideas, and even our illusory moral ideas, are not built round or upon the material substratum of our lives, but are rather embedded within, and constitute an integral part of, the basic ways in which we live. If Marx had only put his case more modestly—particularly if he could have been guided by Montesquieu—Rousseau might not have quarrelled with him at all. Largely because he himself had learnt so much from Montesquieu, Rousseau was as convinced as anyone in the Enlightenment that our moral, legal, and political principles are influenced by forces outside us—by customs and mores beyond the control of individuals, and by such factors as climate and terrain beyond the control of men collectively.[68] But neither Montesquieu nor Rousseau believed that those influences causally determine or functionally explain our moral ideas in any sense supposed by Marx or Cohen; they only, and everywhere, act as fetters upon the dissemination of ideas, in so far as they discourage the application of principles, independently conceived, in places and circumstances to which those principles are not rightly suited.[69] According to Marx it was the relations of production that fettered the forces in ways which prompted a revolutionary transformation of society. For Montesquieu and Rousseau, by contrast, such fetters were a mark of more or less stable, rather than revolutionary, epochs; they operated upon intellectual superstructures and not economic foundations; and they manifested the influence of forces which were divorced from

---

[67] Marx, *Critique of the Gotha Programme*, *SW* III. 14 (*MEW* XIX. 16).

[68] See, for instance, Rousseau's *Contrat social*, III. 8–9, *Considérations sur le gouvernement de Pologne*, chs. 2–3, and *Émile*, V, *OC* III. 414–20, 956–66, and *OC* IV. 850–1.

[69] Hence, Rousseau wrote in the *Contrat social*, III. 8 (*OC* III. 414–15), 'Liberty, as it is not the fruit of all climates, is not within the reach of all peoples. . . . In every climate there are natural factors according to which one may assign the form of government that climate requires, and, we might even say, what sort of inhabitants it must have'.

our will upon our social relations, and not, as Marx contended, the influence of social relations upon forces.

The difference between Montesquieu's and Rousseau's conceptions of such matters, on the one hand, and Marx's theory of the relation between a societal base and its superstructure, on the other, is an important subject which, perhaps fortunately, there is not enough space to consider here. But I think it is worth mentioning Montesquieu in this context, because, according to Rousseau, that illustrious thinker had nevertheless laboured under a misapprehension about the nature of our moral ideas—a misapprehension which I believe he would have held that Marx suffered from too. For Montesquieu, wrote Rousseau in *Émile*,[70] had conflated the interpretation of political principles with a study of actual states, whereas these were incompatible and wholly distinct subjects. He had, that is, confused fact and right, and even if Rousseau were as convinced by Marx's materialist explanation of morality as he was by Montesquieu's view of the spirit of laws, he would still have regarded Marx as mistaken to suppose that our ideals neither need nor could have any independent validity. 'What kind of a right is it which perishes when force fails?', he asked in the *Social Contract*.[71] If force creates right, the effect changes with the cause, and the word 'right', since it has no meaning apart from force, means absolutely nothing.

Rousseau also differed from Montesquieu, and would, I think, have similarly disagreed with Marx, over at least one further point, connected with these matters, about the influence of morality. That difference is expressed most vigorously in his claim, made in the *Social Contract*,[72] that 'what is possible in our moral affairs is less sharply circumscribed than we suppose'. Marx may have had little patience for the groundless idealism and fantasies of other socialist thinkers, but for Rousseau it was in our dreams that we shaped and breathed life into our moral principles, and through our fantasies that we conceived the means for their realization in practice as well. If our social bonds were only manifestations of our abstract notions of obedience under circumstances in which we also supposed ourselves free, then no feature of our material mode of existence could of itself prevent

[70] See *Émile*, V, *OC* IV. 836.
[71] Rousseau, *Contrat social*, I. 3, *OC* III. 354.
[72] Rousseau, *Contrat social*, III. 12, *OC* III. 425.

our abandonment of those notions and hence, too, delivery from our illusions of freedom. However confined is reality, Rousseau observed, the world of imagination, which we inhabit at the same time, is infinite.[73] And whereas in our minds and hearts every one of us may perceive a world without limits—whereas in masturbation, to which Rousseau succumbed all his life, we picture ourselves in the arms of a lover possessing any of the qualities we desire—so he imagined the possibility of mankind collectively achieving new bliss, acquiring a new corporate identity, under institutions of popular self-rule.

Just as reverie constitutes the free association of ideas never before conceived, democracy, as Rousseau pictured it, might be said to comprise a free association of people such as had never been truly envisaged before. The imagery of public participation in all facets of social life was deeply felt and richly drawn by Rousseau, around such aesthetic, religious, and cultural symbols of solidarity as he portrays in the military dance of the regiment of Saint-Gervais in his *Letter on the Theatre*, or the uplifting song of the grape pickers in *The New Héloïse*.[74] Democratic politics as he saw it was infused with the charm and gaiety of a cultural festival, a popular banquet, a theatrical display of all the people, held in the open air, under the sky.[75] Shakespeare's melancholic Jacques in *As You Like It* may have regretted that 'All the world's a stage', but through the force of his imagination Jean-Jacques aspired to make it so.

We should be mistaken, however, if we were to regard Rousseau's images of freedom as utopian ideals of a kind which Marx thought irrelevant to the main course of human history. Time and again Rousseau insisted that fictitious and imaginary states of the past or future were not his concern. Plato's *Republic* and More's *Utopia*, he reflected in his *Letters from the Mountain*, may have been chimeras, but he had attempted in the *Social Contract* to lay the theoretical foundation of an object which was real, that is, the constitution of Geneva, and it was because he had set his sights too close to home rather than too far away that he had not been forgiven by his critics.[76] Of course the Geneva he

[73] See *Émile*, II, *OC* IV. 305.
[74] See Rousseau's *Lettre sur les spectacles*, ed. M. Fuchs (Geneva, Droz, 1948), pp. 181–2n., and *La Nouvelle Héloïse*, V. 7, *OC* II. 607.
[75] See the *Lettre sur les spectacles*, pp. 168–9.
[76] See the *Lettres de la montagne*, VI, *OC* III. 810.

portrayed was not exactly real either, and its history is recounted by him in hypothetical terms not unlike his speculative reconstruction of the history of mankind in the *Discourse on Inequality*, where, in order to get at the truth, it had proved necessary to lay the facts aside. But in all his political works I believe Rousseau was determined to show that what we suppose to be real in public affairs is in fact abstract, artificial, illusory. They think that I am swayed by chimeras, he remarked about his critics in *Émile*; I see that they are moved by prejudice.[77] His political doctrines were framed, as he put it in the introductory chapter of the *Social Contract*, to construct a system of laws as they might be, taking men as they are, and, in my view, his arguments have always drawn much of their appeal from the conviction underlying them—that our political and social institutions, being human contrivances, *can* be changed, and that, once they are changed properly, the despair and decadence of our lives, which is attributable to them, may be overcome as well.

How odd it seems, in the light of these differences, that it was Marx who was the revolutionary, while Rousseau always counselled restraint. Despite espousing the thesis that no social order ever perishes until all the productive forces for which there is room in it have matured, Marx felt little hesitation about advocating a communist revolution in Germany, before the fruits of capitalism had really been harvested, and in Russia, before the seeds had even been sown.[78] Rousseau, for his part, foresaw a century of revolutions which would bring down the monarchies of Europe,[79] and yet the liberty of the whole of humanity, he insisted, could not justify shedding the blood of a single man.[80] He had drafted his political writings about Geneva not to foment revolution but to arrest it,[81] and whereas Marx was later to try,

[77] See *Émile*, IV, *OC* IV. 549.

[78] Marx encouraged a communist revolution in Germany most vigorously in his *Address to the Communist League* of 1850. His endorsement of a Russian revolution based upon an indigenous form of peasant communism, which might signal proletarian uprisings in the West, appears or is implied in at least three places: a letter on Mikhailovsky of 1877, a letter to Vera Zasulich of 1881, and the preface to the 1882 Russian edition of the *Communist Manifesto*.

[79] See *Émile*, III, *OC* IV. 468–9 and n.

[80] See Rousseau's letter to the comtesse de Wartensleben, 27 Sept. 1766, *Correspondance complète de Rousseau,* ed. R. A. Leigh (Geneva, Institut et Musée Voltaire, and Oxford, The Voltaire Foundation, 1965–), 5450, XXX. 384–8.

[81] See the *Lettres de la montagne*, VI, *OC* III. 809.

but fail, to direct the revolutionary fortunes of his contemporaries in the Communist League and the First International, Rousseau actually managed, quite by himself—not only on his own testimony but also on that of other witnesses—to prevent the outbreak of a revolution in Paris which would have occurred but for the fact that the publication of one of his works so incensed the crowd that its hostility was turned instead upon him.[82]

Marx may have been committed to the shortening of the working day, and to increasing the free time of the working classes, but if his doctrine of historical materialism ensured that time was so much on their side, we may well wonder why both he and the proletariat did not have at least a little more time on their hands, while awaiting the full evolution of the economic system they must eventually bring down. Rousseau, whose rage against the corruption of the *ancien régime* was matched only by Marx's contempt for fellow socialists, sought nothing so passionately as a life of solitude and isolation, which, however, was constantly upset by political turmoil of a kind Marx was never able to incite. All this is most baffling, and to my mind it confirms the conclusion of Plamenatz, specifically about Marx but which I believe he thought equally true of Rousseau—that each author, while pointing with one hand in the direction in which he wished us to go, was with the other throwing dust in our eyes.[83] If Rousseau had lived in Marx's day he would most likely have been inspired to think afresh about the material or economic forces that shape human history and their connection with those ideas by which, he supposed, men are moved too. If he had lived in our day he might well have looked at Marx's putatively scientific account of our historical epochs and wondered whether it was not really an expression of just that naïve faith in humanity which had been held against him, and whether his own bleaker conception of our decline was not more justified than Marx's optimism. Of this profoundly significant difference between their respective philosophies of history I have hardly taken any note at all here.

Stemming from what I have said, however, one thing does seem to me clear—and this is that Marxists now are in need of some of the light, and certainly more of the fire, of Rousseau's

---

[82] See Rousseau's *Confessions*, *OC* I. 384, and my 'Rousseau on Rameau and Revolution', pp. 251–5.

[83] Plamenatz, *Karl Marx's Philosophy of Man*, p. 472.

vision to keep their movements out of the cold. Marx was in my view mistaken, or at any rate misleading, in his famous eleventh thesis on Feuerbach that philosophers had only interpreted the world, whereas the point was to change it. In a sense Rousseau anticipated this remark when, in a reply to one of his early critics he had agreed, 'Let us correct ourselves, and speculate no more.'[84] But he also perceived, even if it seems Marx occasionally did not, that when we reinterpret the world we *do* come to change it, since a world of abstract images cannot survive as it is if men no longer accept the illusions of their place within it. In *Émile* he claimed that however much the golden age might be a chimera, to bring it to life it was only necessary to love it.[85] An impossible task, no doubt, as he himself recognized. Yet by exciting such love, and by envisaging our release from bondage of our own making, Rousseau captivated the revolutionary imagination of mankind in fervent ways which Marxists have also managed to achieve, but only by abandoning the doctrines they purport to follow. Still in need of reinterpretation, the world they have changed remains much as it was.[86]

[84] 'Dernière réponse' [to Borde], *OC* III. 94.

[85] See *Émile*, V, *OC* IV. 859.

[86] My remarks about Rousseau in this final section are much inspired by the work of Ralph Leigh, Jean Starobinski, and Bronislaw Baczko, as well as Plamenatz. I am also grateful to several colleagues and other scholars who have read an earlier draft of the whole text, and whose expert knowledge, especially on Marx, has saved me from more errors than those that remain: Jerry Cohen, Michael Evans, Norman Geras, David McLellan, John Hope Mason, David Miller, Hillel Steiner, and William Weinstein. To Terrell Carver, who differs sharply from the bulk of my statements about Marx, my greatest thanks are due. If I have not managed always to be persuaded by him or others I take some comfort at least from their lack of an agreed alternative interpretation.

John Petrov Plamenatz: an appreciation*

John Plamenatz often struck those who met him for the first time as pre-eminently English and Oxonian. His soft and refined voice, the playful irony of his mind, and his taste for concise statement—all seemed to conjure up the intellectual tradition of his ancient university and the conversation of its common rooms.

Nor was the appearance altogether misleading. Oxford, where he was an undergraduate and where he taught for more than thirty years, had, indeed, a profound influence on him.

Most notably, Oxford in the 1930s shaped his conception of philosophy and, by implication, political theory. He learned to disentangle the most complicated writings into distinct arguments, and to consider each argument on its own merits. He proceeded by identifying assumptions and definitions, and scrupulously considered whether the conclusions which were claimed to follow from them, did really follow from them. The subtlety or plausibility of one argument did not prevent him from pointing out the inadequacies of another. He was always wary of system-builders. Using the principle of non-contradiction as a fine scalpel, he was analytical without being reductionist. His earliest work, *Consent, Freedom and Political Obligation*, gives perhaps the clearest view of the impression made on him by Oxford philosophy. Yet it entirely lacks the positivistic fervour which led some writers at that time to look forward to the virtual abolition of traditional political philosophy.

That book represents the high-water mark of Oxford philosophy's influence on John Plamenatz. In later works his own remarkable family background and personal instincts came gradually to the fore.

John Plamenatz sprang from an old and distinguished family in Montenegro, a principality which was absorbed into the new state of Yugoslavia at the end of the First World War. The Plamenatz family had provided the Princes of Montenegro with ministers in the decades prior to 1914. Yet central government in that rugged, upland region of the Balkans was very limited. Montenegro remained an almost tribal society. It was never subjugated by the Turks; nor did the feudal system really take root there. It was a society of villages and of large, clannish families. This was the background of John Plamenatz's life. Although his parents fled from Montenegro when it was overrun (in 1917), settling first in Paris and then in Vienna, John Plamenatz never forgot his origins.

Because of a curious encounter between his father and some British officers before the First War, John Plamenatz was sent to a small public school in Dorset in the early 1920s. From there he went up to Oriel College, Oxford. In Oxford, academic success led, in turn, to his election as a Fellow of All Souls. The future course of his life was established.

Yet he resisted assimilation. Or, perhaps, it would be more accurate to say that he was incapable of it. He remained essentially an observer of the English and their ways—and was keenly aware that he was living in a more complex, hierarchical and mannered society than any of his ancestors had done. Into that society he carried a simplicity and directness, together with a concern for the enduring problems of human existence, which set him apart. Perhaps that is why, as the years went by, he was increasingly attracted to the writings of Rousseau. Rousseau's exploration of the effects of social structure on human needs and wants, and his concern with the consequences of social inequality, were highly congenial to John Plamenatz's mind. The social nature of man became the leitmotiv of his work.

There were other reasons why he was drawn to Rousseau. He had spoken French before learning to speak English. And throughout his life he retained an affection for French literature of the seventeenth and nineteenth centuries—reading writers such as Racine, Pascal, Diderot, and Balzac with extreme pleasure. In part, his taste reflected the hold of French culture on leading Balkan families before 1914. But it also reflected the hold of the introspective tradition in French philosophy and literature on a mind such as his.

John Plamenatz was a solitary worker. Although much of his academic life was devoted to lecturing and the conscientious supervision of graduate students, he did not take naturally to group life. He was perhaps only completely himself in his study.

The arguments in his books were hammered out, not in the interchange of seminars or in conversation, but in an intensely private encounter with the writings of the major social and political thinkers of modern Europe. With them he carried on a kind of *tête à tête*.

He once remarked to a friend that he had to write down the arguments he encountered in his own terms, if he was to understand them at all. And that was what he did. He brought to bear on the classical texts of social and political theory a fiercely independent spirit and yet a wonderfully simple concern to establish the truth. The shyness and restraint which marked him in public settings, gave way, in his study, to vigorous combat. In that way the pride, simplicity, and independence of his Montenegrin forebears were transmuted into a distinctive intellectual quest. Social and political theory was no mere academic exercise for John Plamenatz. It was a passionate exercise in self-discovery and self-definition.

Thus, while Oxford provided him with philosophical standards, the spirit underlying his work had more to do with his Montenegrin origins and the need of a precocious but uprooted boy to understand an alien society. In that light, the title of one of his books, *On Alien Rule and Self-Government*, may be seen to have more meaning than he perhaps intended. Social and political theory was for John Plamenatz the means of analysing and bringing under some control powerful social influences, to which we are all subject, but which few of us disentangle with such subtlety and disinterestedness.

Larry Siedentop

Bibliography of the Published Work of John Plamenatz

This bibliography could not have been compiled without the help of Marjorie Plamenatz, who provided the original sources of most of the references from her late husband's papers. I owe her an immense debt of gratitude. I should also like to thank Robert Wokler, Phillip Darby, and several others who helped to track down some out-of-the-way items. Even so several pieces, mostly book reviews, have continued to elude my searches. I have included all the published work that I have found, with the exception of two unsigned reports published as special supplements to the *National News-Letter* in 1946—'Exports and Britain's Life' and 'What is Democracy?'—which appear to have been largely if not wholly Plamenatz's work. Encyclopaedia entries have been listed only on their first appearance.

David Miller

1938
Consent, Freedom and Political Obligation (London, Oxford University Press, 1938).

1944
The Case of General Mihailovitch, private edition (Gloucester, John Bellows, 1944).

1945
'L'Industrie du Charbon en Grande-Bretagne', *La France Libre,* 9, No. 53 (March 1945), 341–5.
'Chambre des Communes et Commissions Parlementaires', *La France Libre,* 11, No. 61 (Nov. 1945), 30–3.

1946
'Économie Nouvelle', *La France Libre,* 11, No. 64 (Feb. 1946), 297–302.
'Toujours le prêt américain', *La France Libre*, 12, No. 69 (July 1946), 184–9.
Review of E. Mantoux, *The Carthaginian Peace* in *La France Libre*, 12, No. 70 (Aug. 1946), 333–6.

1947
What is Communism? (London, National News-Letter, 1947).

1948

'Soviet Communism: its Theoretical Basis', *The Listener,* 39, No. 1013 (24 June 1948), 1001–2.

'Communism and the Western Tradition', *The Listener,* 40, No. 1022 (26 Aug. 1948), 308–9.

Review of F. Hertz, *The Economic Problem of the Danubian States* in *International Affairs,* 24 (1948), 132–3.

1949

The English Utilitarians (Oxford, Blackwell, 1949).

1950

'Deviations from Marxism', *Political Quarterly,* 21 (1950), 40–55.

'Rights', *Proceedings of the Aristotelian Society,* Supplementary Vol. 24 (1950), 75–82.

1951

'Hobbes's Leviathan', *Manchester Guardian,* 16 Apr. 1951, 4.

'The Communist Ideology', *Political Quarterly,* 22 (1951), 16–26.

Contribution to R. McKeon (ed.), *Democracy in a World of Tensions* (Paris, UNESCO, 1951).

Review article on theories of party from Burke to Schattschneider in *Parliamentary Affairs,* 5 (1951–2), 211–22.

Review of R. H. Soltau, *An Introduction to Politics* in *Political Quarterly,* 22 (1951), 298–9.

Review of A. Mousset, *The World of the Slavs* in *International Affairs,* 27 (1951), 247.

1952

The Revolutionary Movement in France, 1815–1871 (London, Longman, 1952).

Review of K. Popper, *The Open Society and its Enemies* in *British Journal of Sociology,* 3 (1952), 264–73 (reprinted in R. Bambrough, *Plato, Popper and Politics* (Cambridge, Heffer, 1967)).

Review of H. Cairns, *Legal Philosophy from Plato to Hegel* in *Mind,* 61 (1952), 578–81.

1953

From Marx to Stalin (London, Batchford Press, 1953).

'Stalin as a Theorist', *Manchester Guardian,* 13 Mar. 1953, 6, 14.

'The Open Society—A Rejoinder', *British Journal of Sociology,* 4 (1953), 76–7 (reprinted in R. Bambrough, *Plato, Popper and Politics* (Cambridge, Heffer, 1967)).

Review of G. Davy, *Thomas Hobbes et J. J. Rousseau* in *Political Studies,* 1 (1953), 282–3.

1954

German Marxism and Russian Communism (London, Longman, 1954).

'Interests', *Political Studies,* 2 (1954), 1–8.

Review of J. Bowle, *Politics and Opinion in the Nineteenth Century* in *Manchester Guardian,* 3 Aug. 1954, 2.

Review of R. N. Carew Hunt, *Marxism Past and Present* in *Manchester Guardian,* 21 Dec. 1954, 4.

Review of G. E. Fasnacht, *Acton's Political Philosophy* in *Philosophy,* 29 (1954), 85–6.

1955

'Nikola Pasic' in *Encyclopaedia Britannica* (London, Encyclopaedia Britannica, 1955).

Review of M. M. Drachkovitch, *De Karl Marx à Leon Blum* in *English Historical Review,* 70 (1955), 345–6.

Review of A. G. Meyer, *Marxism: The Unity of Theory and Practice* in *Annals of the American Academy of Political and Social Science,* 298 (March 1955), 210–11.

Review of L. Strauss, *Natural Right and History* in *Philosophical Review,* 64 (1955), 300–2.

Review of M. B. Swabey, *The Judgement of History* in *Political Studies,* 3 (1955), 279–80.

1956

'Cultural Prerequisites to a Successfully Functioning Democracy: A Symposium' with E. S. Griffith and J. Roland Pennock, *American Political Science Review,* 50 (1956), 101–38.

'Russia's Basic Strategy: Facts versus Illusions', *The Nation,* 183 (1956), 491–4.

Review of H. B. Acton, *The Illusion of the Epoch* in *British Journal of Sociology,* 7 (1956), 154–6.

Review of F. C. Green, *Jean-Jacques Rousseau* in *Times Literary Supplement,* 2820 (16 Mar. 1956), 157–9.

1957

'Matija Nenadovitch' in *Encyclopaedia Britannica* (London, Encyclopaedia Britannica, 1957).

'Equality of Opportunity' in L. Bryson *et al.* (eds.), *Aspects of Human Equality, Fifteenth Symposium of the Conference on Science, Philosophy and Religion* (New York, Harper, 1957).

'Mr. Warrender's Hobbes', *Political Studies,* 5 (1957), 295–308 (reprinted in K. Brown (ed.), *Hobbes Studies* (Oxford, Blackwell, 1965)).

Review of F. E. Manuel, *The New World of Henri Saint-Simon* in *Political Studies,* 5 (1957), 105.

Review of R. V. Sampson, *Progress in the Age of Reason* in *Political Studies,* 5 (1957), 330–2.

1958

The English Utilitarians, 2nd edn. with additional chapter (Oxford, Blackwell, 1958).

The place and influence of political and social philosophy, prepared for the congress of the International Political Science Association, Rome, September 1958 (Mimeo).

'Jean-Jacques Rousseau' in *Encyclopaedia Britannica* (London, Encyclopaedia Britannica, 1958).

'World War, Communism and Social Democracy' in J. Bowle (ed.), *The Concise Encyclopaedia of World History* (London, Hutchinson, 1958).

'Electoral Studies and Democratic Theory. A British View', *Political Studies,* 6 (1958), 1–9.

Review of A. B. Spitzer, *The Revolutionary Theories of Louis Auguste Blanqui* in *Political Studies,* 6 (1958), 278–9.

1959

'Jeremy Bentham' in *Encyclopaedia Britannica* (London, Encyclopaedia Britannica, 1959).

'The Legacy of Philosophical Radicalism' in M. Ginsberg (ed.), *Law and Opinion in England in the 20th Century* (London, Stevens and Sons, 1959).

'El lugar y la influencia de la filosofía política y social', *Revista de Estudios políticos,* 108 (1959), 109–30.

Review of C. Guyot, *Un ami et défenseur de Rousseau, Pierre-Alexandre Du Peyrou* in *Times Literary Supplement,* 3005 (2 Oct. 1959), 558.

Review of S. Mellon, *The Political Uses of History* in *Political Studies,* 7 (1959), 87.

Review of G. G. Iggers, *The Cult of Authority* in *Political Studies,* 7 (1959), 308.

Review of L. C. Webb (ed.), *Legal Personality and Political Pluralism* in *Political Science Quarterly,* 74 (1959), 300–2.

1960

On Alien Rule and Self-Government (London, Longman, 1960).

'In What Sense is Freedom a Western Idea' in R. St. J. Macdonald (ed.), *Current Law and Social Problems* (Toronto, University of Toronto Press, 1960).

'The Use of Political Theory', *Political Studies,* 8 (1960), 37–47 (reprinted in A. Quinton (ed.), *Political Philosophy* (London, Oxford University Press, 1967)).

Review of J. Touchard *et al., Histoire des Idées Politiques* in *Political Studies,* 8 (1960), 214–15.

Review of E. Durkheim, *Socialism and Saint-Simon* in *Political Studies,* 8 (1960), 308–9.

1961

'Heroic Leadership?', *Encounter,* 17, No. 3 (Sept. 1961), 64–6.

Review of M. Curtis, *Three Against the Third Republic* in *History,* 46 (1961), 163–4.

Review of J. C. Talmon, *Political Messianism: The Romantic Phase* in *Political Science Quarterly,* 76 (1961), 593–5.

1962

Introduction to Hobbes, *Leviathan* (London, Collins, 1962).

'Socialist thought from Owen to Marx' in *Chapters on Western Civilization,* 3rd edn., Vol. II (New York, Columbia University Press, 1962).

'What Principles Should Guide us in Seeking to Influence Foreign Governments and Peoples' in H. D. Lasswell and H. Cleveland (eds.) *The Ethic of Power* (New York, Harper, 1962).

'Pascal and Rousseau', *Political Studies,* 10 (1962), 248–63.

1963

Man and Society (London, Longman, 1963).

'Self-Government Reconsidered' in K. Robinson and F. Madden (eds.), *Essays in Imperial Government, presented to Margery Perham* (Oxford, Blackwell, 1963).

Review of M. Oakeshott, *Rationalism in Politics* in *British Journal of Sociology,* 14 (1963), 284–6.

Review of M. Mack, *Jeremy Bentham* in *The Economist,* 206 (Jan.–Mar. 1963), 328.

Review of F. E. Manuel, *The Prophets of Paris* in *History,* 48 (1963), 232.

Review of G. Lichtheim, *Marxism: An Historical and Critical Study* in *English Historical Review,* 78 (1963), 342–5.

Review of R. Tucker, *Philosophy and Myth in Karl Marx* in *English Historical Review,* 78 (1963), 410–11.

Review of M. Malia, *Alexander Herzen and the Birth of Russian Socialism, 1812–1855* in *English Historical Review,* 78 (1963), 808–9.

Review of H. D. Lewis, *Freedom and History* and of S. Hook, *The Paradoxes of Freedom* in *Political Studies,* 11 (1963), 217–18.

1964

'General Will', 'Interest', 'Justice', and 'Utilitarianism' in J. Gould and Wm. L. Kolb (eds.), *Dictionary of the Social Sciences* (London, Tavistock Publications, 1964).

'La pensée Communiste' in M. Beloff, P. Renouvin, F. Schnabel, and F. Valsecchi (eds.), *L'Europe du xixe et du xxe Siècle (1914–Aujourd'hui),* Part I (Milan, Marzorati, 1964).

Review of D. G. Charlton, *Secular Religions in France, 1815–1870* in *History,* 49 (1964), 97.

1965

Introduction to *Readings from Liberal Writers: English and French* (London, Allen and Unwin, 1965).

'Ce qui ne signifie autre chose sinon qu'on le forcera d'être libre', *Annales de Philosophie Politique 5: Rousseau et la philosophie politique* (Paris, Presses Universitaires de France, 1965), 137–52 (reprinted in M. Cranston and R. S. Peters (eds.), *Hobbes and Rousseau: a collection of critical essays* (New York, Doubleday, 1972)).

'Srbi i Velike Sile', *Nasa Rec,* 18, No. 163/4 (1965), 2–3.

'Srbija Izmedju Austrije i Rusije', *Nasa Rec,* 18, No. 165/6 (1965), 2–3, 9.

'Strangers in Our Midst', *Race,* 7 (1965), 1–16.

'La Classe Dirigeante', *Revue Française de Science Politique,* 15 (1965), 28–39.

Review of L. J. Halle, *The Society of Man* in *The Guardian,* 15 Oct. 1965, 8.

Review of S. A. Lakoff, *Equality in Political Philosophy* in *History,* 50 (1965), 281–2.

1966

'Srbija—Nezavisna Suverena Drzava 1878', *Nasa Rec,* 19, No. 168 (1966), 2–3.

Review of Jean Guéhenno, *Jean-Jacques Rousseau* in *New York Review of Books,* 7 (11) (29 Dec. 1966), 8–10.

Review of Z. A. Pelczynski (ed.), *Hegel's Political Writings* in *Philosophical Quarterly,* 16 (1966), 182–3.

1967

'Diversity of Rights and Kinds of Equality' in J. R. Pennock and J. W. Chapman (eds.), *Nomos IX: Equality* (New York, Atherton Press, 1967).

'Responsibility, Blame and Punishment' in P. Laslett and W. G. Runciman (eds.), *Philosophy, Politics and Society* (3rd series) (Oxford, Blackwell, 1967).

'Communist Ideology Seen Through Western Eyes', *Review* (London, Study Centre for Jugoslav Affairs), vol. 1, No. 6 (1967), 383–402.

Review of L. Goldmann, *The Hidden God* and of J. Steinmann, *Pascal* in *New York Review of Books,* 8 (8) (4 May 1967), 31–4.

Review of R. Niebuhr, *Man's Nature and His Communities* in *Political Science Quarterly,* 82 (1967), 139–41.

Review of J. P. Nettl, *Rosa Luxemburg* in *Political Studies,* 15 (1967), 221–2.

Review of P. H. Vigor, *A Guide to Marxism,* M. M. Drachkovitch (ed.), *Marxism in the Modern World,* and G. H. Hampsch, *The Theory of Communism* in *Slavonic and East European Review,* 45 (1967), 262–4.

1968

Consent, Freedom and Political Obligation, 2nd edn. with new postscript (Oxford, Oxford University Press, 1968).

'Some American Images of Democracy' in O. Bird (ed.), *The Great Ideas Today, 1968* (Chicago, Encyclopaedia Britannica, 1968).

1969
Review of S. Avineri, *The Social and Political Thought of Karl Marx* in *Political Science Quarterly*, 84 (1969), 512–13.
Review of T. L. S. Sprigge (ed.), *The Correspondence of Jeremy Bentham* in *Times Literary Supplement*, 3491 (23 Jan. 1969), 85–6.

1970
Ideology (London, Pall Mall, 1970).

1971
'History as the Realization of Freedom' in Z. Pelczynski (ed.), *Hegel's Political Philosophy: Problems and Perspectives* (Cambridge, Cambridge University Press, 1971).

1972
Preface to E. Halevy, *The Growth of Philosophic Radicalism* (London, Faber and Faber, 1972).
Introduction to Machiavelli, *The Prince, Selections from the Discourses and other writings* (London, Collins, 1972).
'In Search of Machiavellian Virtu' in A. Parel (ed.), *The Political Calculus* (Toronto, University of Toronto Press, 1972).
' "Separate but Equal" ' in J. Floud *et al.* (eds.), *Problems and Prospects of Socio-Legal Research* (Oxford, Nuffield College, 1972).
'Nationalism, Western and Eastern', *Hemisphere*, 16 (1972), 12–14.
'Rousseau: The Education of Émile', *Proceedings of the Philosophy of Education Society of Great Britain*, 6 (1972), 176–92.
Review of N. V. Riasanovsky, *The Teaching of Charles Fourier* in *English Historical Review*, 87 (1972), 212–13.

1973
Democracy and Illusion (London, Longman, 1973).
'Liberalism' in P. P. Wiener (ed.), *Dictionary of the History of Ideas*, Vol. III (New York, Charles Scribner's Sons, 1973).
'Two Types of Nationalism' in E. Kamenka (ed.), *Nationalism: The Nature and Evolution of an Idea* (Canberra, Australian National University Press, 1973; corrected edn, London, Edward Arnold, 1976).
Review of J. Franklin, *Jean Bodin and the Rise of Absolutist Theory* in *Political Theory*, 1 (1973), 345–6.

1974
'On Preserving the British Way of Life' in B. Parekh (ed.), *Colour, Culture and Consciousness: Immigrant Intellectuals in Britain* (London, Allen and Unwin, 1974).
'Privacy and Laws Against Discrimination', *Rivista Internazionale di Filosofia del Diritto*, 51 (1974), 443–55.
'Beaumarchais's *The Marriage of Figaro*', programme note for National Theatre production, 9 July 1974.

Review of H. M. Drucker, *The Uses of Ideology* in *Political Studies,* 22 (1974), 507–8.

1975

Karl Marx's Philosophy of Man (Oxford, Clarendon Press, 1975).
'Public Opinion and Political Consciousness', *Political Studies,* 23 (1975), 342–51.
Review of P. Singer, *Democracy and Disobedience* in *American Political Science Review,* 69 (1975), 257.

1977

'Persons as Moral Beings' in G. Dorsey (ed.), *Equality and Freedom: International and Comparative Jurisprudence* (Dobbs Ferry, N.Y., Oceana Publications, 1977), Vol. I.

1983

'The Philosophical Element in Social Theory and Practice' in A. Parel (ed.), *Ideology, Philosophy and Politics* (Waterloo, Ontario, Wilfrid Laurier University Press, 1983).

Index of Names